# DEFEND OF FAITH

## THE BOOK OF MORMON FROM A SOLDIER'S PERSPECTIVE

# DEFENDERS OF FAITH

## THE BOOK OF MORMON FROM A SOLDIER'S PERSPECTIVE

## DOUGLAS J. BELL

CFI
An imprint of Cedar Fort, Inc.
Springville, Utah

ISBN 13: 978-1-59955-987-2

Published by CFI, an imprint of Cedar Fort, Inc., 2373 W. 700 S., Springville, UT 84663
Distributed by Cedar Fort, Inc., www.cedarfort.com

LIBRARY OF CONGRESS CATALOGING-IN-PUBLICATION DATA

Bell, Douglas J. (Douglas Josiah), 1946- author.
  Defenders of faith : the Book of Mormon from a soldier's perspective /
Douglas J. Bell.
    pages cm
  ISBN 978-1-59955-987-2
  1.  Book of Mormon--Criticism and interpretation. 2.  Book of
Mormon--Commentaries. 3.  Church of Jesus Christ of Latter-day
Saints--Doctrines. 4.  Mormon Church--Doctrines. 5.  United States.
Army--Military life. 6.  Christian life. I. Title.

  BX8627.B33 2012
  289.3'22--dc23

                        2011050120

Cover design by Brian Halley
Cover design © 2012 by Lyle Mortimer
Edited and typeset by Melissa J. Caldwell
Map illustrations by Crystal Oftedahl

Printed in the United States of America

10  9  8  7  6  5  4  3  2  1

Printed on acid-free paper

*To my wife Caryl,*
*who has been so patient during this project*
*and was a marvelous support while I was away in Iraq.*

*To my fellow soldiers of the 142nd Military Intelligence Battalion,*
*who served with me in Kuwait and Iraq. They performed their duties*
*flawlessly and will be my friends for eternity.*

*To the amazing prophet-warriors of the Book of Mormon—*
*their dedication to God, to freedom, and to their families*
*give us wonderful examples to examine and emulate.*

*To a loving Father in Heaven and a Savior,*
*who have given me the opportunity to learn*
*and have blessed me with the ability to communicate*
*my heartfelt love of the Book of Mormon.*

# Contents

# CONTENTS

# Introduction

# THE BOOK OF MORMON—AN ESSENTIAL ELEMENT IN OUR LIVES

This commentary on the Book of Mormon is undertaken with a deep love for its contents. My training as a soldier in the United States Army has given me a unique perspective on the book and explains the subtitle, "The Book of Mormon from a Soldier's Perspective." I have read the Book of Mormon many times and have taught courses on the Book of Mormon at Brigham Young University. However, the book's influence on me was magnified many times over when I served as a soldier in Iraq with the 142nd Military Intelligence Battalion during 2003. While I was stationed in Baghdad during Operation Iraqi Freedom, I had an opportunity to study the Book of Mormon while serving in a war zone. The prophet-warriors came alive as never before. Their actions took on a new meaning because I saw them as military commanders and not just warriors. The wonder and significance of the "war chapters" seemed to leap off the pages. The dangers of living in a war zone gave new and cherished meaning to life. People generally don't understand the life of a soldier and his confrontation with possible death and the faith that springs from it. People would often say to me when they discovered that I had been to Iraq: "How dreadful, terrible, or awful." They seemed shocked when I would say, "On the contrary, my opportunity

to serve was an honor and a great adventure." It is with this same sense of adventure that this soldier's commentary on the Book of Mormon is undertaken.

Modern prophets have told us that the Book of Mormon can have a marvelous influence in our lives. The promise that life can take on new meaning as we study the Book of Mormon has been given to us multiple times. The promised blessings are there for all of us, and it is helpful to review these prophetic statements periodically to refresh our memories. Joseph Smith, translator of the Book of Mormon and the prophet most familiar with its contents, gave us the most definitive statement regarding the value of the book.

> I told the brethren that the Book of Mormon was the most correct of any book on earth, and the keystone of our religion, and a man would get nearer to God by abiding by its precepts, than by any other book (Introduction: Book of Mormon).

Ezra Taft Benson, former president and prophet of The Church of Jesus Christ of Latter-day Saints, was concerned about the role of the Book of Mormon in the lives of the members of the Church. It is clear that as the spokesman for God, President Benson wanted us to increase our interest in the Book of Mormon when he made the following statement.

> The Lord is not pleased with us in the manner of attention we're giving the Book of Mormon, a new witness for Christ. We need it in our homes; we need it in our families. It was written for us today.[1]

It is difficult to take such a declarative statement lightly. In an October 1986 General Conference address, President Benson stated the following regarding the Book of Mormon in our lives.

> There is a power in the book which will begin to flow into your lives the moment you begin a serious study of the book. You will find greater power to resist temptation. You will find the power to avoid deception. You will find the power to stay on the strait and narrow path. The scriptures are called "the words of life" (D&C 84:85), and nowhere is that more true than it is of the Book of Mormon. When you begin to hunger and thirst after those words, you will find life in greater and greater abundance. . . . [You will also enjoy] increased love and harmony in the home, greater respect between parent and child, [and] increased spirituality and righteousness. These promises are not idle promises, but exactly what the Prophet Joseph Smith meant when he said the

Book of Mormon will help us draw nearer to God.[2]

These statements from modern prophets leave no doubt that it is our duty to study the Book of Mormon regardless of our circumstances, and to learn its principles. Most important, however, is for us to apply them to our lives.

## A Comparison of Christians and Warriors

Consider for a moment an observation about Christians and warriors. A person truly devoted to Christ is often called a disciple. The root word for *disciple* is the same as for the word *discipline*. Just as the word *disciple* describes a true Christian, the word *discipline* describes the core value of a soldier or warrior. A true Christian must be like a warrior and demonstrate strong self-control, a life of order, and obedience to core values.

The Book of Mormon describes many great military commanders who were also courageous Christians and warriors. The commanding generals of their armies were called chief captains. Sixteen years before the appearance of the Savior in the Americas, a great prophet named Nephi

put the role of Nephite Chief Captain into perspective when he wrote the following:

> *Now the chiefest among all the chief captains and the great commander of all the armies of the Nephites was appointed, and his name was Gidgiddoni.* **Now it was the custom among all the Nephites to appoint for their chief captains, (save it were in their times of wickedness) some one that had the spirit of revelation and also prophecy;** *therefore, this Gidgiddoni was a great prophet among them, as also was the chief judge.* (3 Nephi 3:18–19; emphasis added)

The leaders of their armies were much more than military commanders—they were also prophets. Knowing this, one can see why Mormon wanted us to study these awe-inspiring men. While we explore the lives of these marvelous prophets in the Book of Mormon, it will become evident that the skills of a warrior, such as self-control and obedience, also played a role in making them more loyal disciples of Christ. As I discuss their thrilling stories, it is my hope that their personal qualities and values will give you marvelous examples to emulate and energize your faith in Christ.

### My Days in Kuwait:
### Murmuring and Then Awakening

In 2003, my military unit was flown into Kuwait and sent to live in tents in the desert. During this experience, I had a spiritual awakening that is explained through the Book of Mormon. Our unit was not happy. The cause of our displeasure was much more than just being away from home. Our mission had been changed, and the uncertainty of where we would go and what we would do created dreadful anxiety. We had been trained to set up a prisoner of war detention facility in northern Iraq and carry out screenings and interrogations. That mission had been scrapped and appeared to have been a waste of time. It was so hot in Kuwait that we couldn't sleep until after eleven o'clock at night, and during the day the wind would stir up dust and leave a fine film over all of our gear in the tent. The dust had the consistency of flour and would stick to everything, especially our perspiring bodies. I attended meetings with good people who had changed their normally first-class demeanor to a bearing of distasteful irritability. Most of us had become angry, bad tempered, and quite dysfunctional. As I was reading the Book of Mormon, I realized that I had become just like the wayward sons of the prophet Lehi—Laman and Lemuel: (1) I wanted the comforts of home, (2) I hated the desert and intense heat, (3) I didn't understand where I was destined to go, and (4) I resented the people who brought me there. It became clear to me that I was murmuring, and I had become very good at it. My behavior was almost identical to these two sons of Lehi who didn't want to leave their home in Jerusalem. They were in the deserts near the Red Sea and rebelled against their father (see *murmurings* in 1 Nephi 3:5–6; 7:6–7,16; 15:7–8; 16:20, 36–37; 17:17, 45–49; 18:9–11).

This recognition was an awakening for me, and I decided to make a serious change in behavior. The first step I took was to stop focusing on my own discomfort and begin inviting people into my life. I began with the chow line, which was several hundred yards long. The wait for each meal gave me time to talk to other soldiers. I would ask the following questions: "Where are you from?" "What is your MOS (military job)?" "Do you have children?" "Do you a have a life outside the army?" Their responses were marvelous and insightful. My journal is full of stories about the people I met: mechanics, infantrymen, tank commanders, pilots, and surgeons—just to name a few. They were high-quality people, and it was clear that they were sacrificing much more than me. My attitude almost immediately changed toward hope and appreciation for the others who were suffering through that dreadful experience with me.

## A Walk on Sacred Ground

My attitude also changed by an interesting incident that again brought the Book of Mormon close to my heart. I noticed some small, white rocks mixed in with the sand and dust that made up the desert floor. I began to collect a few. The rocks were just smaller than golf balls and worn smooth from centuries of wind and grinding dust. One night in the tent, I took one of these rocks from my pocket and put my flashlight under it. The rock absorbed the light and it glowed! I was stunned. My mind was immediately directed to a Book of Mormon story about the experience of the brother of Jared. He was the leader of a small group that God separated and led away from the land of the Tigris and Euphrates valley at the time of the Tower of Babel. The brother of Jared needed light for the ships he had built to cross the ocean, and his solution was to ask the Lord to touch some stones, knowing that they would glow from His touch and bring continuous light for his ships. The Lord was pleased with the solution and touched the stones, which glowed and provided light for the Jaredite voyage. When my stones glowed easily, I suddenly recognized that I was geographically near the site where Jared and his small band had traveled over four thousand years earlier. I was camped on hallowed ground that had been blessed by the footsteps of prophets (see Ether 2:18–24; 3:1, 4–6).

From that time on, I was energized by the idea that I was traveling in a region blessed by God. When in Kuwait, I was near the place where the Jaredites had gone to escape from the Tower of Babel. When I eventually went to Iraq, I was in the land of Abraham, Daniel, Ezekiel, Ester, Jonah, and many others. My interest in Old Testament scriptural accounts intensified. The book of Daniel was most inspirational to me because it told of ancient Babylon and the captive Jews. Knowing that I was near the birthplace of Abraham, the founding patriarch of Israel, added depth and understanding to every trip I took.

## My Days in Iraq: A Great Adventure

In 2003, I spent nine months in Iraq. During this time ,I was stationed in an unstable and dangerous war zone. My reading of the war chapters in the Book of Mormon spoke to me as never before. It was almost as if these great prophet-warriors joined me and my fellow soldiers. They helped me understand the need for soldiers to love the Lord, their country, and their families. Moreover, I came to understand the wonder of a nation being liberated. The Iraqi people had been dreadfully oppressed for decades by the wicked dictator Saddam Hussein. The war was devastating to them but the opportunity to be free from tyranny brought impressive energy to their lives. The work I did with the Iraqi people became the adventure of a lifetime.

I was permanently stationed in Baghdad and had the opportunity to travel throughout the surrounding area. The city and its suburbs have over six million people. Laced with freeways, it is quite modern. Very little of Baghdad had been destroyed by bombing. It was, however, ravaged by its own people. When the Iraqi armies were told to stop fighting and go home, there was no law or policing authority in most of the country. Consequently, nearly all government buildings and schools were looted. It was sad to enter beautiful, stately buildings and see rooms without furniture and strewn with waste and paper. The light fixtures, switches, and outlets were taken, and even the toilets and sinks were cut from the walls. This looting highlighted a people who had been so oppressed and dominated by an evil dictator that they felt justified in stealing property back from the government. We were all dismayed by this self-destructive behavior. The ravages of war can take many forms, and they permanently touch every soldier. This behavior had a resounding effect on me.

I mentioned earlier that while in the Middle East, I felt I was walking on sacred ground. To gain a better perspective, I read and reread the stories of Abraham and Daniel many times. As I read the book of Daniel, I checked the Bible Dictionary and found out that the ancient city of Babylon was surrounded by a wall 335 feet high, 85 feet wide, and 56 miles long. I was stricken by the enormity of the area and began to see the spiritual as well as the historical significance of this remarkable land. In short, faith in the Lord and knowledge of the history of Chaldea, the biblical name for Iraq, made my journey among the people more meaningful.

Traveling in Iraq was dangerous because of improvised explosive devices, commonly called "IEDs." These explosive charges would be placed on the roadside and exploded by remote control devices (usually cell phones) as US military convoys or vehicles drove by. In spite of the danger, it was satisfying to travel through the cities and take the opportunity to meet with interesting people. I met with impressive Iraqi generals, university presidents, scientists, and many other influential Iraqi citizens. They loved and appreciated their newfound freedom and helped us at the peril of their own lives. If loyalists to Saddam Hussein found out they helped the United States Army, thy could still attack them or their families.

One of the former Iraqi generals became a close friend, a friendship illustrated by a hug as a greeting before we would begin our discussions. He was an honorable man and always showed us respect. At the end of our meetings, we would often spend time talking about family, economic conditions, or the government. After one very productive meeting, I asked the general if he was a descendent of Abraham. His countenance brightened as he said, "Yes, I am." I said, "A descendent of Ishmael, right?" He replied with even greater interest. "Yes, indeed." In a way, I think his interest and excitement was sparked because I knew his ancestry. I then stated, "I am also a descendant of Abraham." At this point, the translator became very concerned because he thought I had told him I was a Jew. I quickly stated, "I am a descendent of Ephraim." My great Iraqi friend rose up and said, "We are cousins." Friendship and freedom are so wonderful! Only a few months earlier, we were possible battlefield enemies, and now we were friends and soldiers with deep admiration for each other.

Captain Moroni, perhaps the greatest of all Book of Mormon generals, illustrated this same respect for a former enemy. Readers of the Book of Mormon may wonder how Captain Moroni could be so bold as to allow his defeated battlefield enemies to return home after giving an oath. After my experience, Moroni's actions become especially understandable. Moroni was a battle-hardened veteran, who had learned to respect the valor of his enemy. Moroni always showed mercy to his enemy when his army had a distinct advantage. He avoided slaughter and allowed his archenemy relief and freedom if the enemy soldiers would put down their weapons and take an oath never to return. Just as Captain Moroni, we Americans were able to set our enemies free, and they worked with us to end the war and to establish freedom and peace in their newly liberated nation.

## The War Zone: A Time to Seek the Lord

The large base where we were stationed in Iraq had several hundred LDS soldiers from Utah, so forming a group for church meetings was rather easy. We met three times a week for church—once on Friday (the Muslim holy day) and twice on Sunday. It seemed to me that no matter what talk or testimony was given, the message moved to a central theme: "The Lord is in charge of our lives and the welfare of our families." We knew that the Lord loved us. Moreover, we knew that He would care for our families no matter what happened to us. It was an experience that dramatically increased my faith and changed my life. I doubt I will ever forget the role of the Lord played in my life while I was in the

Iraqi war zone. If we were faithful, he gave us understanding and hope. One example was when a group of LDS soldiers gathered in the evening to listen to general conference, which was streamed to us over the Internet. We were so excited to hear the Lord's chosen prophets and felt that it was perhaps the first time in over 2,000 years that their voices were heard in Babylon (Iraq).

Each morning I would run five miles following the walls that surrounded the compound. I would often run with fellow warrant officers, who were also very dear friends. Discussions about religion, matters of the day, and family were very cathartic. Other times, I would run alone with an MP3 player of my favorite music. Among the songs were a number of pieces from the Mormon Tabernacle Choir. This time alone was very personal and reflective, even spiritual. I can clearly remember in "Come, Come, Ye Saints" the exact spot where I was when the choir sang, "And should I die before my journey's through, Happy day! All is well!" While I was not a pioneer, I certainly had similar feelings in a very difficult and dangerous situation. It was such a blessing to be in Iraq, to come closer to the Lord, and to play a role in bringing liberty to a part of the world that had been so devastated by terrible and wicked rulers.

## Coming Home Was Wonderful But Difficult

Upon returning home, I encountered a difficult transition—most of the normal activities of life seemed trivial and unimportant. Since that time I have spoken with many of my friends that went with me to Iraq, and most have had a similar experience. Family, friends, and church became the central focus of life. Everyday life, including work and the news, became inconsequential. Complaints about the difficulties of life seemed trivial. For example, student complaints about the stress of life or school was hard to hear when compared to life in a war zone. It was as if students couldn't possibly know how truly wonderful it was to just be at BYU. Before I left for Iraq, my life was focused on personal finance, school, employment, or cultural activities, such as movies and sports. Upon my return, those parts of life seemed so simple and insignificant. I remember walking across the BYU campus and watching the students, all busy and hurrying to various buildings or activities. I wanted to stand on a wall and yell at the top of my voice, "Wake up! Be grateful the Lord lives! He is in charge! He is blessing us every day! We need to honor Him!" I'm sure most of the students were grateful and mindful of the Lord, but I assumed they were much like me before my experience with war—consumed every day

by the need to improve my personal situation in the temporal world.

While living in a war zone, the proximity to my Savior, the attention to family, and a concern for the principles of freedom became the focus of my emotions. Personal liberty is paramount! It may seem commonplace to Americans at home, but it is not commonplace to the soldier fighting for this precious principle at the peril of his or her life. Referring to our God-given agency and our inalienable rights, Thomas Jefferson said it best in the American Declaration of Independence: "We hold these truths to be self-evident, that all men are created equal, that they are endowed by their Creator with certain unalienable Rights, that among these are Life, Liberty and the pursuit of Happiness." This statement alone is worth fighting for. While in the Middle East, the concept of freedom was paramount in my thoughts. My heart and mind were filled with a love of liberty. Being free to use our agency is the governing principle of the gospel of Jesus Christ. Without freedom, the purpose of the world would come to naught.

Coming home took me away from this emotional concern for liberty. The awkward feeling that the normal pursuits of life were mundane took months of reflection to understand. I have now finished the reentry process and have a new appreciation for life. My conclusion is this—in a war zone—every soldier is confronted with danger and the possibility that any day may be his last. When a soldier comes home, the danger is gone, but the spotlight on the importance of life remains. Hence, he or she is confronted with the trivial nature of our day-to-day lives and the improper focus on the temporal self-centered world. With months of reflection, it becomes possible to live in the midst of this worldly conflict and still focus on the most important principles: God, family, and country.

## The Book of Mormon and My Experience with War

Having given you this personal background, I hope you understand how I was touched by war in the Middle East. The Book of Mormon played a major part in my understanding of war and the need to have the Lord by my side. Many people find the Book of Mormon war chapters difficult to understand. It is my prayer that my commentary will help Book of Mormon readers overcome that aversion.

The Book of Mormon was named after its principal editor and compiler. Mormon took his account from the writings of others and relied on the Spirit to tell him what was most important for our day. He would often interject an editorial within a story he was writing. On one occasion, he interrupted the story and made this comment.

*And now there are many records kept of the proceedings of this people, by many of this people, which are particular and very large, concerning them.* **But behold, a hundredth part of the proceedings of this people,** *yea, the account of the Lamanites and of the Nephites, and their wars, and contentions, and dissensions, and their preaching, and their prophecies, and their shipping and their building of ships, and their building of temples, and of synagogues and their sanctuaries, and their righteousness, and their wickedness, and their murders, and their robbings, and their plundering, and all manner of abominations and whoredoms,* **cannot be contained in this work.** *But behold, there are many books and many records of every kind, and they have been kept chiefly by the Nephites. (Helaman 3:13–15; emphasis added)*

If Mormon could not even include "a hundredth part" then why would he spend so much time on the periods of war? There is a section of the Book of Mormon that people commonly call the war chapters (Alma 43–62). If one includes several other accounts of times when war was prevalent, the chapters on war total more than 140 pages. This is over 25 percent of the Book of Mormon. Considering the difficulty Mormon had etching the history on gold plates, there must be a very serious and important message given on those precious pages. A vital part of this study will be to discover the messages delivered by the prophet-warriors in the Book of Mormon.

Mormon used an interesting literary device, the phrase "thus we see," to insert editorial messages. There are over twenty instances of this wording, which begins reflective comments on the situation or on the behavior of the people. Other times Mormon simply interjected comments in the middle of a story. An example is found in Alma 28, following an awful war in which "many thousands were slain." Mormon, a great military general, had personally experienced the ravages of war and felt inclined to make this statement after recording the history of a terrible conflict 400 years before his time.

***And thus we see*** *how great the inequality of man is because of sin and transgression, and the power of the devil,* *which comes by the cunning plans which he hath devised to ensnare the hearts of men.*

*    **And thus we see** the great call of diligence of men to labor in the vineyards of the Lord; **and thus we see** the great reason of sorrow, and also of rejoicing— sorrow because of death and destruction among men, and joy because of the light of Christ unto life. (Alma 28:13–14; emphasis added)*

It is clear that Mormon was looking forward to our time and wanted us to learn an important lesson from his historical account. Moroni, son of Mormon, was also a prophet-warrior. He finished the recorded history on the golden plates and later buried them about in AD 400. Moroni looked forward to our day and wrote the following editorial near the end of his writings. He had been blessed to see a vision of the future when the Book of Mormon would come forth. Moroni followed this proclamation with a warning, which I will quote later in the text.

*    Behold, the Lord hath shown unto me great and marvelous things concerning that which must shortly come, at that day when these things shall come forth among you. Behold, I speak unto you as if ye were present, and yet ye are not. But behold, Jesus Christ hath shown you unto me, and I know your doing. (Mormon 8:34–35)*

These great prophets saw our day and tried to inspire us to learn from their experience. The faith-inspiring heroes of the Book of Mormon have changed my life. Their poignant expressions were magnified and became especially clear while I was serving as a soldier. My meager efforts to help a captive and impoverished nation become free took on an even greater significance as I read about the incredible efforts of the Book of Mormon warriors to establish and maintain freedom in their ancient land. My study brought to light the depth of their convictions and the role that war played in their history. My purpose in writing this commentary can be simply stated: the great Book of Mormon prophets speak directly to us from their hearts and want us to see the dangers confronting us today. They lived in wicked and perilous times that required incredible faith, obedience, and sacrifice. They want us to learn from their experience and avoid the mistakes and pitfalls of their day.

I am humbled by the truths taught by the Book of Mormon authors. While writing this book, I had one primary concern: I prayed that what I wrote would increase the reader's appreciation for these marvelous prophets and their military acumen. Above all, I want to give the reader an additional opportunity to see their testimonies of Christ. With that goal in mind, I humbly present *Defenders of Faith: The Book of Mormon from a Soldier's Perspective*.

## Notes

1. *Church News*, 9 Nov. 1986, 10.
2. Conference Report, Oct. 1986; or *Ensign*, Nov. 1986.

# One

# NEPHI—PROPHET AND PROTECTOR

*I will go and do the things which the Lord hath commanded,*
*for I know that the Lord giveth no commandments*
*unto the children of men, save he shall prepare a way for them*
*that they may accomplish the thing which he commandeth them.*
YOUNG NEPHI, SON OF LEHI—1 NEPHI 3:7

*The people having loved Nephi exceedingly, he having been a great protector*
*for them, having wielded the sword of Laban in their defence,*
*and having labored in all his days for their welfare.*
JACOB, YOUNGER BROTHER OF NEPHI—JACOB 1:10

It is most appropriate that any work that discusses the characters of the Book of Mormon begin with Nephi. He is not often seen as a warrior. However, as we review his life, it will become clear that he was indeed a warrior fighting for the purposes of the Lord. Moreover, he has was the first great military commander of his people. Nephi was incredibly loyal to his father, Lehi, and dedicated to the Lord. He set the stage for the entire history of his people. In 1 Nephi 3:7, Nephi is quoted from his youth, knowing that the Lord would prepare a way if he was obedient. In Jacob 1:10, the statement is from Nephi's younger brother Jacob regarding the lifelong dedication of the beloved prophet. Nephi was not only a leader and prophet; he was also a warrior who defended his people with the sword of Laban. Indeed, Nephi was so loved that the entire nation was named after him: *the Nephites.*

## The Setting

This one-thousand-year epic story began with Lehi, a prophet of the Lord, being told through revelation that Jerusalem would be destroyed. To escape the impending devastation from Babylon, he left Jerusalem with his family in approximately 600 BC. They traveled south toward the land bordering the Red Sea. After traveling a short time, Lehi received another revelation.

> *Wherefore, the Lord hath commanded me [Lehi] that thou [Nephi] and thy brothers should go unto the house of Laban, and seek the records, and bring them down hither into the wilderness.*
>
> *And now, behold thy brothers murmur, saying it is a hard thing which I have required of them; but behold I have not required it of them, but it is a commandment of the Lord. Therefore go, my son, and thou shalt be favored of the Lord, because thou hast not murmured.*
>
> **And it came to pass that I, Nephi, said unto my father: I will go and do the things which the Lord hath commanded, for I know that the Lord giveth no commandments unto the children of men, save he shall prepare a way for them that they may accomplish the thing which he commandeth them.** (1 Nephi 3:4–7; emphasis added)

This verse is often quoted from LDS scripture. It reflects Nephi's humility and obedience, hallmarks of his character. Not only did he move forward as a younger brother with a difficult task that his older brothers shunned, he illustrated obedience and leadership that would continue throughout his life. Following the revelation and the positive response of Nephi, Lehi sent his sons back to Jerusalem to retrieve the records, which were kept on brass plates. This was not a simple task because Laban was a powerful man and commander of fifty guards and would not give up the plates willingly. The boys returned to Jerusalem. Laman, the eldest son of Lehi, went to Laban to request that he be given the plates and was summarily rejected by Laban, who threatened to kill him. In a second attempt, they tried to buy the plates with some of the wealth and property of their father (1 Nephi 3). After this attempt, Laban forcibly took those possessions and sent his guards after them with orders to slay them. Laman and Lemuel wanted to quit and return to their father. They even beat their younger brothers, Nephi and Sam. The beating was interrupted by an angel, who chastised them and said, "Why do ye smite your younger brother with a rod? Know ye not that the Lord hath chosen him [Nephi] to be a ruler over you, and this because of your iniquities? Behold ye shall go up to Jerusalem again, and the Lord will deliver Laban into your hands" (1 Nephi 3:29). Following this admonition, they made one more attempt to secure the plates. Nephi entered the city alone while his brothers remained hidden outside the walls of Jerusalem. Nephi wrote about this final attempt:

> And it came to pass that I spake unto my brethren, saying: Let us go up again unto Jerusalem, and let us be faithful in keeping the commandments of the Lord; for behold he is mightier than all the earth, then why not mightier than Laban and his fifty, yea, or even than his tens of thousands? . . .
>
> Now when I had spoken these words, they were yet wroth, and did still continue to murmur; nevertheless they did follow me up until we came without the walls of Jerusalem. And it was by night; and I caused that they should hide themselves without the walls. And after they had hid themselves, I, Nephi, crept into the city and went forth toward the house of Laban. And I was led by the Spirit, not knowing beforehand the things which I should do. . . .

> I beheld a man, and he had fallen to the earth before me, for he was drunken with wine. And when I came to him I found that it was Laban. **And I beheld his sword, and I drew it forth from the sheath thereof; and the hilt thereof was of pure gold, and the workmanship thereof was exceedingly fine, and I saw that the blade thereof was of the most precious steel.** (1 Nephi 4:1, 4–9; emphasis added)

It is interesting that Nephi was commanded by the Spirit to slay Laban. Nephi, being young and inexperienced, hesitated to obey. It took two admonitions by the Spirit and some serious thought before Nephi finally complied.

> And it came to pass that I was constrained by the Spirit that I should kill Laban; but I said in my heart: Never at any time have I shed the blood of man. And I shrunk and would that I might not slay him.
>
> And the Spirit said unto me again: Behold the Lord hath delivered him into thy hands. Yea, and I also knew that he had sought to take away mine own life; yea, and he would not hearken unto the commandments of the Lord; and he also had taken away our property. And it came

*to pass that the Spirit said unto me again: Slay him, for the Lord hath delivered him into thy hands;*

*Behold the Lord slayeth the wicked to bring forth his righteous purposes. It is better that one man should perish than that a nation should dwindle and perish in unbelief. **And now, when I, Nephi, had heard these words, I remembered the words of the Lord which he spake unto me in the wilderness, saying that: Inasmuch as thy seed shall keep my commandments, they shall prosper in the land of promise.***

*Yea, and I also thought that they could not keep the commandments of the Lord according to the law of Moses, save they should have the law. And I also knew that the law was engraven upon the plates of brass. And again, I knew that the Lord had delivered Laban into my hands for this cause—that I might obtain the records according to his commandments.*

*Therefore I did obey the voice of the Spirit, and took Laban by the hair of the head, and I smote off his head with his own sword. (1 Nephi 4:10–18; emphasis added)*

Without question, Nephi was the protector of his people beginning at very young age.

When he was only a teenager, he took on enormous responsibility. He understood the need to have the records to keep his descendants from dwindling in unbelief. Moreover, Nephi could clearly recognize the power and influence of Laban to thwart the migration of his people to a promised land. Nephi's obedience to the Lord wavered momentarily at this critical time because of the enormity of the task before him and because he regretted taking a life. Once he knew the desire of the Lord and could see the purpose behind the command, he obeyed. This is similar to all defenders of liberty. I saw this in my military experience. All soldiers want to support their freedom-loving people but none want to take a life. The wickedness of those who would take liberty and control the people is so strong that it forces patriots to defend that freedom with their lives.

Certainly, the decision to take the life of Laban was a defining moment in Nephi's life. Internally, he had previously made a commitment to follow the Spirit, and this was the first major test of his loyalty to his Lord (1 Nephi 3:7 and 4:6). Nephi took the brass plates, and the sword of Laban, and one of Laban's servants, Zoram, and returned to his father (1 Nephi 4).

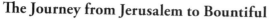

## The Journey from Jerusalem to Bountiful

The brothers returned a second time to Jerusalem to convince the family of Ishmael to come with them. Ishmael's family was large and had faithful women for the sons of Lehi to marry.

At the beginning of this impressive journey, Lehi and Nephi had marvelous visions. First, Lehi had a vision of the tree of life (1 Nephi 8). The children of Lehi had difficulty understanding the dream. In the vision, a glorious tree with fruit and a fountain of living waters was reachable by taking hold of and following a rod of iron. The rod symbolized the word of God, and the tree represented the love of God. If people grasped the rod and followed the words of God, they reached the tree and partook of the fruit. The influence of Satan and the pride of the world were represented by a large building filled with people mocking the followers of the word of God. If followers let go of the rod, they would be lost in a mist of darkness, which represented the influence of Satan. Ultimately, the lost souls would fall into a fountain or river of filthy water, which represented the depths of hell (see 1 Nephi 8, 11, 12). The vision brought both joy and sorrow to Lehi because he saw each of his sons and their future faithfulness. Nephi and Sam were faithful and partook of the fruit, while Laman and Lemuel were not faithful and drifted into unrighteousness.

Nephi wanted to understand Lehi's dream and requested help from the Lord. In response, he was given the same vision by an angel, who also gave him the interpretation. Moreover, Lehi and Nephi were both given a vision of the Savior's visit to the world. Nephi was also shown the latter days, when the gospel would come forth among the Gentiles. In addition, Nephi saw the coming forth of the Bible and the Book of Mormon (1 Nephi 11, 12, 13). Lehi was saddened to find out that Laman and Lemuel would not be faithful but was consoled somewhat because he saw his descendants who had dwindled in unbelief receive the gospel in the latter-days (1 Nephi 15).

The strength of Nephi's character is illustrated here in that the Lord blessed him at a young age with a witness of the Savior and a vision of the future. When Lehi tried to explain the visions, Laman and Lemuel complained that they could not understand. Nephi was concerned and confronted them with an age-old question:

*And I said unto them: Have ye inquired of the Lord? And they said unto me: We have not; for the Lord maketh no such thing known unto us. Behold, I said unto them: How is it that ye do not keep the commandments of the Lord? How is it that ye will perish, because of the hardness of your hearts?*

*Do ye not remember the things which the Lord hath said?—If ye will not harden your hearts, and ask me in faith, believing that ye shall receive, with diligence in keeping my commandments, surely these things shall be made known unto you. (1 Nephi 15:8–11)*

This short story at the beginning of a momentous journey is a sad but true example of a common chronicle. Failing to keep the commandments and then complaining about the consequence is a depressing narrative that is repeated many times in the forthcoming story of Lehi's descendants. This should be a lesson for all of us. The visions given to us in scripture are often difficult to understand, especially when the Spirit is not there to help us. When we are not actively following the commandments, the Spirit departs from us, and we are left to our own understanding, which is grossly inadequate. It seems ridiculous because we then complain when we create the problems.

The journey in the wilderness was difficult and lasted eight years (1 Nephi 16–17). Travel was aided by a miraculous device—the Liahona—given to Lehi by the Lord. This "curious" ball was made of brass and functioned much like a compass to tell Lehi and his family the direction to travel (1 Nephi 16:10). It also gave them messages that were periodically written it. The Liahona, however, would only function properly if they were faithful and diligent (1 Nephi 16:28–29).

Several times during the journey, tension grew into episodes of anger, during which Laman and Lemuel accused Nephi of lying about his visions. They were annoyed with the stresses of the desert and wanted to return to the good life in Jerusalem but knew that was impossible. If they returned, they would all most certainly be blamed for the death of Laban, which Nephi had caused. Anger, complaints, and murmurings happened many times (see 1 Nephi 3:5–6; 7:6–7,16; 15:7–8; 16:20, 36–37; 17:17, 45–49; 18:9–11).

In the introduction to this book, I told of my military experience in the Middle Eastern deserts of Kuwait. The heat is unbelievably harsh, and the wind and dust is unrelenting. There is no shade, and living in a hot tent with very little water becomes almost unbearable. Your body sweats constantly, and the dust sticks to you like flour to a wet hand. Under these conditions, my fellow soldiers and I became excellent complainers. It was easy to blame those who sent us there—we had left a pleasant and fruitful life, and the conditions we had come to were physically demanding. I watched good people become angry and unbearably difficult. They wanted to return home and were relentless in their complaints to the commander. This Book of Mormon story helped me see that I had become just like Laman and Lemuel: I wanted to return to the comforts of home; I resented the desert and the intense heat; I didn't know where I was being sent; and I was angry with those who brought me there. It was clear I was murmuring. In short, I can appreciate how demanding life in the desert can be, and I have come to personally understand why Laman and Lemuel complained so much. It is easy to condemn Laman and Lemuel without having had a similar experience. Having been there, I can comprehend their behavior and generate some empathy in their behalf. In difficult and perplexing conditions, people come face-to-face with difficult choices. Great literature is full of stories about the complex conflicts of life and how people learn to adjust and control their responses. When we examine our own lives, we can see how stress and difficulty have affected our behavior and how easily we can change from a pleasant person to an unpleasant one. When times are tough, it is easy to blame others, become angry, and rebel. Moreover, in harsh conditions, it is very difficult to become

humble, to listen, and to learn self-control. This expedition of approximately 1,500 miles through the desert by Lehi, Ishmael, and their families was demanding and dangerous, especially at that time. They traveled a trade route that ran along the Red Sea between Jerusalem and the southern tip of the Arabian Peninsula. There would be many thieves waiting to take not only their valuables but also their lives. The heart of this problem was that they would travel hundreds of miles in a lawless wilderness. There was only one major population center near the Indian Ocean. Consequently, they needed to travel many hundreds of miles in dangerous, harsh desert regions. The law of the desert was called "retribution." Tribes and extended families protected each other by vengeance and retribution for murder and theft. Without a tribe who knew the desert regions, travelers were in danger. The fact that the families of Lehi and Ishmael were in constant peril is illustrated by the fact that they were not able to build fires to cook their food. Fires could be seen for many miles and would alert their enemies of their presence in the area (1 Nephi 17:12). Nephi explained how the Lord helped them.

*And it came to pass that we did again take our journey in the wilderness; and we did travel nearly eastward from that*

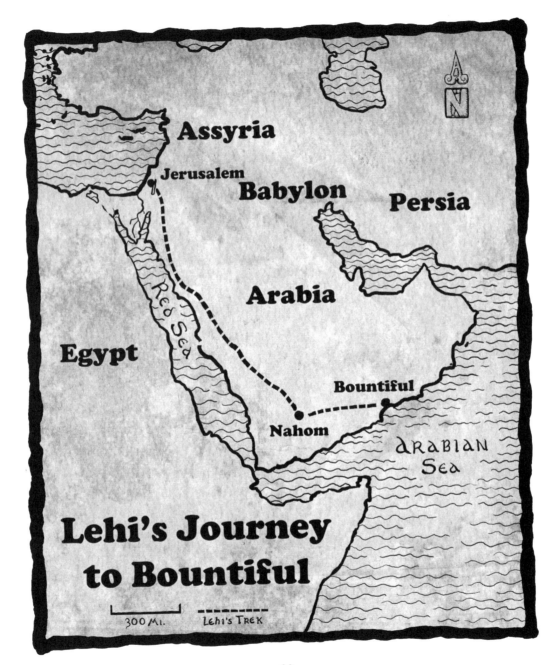

Lehi's Journey to Bountiful

*time forth. And we did travel and wade through much affliction in the wilderness; and our women did bear children in the wilderness.*

*And so great were the blessings of the Lord upon us, that while we did live upon raw meat in the wilderness, our women did give plenty of suck for their children, and were strong, yea, even like unto the men; and they began to bear their journeyings without murmurings.*

**And thus we see that the commandments of God must be fulfilled. And if it so be that the children of men keep the commandments of God he doth nourish them,** *and strengthen them, and provide means whereby they can accomplish the thing which he has commanded them; wherefore, he did provide means for us while we did sojourn in the wilderness.*

*And we did sojourn for the space of many years, yea, even eight years in the wilderness. (1 Nephi 17:1–4; emphasis added).*

Knowing how demanding the desert can be I can also appreciate how magnificent the help of the Lord must have been. My murmuring experience in the desert didn't include taking care of women and children. It is difficult to imagine how hard it would be to care for small children in those conditions. Bearing children in the harsh wilderness is certainly a miracle and speaks highly of the honorable women who bore that burden. The two families continued to journey south to somewhere near the southern part of the Arabian Peninsula. Ishmael died and was buried in a place called "Nahom" (1 Nephi 16:34). Subsequently, they traveled east to a point on the most southern tip of the peninsula near the Arabian Sea, which they called "Bountiful" (1 Nephi 17). This was a restful place with fruit to eat and trees for lumber. The scriptures tell us that Nephi was called into the mountains and told by the Lord to build a ship under His direction. During this hectic time of construction, Nephi explains that he went often into the mountains to seek guidance from the Lord: "And I, Nephi, did go unto the mountains oft, and I did pray oft to the Lord; wherefore the Lord showed unto me many great things" (1 Nephi 18:3). The Lord revealed where he could find ore to make tools and gave him directions on how to build the ship (1 Nephi 17:6–11). Laman and Lemuel thought this project was complete folly. They complained and even plotted to kill Nephi and his father.

*And it came to pass that the daughters of Ishmael did mourn exceedingly, because* of the loss of their father, and because of their afflictions in the wilderness; and they did murmur against my father, because he had brought them out of the land of Jerusalem, saying: Our father is dead; yea, and we have wandered much in the wilderness, and we have suffered much affliction, hunger, thirst, and fatigue; and after all these sufferings we must perish in the wilderness with hunger.

And thus they did murmur against my father, and also against me; and they were desirous to return again to Jerusalem. And Laman said unto Lemuel and also unto the sons of Ishmael: Behold, let us slay our father, and also our brother Nephi, who has taken it upon him to be our ruler and our teacher, who are his elder brethren.

Now, he says that the Lord has talked with him, and also that angels have ministered unto him. But behold, we know that he lies unto us; and he tells us these things, and he worketh many things by his cunning arts, that he may deceive our eyes, thinking, perhaps, that he may lead us away into some strange wilderness; and after he has led us away, he has thought to make himself a king and a ruler over us, that he may do with us according to his will and pleasure. And after this manner

did my brother Laman stir up their hearts to anger. (1 Nephi 16:35–38)

These statements present a pattern of complaints that lasted for centuries—complaints that generated so much hate that Laman and Lemuel justified their plan to murder Lehi and Nephi. However, at this point, the Lord was not willing to let this anger stop the migration of His chosen people to a new and promised land. Nephi spoke with great strength, and Laman and Lemuel were given a sign to bring them back to reality and some sense of righteousness.

Behold, my soul is rent with anguish because of you, and my heart is pained; I fear lest ye shall be cast off forever. Behold, I am full of the Spirit of God, insomuch that my frame has no strength.

And now it came to pass that when I had spoken these words they were angry with me, and were desirous to throw me into the depths of the sea; and as they came forth to lay their hands upon me I spake unto them, saying: In the name of the Almighty God, I command you that ye touch me not, for I am filled with the power of God, even unto the consuming of my flesh; and whoso shall lay his hands upon me shall wither even as a dried reed; and he shall be as naught before the power *of God, for God shall smite him.*

**And it came to pass that I, Nephi, said unto them that they should murmur no more against their father; neither should they withhold their labor from me, for God had commanded me that I should build a ship. . . .**

*And it came to pass that I, Nephi, said many things unto my brethren, insomuch that they were confounded and could not contend against me; neither durst they lay their hands upon me nor touch me with their fingers, even for the space of many days. Now they durst not do this lest they should wither before me, so powerful was the Spirit of God; and thus it had wrought upon them.*

*And it came to pass that the Lord said unto me: Stretch forth thine hand again unto thy brethren, and they shall not wither before thee, but I will shock them, saith the Lord, and this will I do, that they may know that I am the Lord their God.*

**And it came to pass that I stretched forth my hand unto my brethren, and they did not wither before me; but the Lord did shake them, even according to the word which he had spoken.**

**And now, they said: We know of** **a surety that the Lord is with thee, for we know that it is the power of the Lord that has shaken us.** *And they fell down before me, and were about to worship me, but I would not suffer them, saying: I am thy brother, yea, even thy younger brother; wherefore, worship the Lord thy God, and honor thy father and thy mother, that thy days may be long in the land which the Lord thy God shall give thee. (1 Nephi 17:47–49, 52–55; emphasis added)*

Nephi remained close to the Lord, and the Lord worked through him to lead His people. After this shocking experience, Laman, Lemuel, and their families helped Nephi finish building the ship. They placed the vessel in the Arabian Sea and sailed eastward toward the promised land. We are not told much about the voyage, except for another series of complaints by the older brothers. This episode of rebellion was also stopped by an intervention from the Lord (1 Nephi 18). The small ship with a group of about fifty people aboard sailed through the Indian Ocean and across the Pacific Ocean, arriving on the shores of a new promised land. Most analysts who study the geography of the Book of Mormon believe that Lehi landed somewhere on the South American continent, most likely near Mesoamerica.

They named the area where they started their civilization the Land of First Inheritance. Throughout the Book of Mormon, this territory was often referred to as the Land of Nephi. As they explored their new land and moved from place to place, they normally spoke of the mountains as wilderness. The map below gives an idea of the landscape and includes a number of the descriptors used by the authors throughout the Book of Mormon.

## Lands of the Book of Mormon

Nephi was faithful and obedient to his father, their prophet and leader; consequently,

**Promised Land**
**with Nephite Territorial Names**

Land
Northward

NARROW NECK
OF LAND

Land
Bountiful

WILDERNESS

Land of
Jershon

RIVER SIDON

Land of
Desolation

WILDERNESS

Land of
Zarahemla

NARROW STRIP
OF WILDERNESS

Land of First Inheritance
Land of Nephi

the Lord favored them with prosperity. Over time, the older sons of Lehi showed increasing animosity toward Nephi. The initial supporters of Nephi were Lehi and his youngest sons— Sam, Jacob, Joseph—and their families. They called themselves Nephites, while the followers of Laman and Lemuel were called Lamanites.

Throughout nearly one thousand years, these two great civilizations grew and prospered. There were times of peace and growth, but often the animosity between the two nations turned to hatred, which led to armed conflict.

Nephi was a humble person who did not speak of his accomplishments as a nation builder, and we do not have details from his writings about military conflicts or the defense of his people. The reason for this is that a large part of the secular history of the descendants of Lehi from 600 BC to 130 BC is not recorded in the Book of Mormon we have. We do, however, have a record of their spiritual history kept by the prophets. Nephi started writing a separate religious history, and it was continued for approximately 470 years by succeeding Nephite prophets and leaders.

These ancient records were written on metal plates in a reformed Egyptian text. Nephi explained the two records. A secular, historical account was written on what he called the large plates, and a religious history was kept on what Nephi called the small plates. I will not attempt to explain the reasons for this process but will give you Nephi's explanation in his own words.

*And it came to pass that the Lord commanded me, wherefore I did make plates of ore that I might engraven upon them the record of my people. And upon the plates which I made I did engraven the record of my father, and also our journeyings in the wilderness, and the prophecies of my father; and also many of mine own prophecies have I engraven upon them…*

*And after I had made these plates [the large plates of Nephi] by way of commandment, I, Nephi, received a commandment that the ministry and the prophecies, the more plain and precious parts of them, should be written upon these plates [the small plates of Nephi] . . .*

***Wherefore, I, Nephi, did make a record upon the other plates [the large plates of Nephi], which gives an account, or which gives a greater account of the wars and contentions and destructions of my people.*** *(1 Nephi 19:1, 3–4; emphasis added)*

The Book of Mormon originally contained the secular history of Lehi's descendants, but 113 pages were lost by Martin Harris, a friend of Joseph Smith (see Doctrine and Covenants 3). The record of the small plates covered the same period of time and was inserted in the place of the lost portion. Because we only have the history from the small plates, we know very little of the initial wars fought between the descendants and followers of the sons of Lehi. We are told only that the Lord, approximately twenty years after the landing in the promised land, warned Nephi that his older brothers intended to take their lives. Because of the danger, Nephi and his followers migrated to a place north of the Land of First Inheritance (see 2 Nephi 5:1–5).

For several hundred years, there were wars and conflicts with the Lamanites. The wars were reported but details were not given (see Enos 1:20; Jarom 1:7; Omni 1:2). In approximately 280 BC, the Nephites moved farther north and eventually discovered the people of Zarahemla and joined with them. These people were also immigrants from Jerusalem and descendants of Mulek, one of the sons of the Jewish king Zedekiah. However, the Mulekites failed to bring their history with them and didn't keep records. As a result, their faith had dwindled, and their language became corrupted. When joined together, these two nations were eventually called the people of Nephi (see Omni 1:14–19).

Nephi's younger brother Jacob recorded the Nephite efforts to reconcile with the Lamanites and explained the dreadful hatred of their older brothers and their descendants.

*And it came to pass that many means were devised to reclaim and restore the Lamanites to the knowledge of the truth; but it all was vain, for they delighted in wars and bloodshed, and they had an eternal hatred against us, their brethren. And they sought by the power of their arms to destroy us continually. Wherefore, the people of Nephi did fortify against them with their arms, and with all their might, trusting in the God and rock of their salvation; wherefore, they became as yet, conquerors of their enemies. (Jacob 7:24–25)*

Jacob gave the plates to his son Enos, who also described the hatred of the Lamanites and the Nephite attempts to reunite the two nations.

*And I bear record that the people of Nephi did seek diligently to restore the Lamanites unto the true faith in God. But our labors were vain; their hatred was fixed, and they were led by their evil nature that they became wild, and ferocious, and a blood-thirsty people, full of idolatry and filthiness; feeding upon beasts of prey; dwelling in tents, and wandering about in the wilderness with a short skin girdle about their loins and their heads shaven; and their skill was in the bow, and in the cimeter, and the ax. And many of them did eat nothing save it was raw meat; and they were continually seeking to destroy us. (Enos 1:20)*

The hatred of the Lamanites toward the Nephites is illustrated in greater detail by the writings of Zeniff, approximately 400 years after the arrival in the promised land. The animosity had been sustained through many generations based on traditions set forth by Laman and his brother Lemuel.

> *Now, the Lamanites knew nothing concerning the Lord, nor the strength of the Lord, therefore they depended upon their own strength. Yet they were a strong people, as to the strength of men. They were a wild, and ferocious, and a bloodthirsty people, believing in the traditions of their fathers, which is this—*
> * *Believing that they were driven out of the land of Jerusalem because of the iniquities of their fathers, and*
> * *that they were wronged in the wilderness by their brethren, and*
> * *they were also wronged while crossing the sea; and again, that*
> * *they were wronged while in the land of their first inheritance . . .*
> * *they said that he [Nephi] had taken the ruling of the people out of their hands . . .*
> * *they were wroth because he [Nephi] departed into the wilderness as the Lord had commanded him, and took the records which were engraven on the plates of brass, for they said that he robbed them.*
> **And thus they have taught their children that they should hate them [Nephites], and that they should murder them, and that they should rob and plunder them, and do all they could to destroy them; therefore they have an eternal hatred toward the children of Nephi.**
> (Mosiah 10:11–17; emphasis and bullet points added)

This is such a sad commentary. When a person or a people reject the Spirit, the consequences are monumental. Their prosperity is hindered and their lives become driven by satanic animosity for those who are prospering from the Lord's blessings.

## Nephi: Warrior and Protector of the People

While an extended secular history is not available in the records of the small plates, it is clear that there were fierce wars and contentions between these two emerging civilizations. Nephi was undoubtedly in the midst of this contention and was obligated to physically defend his people. Nephi's younger brother Jacob became the prophet and historian after Nephi. He wrote about Nephi as a great warrior who was beloved and honored by his people.

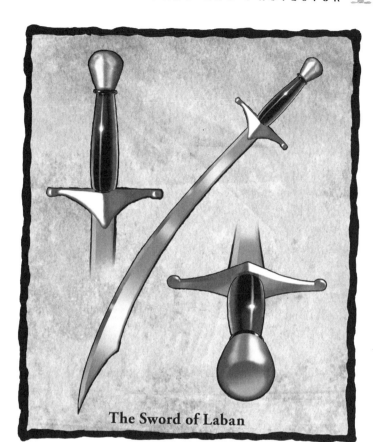

**The Sword of Laban**

Now Nephi began to be old, and he saw that he must soon die; wherefore, he anointed a man to be a king and a ruler over his people now, according to the reigns of the kings. **The people having loved Nephi exceedingly, he having been a great protector for them, having wielded the sword of Laban in their defense, and having labored in all his days for their welfare**—Wherefore, the people were desirous to retain in remembrance his name. And whoso should reign in his stead were called by the people, second Nephi, third Nephi, and so forth, according to the reigns of the kings; and thus they were called by the people. (Jacob 1:9–11; emphasis added)

Nephi was so beloved that the kings following him took upon themselves the name of Nephi, similar to the pharaohs of Egypt. A key part of this passage indicates that Nephi was the "great protector" and had "wielded the sword of Laban in their defence" (Jacob 1:10). The sword of Laban was one of the few possessions from Jerusalem taken to the promised land along with Old Testament scriptures, which were recorded on plates of brass.

To Nephi, the sword of Laban became a symbol of the strength that the Lord would give to his righteous followers, but it also served a practical purpose for the Nephites. In the process of defending themselves against the followers of Laman, Nephi used the sword of Laban as a template to make many swords for use in battle. Using ancient swords and weapons as examples and with the help of a wonderful artist, we made an illustration of how the sword of Laban may have appeared. Hopefully, it presents a picture of how magnificent the sword must have been.

*And it came to pass that we began to prosper exceedingly, and to multiply in the land.* **And I, Nephi, did take the sword of Laban, and after the manner of it did make many swords,** *lest by any means the people who were now called Lamanites should come upon us and destroy us; for I knew their hatred toward me and my children and those who were called my people. (2 Nephi 5:13–14; emphasis added)*

## Nephi's Remorse over the Wrath of War

The small note about Nephi defending his people with the sword of Laban is significant in a military sense because the practice of kings in that era was to advance as the commanding soldier in front of their army. Undoubtedly, Nephi risked his life defending his people. War is terrible in any time, but in Nephi's time it was particularly difficult when fought with swords, spears, and bows. Combat inevitably became face-to-face confrontation. The extreme nature of these first Nephite conflicts is highlighted by the fact that Nephi was forced to defend his family against other family members. It is likely that Nephi had slain people he knew, and perhaps even one or both of his brothers. We know little of Nephi's family or sons, but it is likely that his sons fought at the front line with Nephi and may have been killed. We do know, however, that Nephi did not appoint a son to be the king. If he had a living righteous son, he would have most likely been appointed to follow Nephi as king.

A section in the writings of Nephi may

refer to his remorse for having been forced into armed conflict. These passages are in chapter four of 2 Nephi. These poetic verses are often called "Nephi's Psalm." When reading these passages, I have often wondered how a man of such great stature and righteousness could feel so depressed. Knowing that he had to defend his people with the sword and slay family members may be explain the sorrow expressed in these passages. Another clue as to why Nephi would lament comes from an earlier statement. In the first part of chapter four, Nephi wrote about the blessings given by his father to his brothers, and particularly the blessings of Laman and Lemuel. These chapters were probably written at least thirty years after leaving Jerusalem, and Nephi was possibly reflecting on the needless rebellion that came in a promised land that had plenty for all. While writing this history, Nephi might have been reminded of the hate generated by his brothers and their attempts on his life. Moreover, he probably remembered that Laman and Lemuel had forfeited the blessings given by the hand of Father Lehi. Laman and Lemuel were cursed because of their lack of faith and resulting resentment. Shortly after giving these prophetic blessings to his children, Lehi died. Perhaps Nephi was reflecting on his father's death, which could be another explanation for Nephi's sadness.

The blessings given by Lehi to Laman were recorded in the following verses.

> *Wherefore, after my father had made an end of speaking concerning the prophecies of Joseph, he called the children of Laman, his sons, and his daughters, and said unto them: Behold, my sons, and my daughters, who are the sons and the daughters of my first-born, I would that ye should give ear unto my words.*
>
> *For the Lord God hath said that: inasmuch as ye shall keep my commandments ye shall prosper in the land; and inasmuch as ye will not keep my commandments ye shall be cut off from my presence. (2 Nephi 4:3–4)*

Writing about the blessings Lehi gave to his children most likely deeply concerned Nephi. He had seen the Spirit of the Lord withdraw from his older brothers and their children. Subsequently, he experienced the animosity of his older brothers, which brought them to armed conflict.

## Nephi's Psalm—A Soldier's Prayer

Filled with sadness and remorse from the devastation of war, Nephi wrote his deepest feelings. A close examination reveals that these poetic verses are expressed as a *soldier's* prayer. This will become more evident as we focus on his feelings and expressions. To allow Nephi to speak directly to you, I will include the full text first with some brief headings and highlighted passages. Later, I will discuss highlighted words and their possible meanings. While reading, please take note of the organization of Nephi's thoughts. He praises the Lord, recognizes his personal weaknesses, makes specific requests, and ends with a covenant. This is a wonderful pattern for all prayers.

### A Statement of Appreciation for the Gospel

*For my soul delighteth in the scriptures, and my heart pondereth them, and writeth them for the learning and the profit of my children. Behold, my soul delighteth in the things of the Lord; and my heart pondereth continually upon the things which I have seen and heard.*

### An Expression of Sorrow

*Nevertheless, notwithstanding the great goodness of the Lord, in showing me his great and marvelous works, my heart exclaimeth:* **O wretched man that I am! Yea, my heart sorroweth because of my flesh; my soul grieveth because of mine iniquities.**

**I am encompassed about, because of the temptations and the sins which do so easily beset me. And when I desire to rejoice, my heart groaneth because of my sins; nevertheless, I know in whom I have trusted.**

### An Announcement of Gratitude

*My God hath been my support he hath led me through mine afflictions in the wilderness; and he hath preserved me upon the waters of the great deep. He hath filled me with his love, even unto the consuming of my flesh.* **He hath confounded mine enemies, unto the causing of them to quake before me. Behold, he hath heard my cry by day, and he hath given me knowledge by visions in the night-time.**

*And by day have I waxed bold in mighty prayer before him; yea, my voice have I sent up on high; and angels came down and ministered unto me. And upon the wings of his Spirit hath my body been carried away upon exceedingly high mountains. And mine eyes have beheld great things, yea, even too great for man; therefore I was bidden that I should not write them.*

## A DECLARATION OF REGRET

*O then, if I have seen so great things, if the Lord in his condescension unto the children of men hath visited men in so much mercy, why should my heart weep and my soul linger in the valley of sorrow, and my flesh waste away, and my strength slacken, because of mine afflictions?*

**And why should I yield to sin, because of my flesh? Yea, why should I give way to temptations, that the evil one have place in my heart to destroy my peace and afflict my soul? Why am I angry because of mine enemy?**

*Awake, my soul! No longer droop in sin. Rejoice, O my heart, and give place no more for the enemy of my soul. Do not anger again because of mine enemies. Do not slacken my strength because of mine afflictions.*

## A REQUEST FOR HELP

*Rejoice, O my heart, and cry unto the Lord, and say: O Lord, I will praise thee forever; yea, my soul will rejoice in thee, my God, and the rock of my salvation.* **O Lord, wilt thou redeem my soul?**

**Wilt thou deliver me out of the hands of mine enemies? Wilt thou make me that I may shake at the appearance of sin?** *May the gates of hell be shut continually before me, because that my heart is broken and my spirit is contrite! O Lord, wilt thou not shut the gates of thy righteousness before me, that I may walk in the path of the low valley, that I may be strict in the plain road! O Lord, wilt thou encircle me around in the robe of thy righteousness!*

**O Lord, wilt thou make a way for mine escape before mine enemies! Wilt thou make my path straight before me! Wilt thou not place a stumbling block in my way—but that thou wouldst clear my way before me, and hedge not up my way, but the ways of mine enemy.**

## A PROMISE AND COVENANT WITH THE LORD

**O Lord, I have trusted in thee, and I will trust in thee forever. I will not put my trust in the arm of flesh; for I know that cursed is he that putteth his trust in the arm of flesh. Yea, cursed is he that putteth his trust in man or maketh flesh his arm.**

**Yea, I know that God will give liberally to him that asketh. Yea, my God will give me, if I ask not amiss;**

*therefore I will lift up my voice unto thee; yea, I will cry unto thee, my God, the rock of my righteousness. Behold, my voice shall forever ascend up unto thee, my rock and mine everlasting God. Amen.* (2 Nephi 4:15–35; *emphasis and headings added*)

## A Soldier's Reflection on Nephi's Psalm

As a soldier, this prayer is deeply touching and reflects upon the truly sensitive character of Nephi. Nephi says he is "easily beset"(v. 18) by temptations and sin. With what sin could such a faithful and dedicated person be so easily beset? This wonderful prophet had conversed with angels and seen many visions—only the most righteous could be so blessed. Nephi had survived the lawless Middle Eastern deserts inundated with bands of robbers that would take his life and steal all his possessions with no regard. Nephi was an innovative genius who, with the help of the Lord, built a ship and then took the leap of faith to cross uncharted oceans. Moreover, he had founded a new civilization and was so loved that his people called all the subsequent kings *Nephi*.

Why would this righteous leader and prophet be so sad and repentant? An answer

to this might be found by considering these statements in context with the devastation of their wars and how they were fought. First, kings advanced at the head of their armies. Consequently, Nephi had been the lead warrior in battle against members of his own family who were motivated by resentment and filled with contempt. Second, Nephi fought in hand-to-hand combat with the sword of Laban. Try to imagine this enormous conflict and the contrast between angelic visions from the Lord and the calamities of war. With this knowledge as a backdrop, it is easier to appreciate why Nephi says he was "easily beset" by sin. Think of the rage generated by combat with his "enemies" (v. 22). Nephi states, "And why should I yield to sin, because of my flesh? Yea, why should I give way to temptation, that the evil one have place in my heart to destroy my peace and afflict my soul? Why am I angry because of mine enemy?" (v. 27). Nephi, a prophet of God filled with the love of Christ, was forced to defend himself and his people at the peril of his life. Most people of routine faith could rationalize these emotions and make excuses for their rage and anger. Not Nephi—he had partaken of the fruit of the "tree of life" and seen a vision of the birth and crucifixion of the Savior. Having previously been so touched by prophetic visions, Nephi was concerned about losing the Spirit.

To Nephi, anger was a sin that caused the Spirit to withdraw. In fact, his sorrow would be multiplied many times over what you and I would experience. Nephi asked the question, "Why am I angry because of mine enemy?" Temptation brought the "evil one" into his "heart to destroy [his] peace and afflict [his] soul" (v. 27). Being so close to death in battle and even causing death by the sword may have motivated him to make this sacred request. "Awake, my soul! No longer droop in sin. Rejoice, O my heart, and give place no more for the enemy of my soul. Do not anger again because of mine enemies. Do not slacken my strength because of mine afflictions" (vv. 28–29).

Normally a great military general would rejoice in victory. For Nephi, this was impossible. He had defeated his enemy; however, his achievements on the field of battle were bitter and empty. He said, "And when I desire to rejoice, my heart groaneth because of my sins" (v. 19). It is evident that the conflict with his older brothers, both in battle and in spirit, brought sadness to his soul.

This stunning poetic prayer sounds more like a soldier's prayer when Nephi finishes with this humble, heartfelt request for help on the battlefield.

### O Lord, wilt thou make a way

*for mine escape before mine enemies. Wilt thou make my path straight before me! Wilt thou not place a stumbling block in my way—but that thou wouldst clear my way before me, and hedge not up my way, but the ways of mine enemy.*

*O Lord, I have trusted in thee, and I will trust in thee forever. I will not put my trust in the arm of flesh; for I know that cursed is he that putteth his trust in the arm of flesh. Yea, cursed is he that putteth his trust in man or maketh flesh his arm. (2 Nephi 4:33–34; emphasis added)*

Nephi refused to trust in the arm of flesh. This means that he would not allow pride to poison his soul. He would not take personal credit for victory and believe that his training, skill, or strategy were the reasons for success. He saw this trust in the arm of flesh (personal ability) as a curse. His trust was in the Lord.

Going to war brings many emotions that are difficult to express. I can't pretend to be as poetic as Nephi nor as close to the Lord, but I do remember the sleepless night I had before flying into Baghdad. I sought comfort from the Lord about my role in the war and asked for an assurance that He would care for my family. Nephi's psalm is a profound example of a righteous soldier pouring his heart out to the Lord, asking for support on the battlefield, and seeking a release from the rage and fury brought on by the experience of war. Please take note of his final, prayerful declaration of love and faith in the Lord.

> *Yea, I know that God will give liberally to him that asketh. Yea, my God will give me, if I ask not amiss; therefore I will lift up my voice unto thee; yea, I will cry unto thee, my God, the rock of my righteousness. Behold, my voice shall forever ascend up unto thee, my rock and mine everlasting God. Amen. (2 Nephi 4:35)*

These heroic and emotional passages are a wonderful literary addition to scriptural poetry. They truly belong among the greatest of all scriptural passages wherein men cry for the support of the Lord.

## Nephi: An Outstanding Leader and Example of Courage, Faith, and Obedience

Nephi was one of the most excellent leaders to ever live. His life illustrates almost unbelievable discipline in the midst of terrible circumstances. His loyalty to his God is comparable to all of the great patriarchs and descendants of Abraham.

In an attempt to put this in perspective, let us suppose that we are searching for a person who would complete a series of difficult tasks. This person would take an oath and complete their tasks regardless of the difficulty. These tasks would require that the person would carry out every assignment with explicit detail. The daunting nature of these tasks would bring fear into the hearts of most men and would require infinite courage. Imagine that the tasks would require the utmost bravery—to boldly stand with a mighty sword and look the enraged enemy straight in the eyes. And finally these tasks would call for a person who would be the ideal disciple of Christ—that no matter the circumstance, his faith would not falter. Without question, you would want a person with the character, obedience, and faith of Nephi. As a soldier, I have watched world events unfold and have desired a strong leader with the strength and faith of Nephi to emerge. A truly great commander needs charisma, character, discipline, and knowledge of true principles. I am in awe of the amazing leadership illustrated by the life of Nephi. He was truly a role model for all leaders to emulate.

Nephi played a important role in blessing his people. Imagine for a moment the remarkable accomplishments that Nephi carried out for the Lord. He supported his righteous father

in leading a chosen people in their escape from Jerusalem before it was destroyed in 600 BC. As a teenager, Nephi retrieved a spiritual record from a seemingly invincible foe with a small army of guards. Nephi provided the spiritual force that held a splintered and often unhappy family together for eight years while crossing a treacherous desert—a journey through a wilderness filled with thieves and enemies. Imagine the difficulty that Nephi and his wife shared while bearing children and raising their young family in the intense heat and filth of the Arabian Desert. After crossing the desert and reaching Bountiful, Nephi mined ore and created the metal tools needed to construct a seagoing vessel. He then constructed it to the Lord's exact specifications. At this point, Nephi took an enormous leap of faith and captained the ship over two huge oceans, ultimately arriving in an untamed but beautiful promised land. Nephi was then faced with the task of founding a new nation with the support of his father and three younger brothers while his older brothers complained and sought to take his life. Visualize for a moment the leadership and personal fortitude needed to found and motivate a new civilization based on fair laws and principles of righteousness. As if this were not enough, Nephi was forced to defend his fledgling nation from the armies of his older brothers consumed with animosity and hate. Nephi was truly a monumental leader often seeking and receiving the support of the Lord to carry him through these seemingly impossible tasks. Now, after all this, the Lord asked him to write this story on plates of gold. In this responsibility as an author, Nephi fulfilled perhaps the greatest of all his roles: he was a witness for the Savior, Jesus Christ. The following verses are Nephi's last statements to us.

*And I pray the Father in the name of Christ that many of us, if not all, may be saved in his kingdom at that great and last day.*

*And now, my beloved brethren, all those who are of the house of Israel, and all ye ends of the earth, I speak unto you as the voice of one crying from the dust: Farewell until that great day shall come.*

*And you that will not partake of the goodness of God, and respect the words of the Jews, and also my words, and the words which shall proceed forth out of the mouth of the Lamb of God, behold, I bid you an everlasting farewell, for these words shall condemn you at the last day.*

***For what I seal on earth, shall be brought against you at the judgment bar; for thus hath the Lord commanded me, and I must obey.***

*Amen. (2 Nephi 33:12–15; emphasis added)*

The loyalty of an obedient servant, the discipline of a valiant soldier, and the humility of a prophet is evident in Nephi's last written words, "I must obey. Amen" (v. 15).

## The Great Commander's First Order to Us: Seek the Lord and Obey Him

When discussing each of these great Book of Mormon prophets, it is imperative that I give you their message as stated in their own words. The first major message of Nephi is given shortly after Nephi's father, Lehi, left Jerusalem and took his family into the wilderness. Nephi was distressed over the disobedient and defiant nature of his older brothers, Laman and Lemuel. He turned to the Lord for guidance and was given this answer, which he conveyed to his brothers.

> *And it came to pass that the Lord spake unto me, saying: Blessed art thou, Nephi, because of thy faith, for thou hast sought me diligently, with lowliness of heart.* **And inasmuch as ye shall keep my commandments, ye shall prosper, and shall be led to a land of promise; yea, even a land which I have pre-**

**pared for you; yea, a land which is choice above all other lands.** *(1 Nephi 2:19–20; emphasis added)*

This is much more than personal obedience—this is a covenant. A covenant is a two-way promise that involves the Lord—obedience is imperative. The message is clear and is not just intended for Nephi. All of us who live in the promised land (the Americas) in the latter days are under the obligations of this covenant. We promise to remember Christ and keep the commandments, and the Lord promises to bless the land with prosperity and a flourishing gospel.

This becomes a major theme throughout the Book of Mormon. The land would be blessed far beyond all other lands if the people would just keep the commandments. This promise was echoed by virtually every prophet in the one-thousand-year history of the Nephites. Nephi's father, Lehi, restated this promise in his last sermon.

> *Wherefore, I, Lehi, have obtained a promise, that inasmuch as those whom the Lord God shall bring out of the land of Jerusalem shall keep his commandments, they shall prosper upon the face of this land; and they shall be kept from all other nations, that they may possess this land unto themselves. . . .*

*But behold, when the time cometh that they shall dwindle in unbelief, after they have received so great blessings from the hand of the Lord—having a knowledge of the creation of the earth, and all men, knowing the great and marvelous works of the Lord from the creation of the world; having power given them to do all things by faith; having all the commandments from the beginning, and having been brought by his infinite goodness into this precious land of promise—behold, I say, if the day shall come that they will reject the Holy One of Israel, the true Messiah, their Redeemer and their God, behold, the judgments of him that is just shall rest upon them.* (2 Nephi 1:9–10; emphasis added)

In his two books, Nephi wrote in such a way as to be absolutely certain that we would not miss this covenant and the consequence for our disobedience—keep the commandments or be swept off the land.

### The Commander's Second Order to Us: Read and Ponder the Scriptures

It is certain that Nephi had a great love of the scriptures. He had risked his life to obtain the brass plates from Laban. Thereafter, he had studied and rejoiced in the writings he found on the plates. Addressing his love of the scriptures, Nephi wrote the following:

*And upon these [small plates] I write the things of my soul and many of the scriptures which are engraven upon the plates of brass. **For my soul delighteth in the scriptures and my heart pondereth them, and writeth them for the learning and the profit of my children.*** (2 Nephi 4:15; emphasis added)

Without question, Nephi wants us to "ponder" the scriptures. He often speaks of his "delight" for the written word of God. His comments give us a pattern to follow as we read and study the scriptures. It is essential that we think seriously when we study. His hope, I'm sure, is that we will also learn to "liken them unto us." Nephi's express purpose was to apply the messages and stories to the lives of his family.

*And now I, Nephi, write more of the words of Isaiah, for my soul delighteth in his words. For I will liken his words unto my people, and I will send them forth unto all my children, for he verily saw my Redeemer, even as I have seen him. . . .*

*And my brother, Jacob, also has seen him as I have seen him; wherefore, I will send their words forth unto my children to prove unto them that my words are true. Wherefore, by the words of three, God hath said, I will establish my word. Nevertheless, God sendeth more witnesses, and he proveth all his words.*

*And now I write some of the words of Isaiah, that whoso of my people shall see these words may lift up their hearts and rejoice for all men. Now these are the words, and ye may liken them unto you and unto all men. (2 Nephi 11:2–8)*

Nephi "rejoiced" in the words of Isaiah and encourages us to do the same. In the midst of his writings Nephi included seventeen chapters of Isaiah. Their value, while often overlooked, is unmistakable. Isaiah prophesied of the rise of Babylon and the captivity of the Jews. Moreover, Isaiah told of the coming Savior and His sacrifice. Nephi marveled at the way Isaiah prophesied of the latter days and told us to be aware and watch Isaiah's prophecies happen. Inspired by the writings of Isaiah, Nephi made his own declarations of the latter days.

*But behold, I proceed with mine own prophecy, according to my plainness; in the which I know that no man can err; nevertheless, in the days that the prophecies of Isaiah shall be fulfilled men shall know of a surety, at the times when they shall*

*come to pass.* **Wherefore, they are of worth unto the children of men, and he that supposeth that they are not, unto them will I speak particularly, and confine the words unto mine own people; for I know that they shall be of great worth unto them in the last days; for in that day shall they understand them; wherefore, for their good have I written them.** *(2 Nephi 25:7–8; emphasis added)*

Nephi's visions and prophecies are found throughout his writings and are of great worth to us because of his "plainness." His visions include the birth and the life of Christ. He saw the gathering of Israel in the latter days. He also saw the restoration of the gospel of Jesus Christ and the coming forth of the Book of Mormon.

### The Commander's Final Statement to the People of the Latter Days

The third spiritual message of this prophet and commander was given later in his life and was meant for the people of the latter days. He testified of the value and truth of the words he had recorded. His prophetic witness of Christ and the Book of Mormon is simple and unmistakable.

*Wherefore, these things [the Book of Mormon] shall go from generation to generation as long as the earth shall stand; and they shall go according to the will and pleasure of God; and the nations who shall possess them shall be judged of them according to the words which are written.*

*For we labor diligently to write, to persuade our children, and also our brethren, to believe in Christ, and to be reconciled to God; for we know that it is by grace that we are saved, after all we can do. . . . **And we talk of Christ, we rejoice in Christ, we preach of Christ, we prophesy of Christ, and we write according to our prophecies, that our children may know to what source they may look for remission of their sins.** (2 Nephi 25:22–23, 26; emphasis added)*

The distinct clarity in the writings of Nephi is wonderful. He leaves no room for doubt or confusion. As he finishes his writing, Nephi bears his witness of Christ with delicate precision.

*And now, my beloved brethren, and also Jew, and all ye ends of the earth, hearken unto these words and believe in Christ; and if ye believe not in these words believe in Christ. And if ye shall believe in Christ ye will believe in these words, for they are the words of Christ, and he hath given them unto me; and they teach all men that they should do good.*

***And if they are not the words of Christ, judge ye—for Christ will show unto you, with power and great glory, that they are his words, at the last day; and you and I shall stand face to face before his bar; and ye shall know that I have been commanded of him to write these things, notwithstanding my weakness.** (2 Nephi 33:10–11; emphasis added)*

There is no doubt that the great leader and commander Nephi will be there at the final judgment, where Christ himself will confirm Nephi's testimony.

# Two

# ALMA THE YOUNGER, PROPHET-WARRIOR

*O that I were an angel, and could have the wish of mine heart,*
*that I might go forth and speak with the trump of God, with a voice*
*to shake the earth, and cry repentance to every people!"*
ALMA 29:1

Near the end of his writings, Alma made this grand statement of desire. His life is a reflection of his love of the Lord and his peoples. The touching personal story of Alma begins with his turbulent youth. Knowing about Alma's troubled past illuminates his adult life. Alma and the sons of Mosiah were close friends and children of royalty. The sons of Mosiah were the sons of the righteous king of the Nephites, and Alma was the son of Alma, prophet and leader of the church. To distinguish between the father and the son, modern day readers of the Book of Mormon often call the son Alma the Younger. Alma the Younger and the four sons of Mosiah (Ammon, Aaron, Omner, and Himni) were more than just rebellious; they consciously tried to mislead the faithful Christians and destroy the church. These young friends were members of a defiant group of "unbelievers" led by Alma the Younger. They led many saints astray with their energy for contrary opinion and lies. King Mosiah described their behavior this way.

*Now the sons of Mosiah were numbered among the unbelievers; and also one of the sons of Alma was numbered among them, he being called Alma, after his father; nevertheless, he became a very wicked and an idolatrous man.* **And he [Alma] was a man of many words, and did speak much flattery to the people; therefore he led many of the people to do after the manner of his iniquities.** *And he [Alma] became a great hinderment to the prosperity of the church of God; stealing away the hearts of the people; causing much dissension among the people; giving a chance for the enemy of God to exercise his power over them. (Mosiah 27:8–9; emphasis added)*

The prayers of King Mosiah and the prophet Alma were answered when an angel of the Lord appeared to all of their sons and spoke with a voice of thunder. Alma the Younger was struck dumb, and, subsequently, the group repented. Alma the Younger became a great prophet and Nephite leader, while the sons of Mosiah demonstrated their repentance by going on dangerous missions to the Lamanites. The mission of the sons of Mosiah will be addressed later in this book. For now, the incredible life of Alma the Younger is the focus. Later in his life, Alma taught all of his sons with personal messages that

are recorded in his writings ( see Alma Chapters 36–42). Alma gave a sincere explanation of his experience with the angel when teaching his young son Helaman.

*And now, O my son Helaman, behold, thou art in thy youth, and therefore, I beseech of thee that thou wilt hear my words and learn of me. . . . Now, behold, I say unto you, if I had not been born of God I should not have known these things; but God has, by the mouth of his holy angel, made these things known unto me, not of any worthiness of myself; for I went about with the sons of Mosiah, seeking to destroy the church of God; but behold,* **God sent his holy angel to stop us by the way. And behold, he spake unto us, as it were the voice of thunder, and the whole earth did tremble beneath our feet;** *and we all fell to the earth, for the fear of the Lord came upon us. But behold, the voice said unto me: Arise. And I arose and stood up, and beheld the angel. And he said unto me: If thou wilt of thyself be destroyed, seek no more to destroy the church of God. (Alma 36:3, 5–9; emphasis added)*

This experience is the defining moment in Alma's life and is given to us as an example.

Most, if not all, people of faith have defining moments in their lives that give them meaning and direction. Just as Alma shared his confrontation with the angel to his son Helaman, we should take time with our sons and daughters to tell them about these life changing incidents in our lives. The circumstances that bring about these trials come in many forms, such as accidents, illness, sports, work, scouting, school, family, marriage, military, or church. For example, my children should know how my military experience in the Middle Eastern desert brought me closer to God. Our children deserve to know that life is not all sweet and wonderful and that trials and tribulations shape our characters. These life-changing events usually require great sacrifice and are often personally overwhelming. Moreover, they often cause us to alter our spiritual course in life.

In the following passages, Alma tells his son about his defining moment and how it brought new meaning to his life. With very clear and heartfelt language, Alma tells how the Lord took him through the repentance process and redirected his life.

*And it came to pass that I fell to the earth; and it was for the space of three days and three nights that I could not open my mouth, neither had I the use of my limbs. . . . I was struck with such great fear and amazement lest perhaps I should be destroyed, that I fell to the earth and I did hear no more. But I was racked with eternal torment, for my soul was harrowed up to the greatest degree and racked with all my sins.*

*Yea, I did remember all my sins and iniquities, for which I was tormented with the pains of hell; yea, I saw that I had rebelled against my God, and that I had not kept his holy commandments. Yea, and I had murdered many of his children, or rather led them away unto destruction; yea, and in fine so great had been my iniquities, that the very thought of coming into the presence of my God did rack my soul with inexpressible horror . . .*

*And it came to pass that as I was thus racked with torment, while I was harrowed up by the memory of my many sins, behold, I remembered also to have heard my father prophesy unto the people concerning the coming of one Jesus Christ, a Son of God, to atone for the sins of the world.*

*Now, as my mind caught hold upon this thought, I cried within my heart: O Jesus, thou Son of God, have mercy on me, who am in the gall of bitterness, and am encircled about by the everlasting chains of death.* And now, behold, when I thought this, I could remember my pains no more; yea, I was harrowed up by the memory of my sins no more. And oh, what joy, and what marvelous light I did behold; yea, my soul was filled with joy as exceeding as was my pain!

**Yea, I say unto you, my son, that there could be nothing so exquisite and so bitter as were my pains. Yea, and again I say unto you, my son, that on the other hand, there can be nothing so exquisite and sweet as was my joy.**

*But behold, my limbs did receive their strength again, and I stood upon my feet, and did manifest unto the people that I had been born of God. Yea, and from that time even until now, I have labored without ceasing, that I might bring souls unto repentance; that I might bring them to taste of the exceeding joy of which I did taste; that they might also be born of God, and be filled with the Holy Ghost. (Alma 36:10–14, 17–21, 23–24; emphasis added)*

These few verses are especially meaningful to those of us who have drifted from the path of righteousness even in a minor way. Alma's use of adjectives to describe his experience is particularly beautiful—"There could be nothing so exquisite and so bitter as were my pains. Yea, and again I say unto you, my son, that on the other hand, there can be nothing so exquisite and sweet as was my joy" (Alma 36:21). This passage gives us a clear and finite description of the role of the Atonement in refreshing the repentant soul. Is it any wonder that Alma becomes a key figure for the Lord in establishing the gospel among the Nephites? Knowing this background, the stage is set for us to look further into his great life.

## The Setting— A Turbulent Time of Civil Unrest

Alma's story in the Book of Mormon begins with a segment commonly called the "war chapters." During this time, there were civil wars among the Nephites that grew into international wars between the Nephites and the Lamanites. Often, dissenting or rebellious Nephites would be so distraught and angry that they would unite with the Lamanite armies to attack the Nephites. The story of this turbulent period comes nearly 500 years after the people of Lehi left Jerusalem and approximately 100 years before the birth of Christ. The Nephites had moved several hundred miles north from the site of their first landing. They had totally separated from the Lamanites and lived primarily in the land surrounding a city named Zarahemla.

Alma the Younger became the prophet and was one of the primary characters of this time. The Nephite King Mosiah gave Alma the large plates of Nephi with an assignment to record the Nephite history of his time. The writings of the first part of this period are by Alma the Younger and include an account of public conflict and the associated wars.

This was a time of dreadful civil unrest. The Nephites were attempting to establish a new form of democracy in which the people would elect leaders. All of the sons of King Mosiah had refused to be anointed king. Consequently, a democracy was formed by dividing the Nephite nation into geographic divisions wherein judges were elected for local territories, and a chief judge was chosen over all the Nephite lands. The "chief judge" would be compared to a "president" or a "prime minister" today. The book of Mosiah gives us an understanding of this momentous time and explains that the people "rejoiced because of the liberty which had been granted unto them" (see Mosiah 29:39). Moreover, this movement away from monarchy to democracy was so important that they changed their

calendar. They began to state the years based on the "reign of the judges." They would write, for example; "Thus ended the ninth year of the reign of the judges over the people of Nephi" (Alma 8:2).

It was a difficult time for the people of that day, as in most new democracies, because freedom of speech and civil protest frustrate the people who desire harmony. Kings would not tolerate civil protest, while a democracy must embrace it. Persecution of the people who fostered liberty became commonplace even though they had passed "strict laws" regarding fair treatment and persecution (Alma 1:21).

In the midst of this political unrest, a man named Amlici came among the Nephites and demonstrated an ability to influence the people. He was a fast-talking, eloquent man who desired to be elected chief judge. When he failed, he gathered his followers, started a rebellion, and attempted to take control by force. The exact words as recorded by Alma give us insight into the conflict of the times.

> And it came to pass in the commencement of the fifth year of their reign there began to be a contention among the people; for a certain man, being called Amlici, he being a very cunning man, yea, a wise man as to the wisdom of the world. . . . Now this Amlici had, by his cunning,

*drawn away much people after him; even so much that they began to be very powerful; and they began to endeavor to establish Amlici to be a king over the people.*

*Now this was alarming to the people of the church, and also to all those who had not been drawn away after the persuasions of Amlici; for they knew that according to their law that such things must be established by the voice of the people . . .*

*And thus they did assemble themselves together to cast in their voices concerning the matter; and they were laid before the judges. And it came to pass that the voice of the people came against Amlici, that he was not made king over the people. (Alma 2:1–3; 6–7)*

Alma went on to tell us that Amlici was appointed king by a group of Nephite dissenters who began to call themselves Amlicites. They armed themselves to attack the Nephites led by Alma (Alma 2:9–11). Alma's purpose in telling this story is most likely to give us an example of a cunning leader, Amlici, who, through his deceit took control of the minds of people and consequently brought rebellion and war. The Book of Mormon gives us a significant warning—do not let these wicked men take control.

In the 1900s, there were many world leaders who were this type of cunning leader: Adolf Hitler, Joseph Stalin, Benito Mussolini, Mao Tse-tung, Pol Pot, Slobodan Milošević, and Saddam Hussein. They manipulated their societies and became ruthless leaders that historians record as masters of deceit, responsible for the slaughter of millions of innocent people. A more detailed discussion of these modern-day masters of deceit will be covered in chapter six.

## Alma as a Defender of Freedom

Alma, as chief judge, was faced with few options. Cunning lies and deception escalated into armed aggression. Alma recognized this great problem and took his armies to defend against the Amlicites. The scriptures point out that the Lord supported the Nephites because of their faith. Alma personally led his forces in a major battle fought close to the city of Zarahemla near the River Sidon.

It was commonplace for the armies of this time to be led by their kings and leaders and for the strongest and most experienced warriors to be in the front. Alma was not only the leader, but he went first and was at the front. Where did Alma get the expertise to lead an army and fight against the enemy's best warriors? We are not told specifically, but we do know that Alma was the son of a great Nephite leader and that his best friends were the sons of Mosiah, the former king of the Nephite nation. Alma was the equivalent of a prince and was probably taught in his youth to be a great swordsman and military leader. Knowing that in times of war the leaders would go to the front of the battle as chief captains (generals), the kings would be sure that their sons were well trained in the art of war. Training is the key to successful armies. The armies of the Book of Mormon period were not much different than today. They required knowledge of weapons and discipline.

As a young soldier in the United Stares Army, I was trained in combat and in the use of weapons and battlefield tactics. All soldiers go through what is called basic training. As I progressed and became a warrant officer, I attended formal courses on the history and philosophy of war. Officers are taught the history and strategies of war along with battlefield tactics. With this background, they are then given very detailed training in their specialty, such as infantry, artillery, engineering, armor, and intelligence. As a warrant officer my specialty was military intelligence. This means I was taught how to interrogate prisoners of war, how to collect information from civilians, and then how to analyze the information. Finally, we were required to know how to write reports and make the information usable for the commanding officers who would

direct the battles. The lower ranking officers (lieutenants, captains, and majors) are usually called field-grade officers and conduct the actual battle on the ground. Higher ranking officers (colonels and generals) typically determine the movement of units (companies, battalions, brigades, and armies). These higher ranking officers and army commanders are responsible for the strategies of the overall war and the battlefield movements.

I am sure that Alma was a trained military commander with the highest strategic and battlefield skills. To put it into context, consider a modern professional athlete. Alma would be the football quarterback with incredible agility and athleticism. In his army he would be the most skilled and most capable warrior; his men would have labeled him as a warrior who was the best of the best. Unlike today where the army generals stay in the rear and control unit movements, Alma was responsible for both the strategy and the battle. As the chief captain (Nephite commanding general) he would have gone forward with his army at the very point of the attack along with his guards who were his most excellent soldiers. Alma was not only a man of God and chief judge but also a trained and disciplined military commander and battlefield warrior.

Amlici created an army of rebellious

Nephites that numbered in the thousands. The battle is recorded in the following statement.

> Now Alma, being the chief judge and the governor of the people of Nephi, therefore **he went up with his people, yea, with his captains, and chief captains, yea, at the head of his armies, against the Amlicites to battle.** And they began to slay the Amlicites upon the hill east of Sidon. And the Amlicites did contend with the Nephites with great strength, insomuch that many of the Nephites did fall before the Amlicites.
>
> Nevertheless the Lord did strengthen the hand of the Nephites, that they slew the Amlicites with great slaughter, that they began to flee before them. And it came to pass that the Nephites did pursue the Amlicites all that day, and did slay them with much slaughter, insomuch that there were slain of the Amlicites twelve thousand five hundred thirty and two souls; and there were slain of the Nephites six thousand five hundred sixty and two souls. (Alma 2:16–19; emphasis added]

The numbers tell us that this was not a small battle. It was important enough for the recorders to point out that nineteen thousand souls were lost. It is clear that, by giving us this much detail, the writers wanted to illustrate the grievous consequence of the acts of cunning and wicked men and their lust for power—thousands of lives lost.

After the first battle, Alma was not satisfied to rest on his victory. He sent spies to track the Amlicites and received a surprising report. The Amlicites had joined with an army of Lamanites whose intent was to destroy the city of Zarahemla, the Nephite's capital (see Alma 2:21–24). Haven't there been similar alliances in the world wars of our day? During World War II, Hitler combined with Mussolini, and they in turn joined with Japan to form the Axis powers. Wicked leaders often join with other wicked leaders to successfully seek power.

To distinguish themselves, the Amlicites marked their foreheads with red, and the Lamanites shaved their heads. They moved quickly north with the intention to attack the city of Zarahemla. Alma knew this and countered their attack by intercepting the huge army of Amlicites and Lamanites. The army of the Nephites was severely outnumbered. Two verses give us the key factor in this battle—faith.

> And behold, as they (the Nephites) were crossing the river Sidon, the Lamanites and the Amlicites, being as numerous almost, as it were, as the sands of the sea,

**Alma's Battle with Amlici and His Forces**

*came upon them to destroy them. Nevertheless, the Nephites being strengthened by the hand of the Lord, having prayed mightily to him that he would deliver them out of the hands of their enemies, therefore the Lord did hear their cries, and did strengthen them, and the Lamanites and the Amlicites did fall before them. (Alma 2:27–29)*

Alma was again faced with a daunting task of defeating an enemy with forces greater than his own. War was much more than sending young men into harm's way—it was so serious, as noted earlier, that leaders went first. This custom was an overwhelming statement by the leaders about their faith in their people and in the cause of freedom. Moreover, in both battles, the Nephites under Alma sought help from the Lord. Alma eventually met Amlici on the battlefield, and these two great military captains (generals) went into mortal combat.

*And it came to pass that Alma fought with Amlici with the sword, face to face; and they did contend mightily, . . . **Alma, being a man of God, being exercised with much faith, cried, saying: O Lord, have mercy and spare my life, that I may be an instrument in thy hands to save and preserve this***

***people.*** *Now when Alma had said these words he contended again with Amlici; and he was strengthened, insomuch that he slew Amlici with the sword. And he also contended with the king of the Lamanites; but the king of the Lamanites fled back from before Alma and sent his guards to contend with Alma. But Alma, with his guards, contended with the guards of the king of the Lamanites until he slew and drove them back. (Alma 2:29–33; emphasis added)*

Alma not only defeated this huge military force with superior strategy, but also he defeated Amlici in a hand-to-hand contest. He was prepared for battle and not afraid to literally face his enemy. Note how Alma prayed while in hand-to-hand combat. This prayer is a marvelous indicator of the faith and dignity of Alma. We should be humbled by his closeness to the Lord. Not many of us would seek the Lord's help during a difficult and hate-filled moment.

Mormon, editor and compiler of the Book of Mormon, must have included this piece of history because he was touched by Alma's behavior. He wanted us to see this outstanding example of leadership and preparation. Do we prepare as Alma did? Do we solve our problems head on without wasting time? Do we seek the Lord in our moments of greatest need? Is our courage sufficient to bring us face to face with our problems? Alma's dedication, preparation, and prayer are amazing characteristics to emulate.

A soldier would also notice the brief statement regarding the cowardice of the Lamanite king. When he faced Alma in battle, Amlici turned away and left his guards to fight the battle. It is interesting to observe that guards protected both Alma and the Lamanite kings. Inevitably, these great warriors would find themselves at the center of every battle. A brief study of modern warfare finds similar examples of the best-trained soldiers being at the front. In World War II, the 101st Airborne Division filled this role in battles against Germany. They were on the beaches of Normandy on D-Day and were on the point of the attack with the American army all the way to mountain retreats of Germany. The television movie *Band of Brothers* gives an outstanding portrayal of soldiers who were not afraid to be at the spear's point as the United States Army moved through Europe. Another example of the best taking charge is the 9th Army led by General George S. Patton. When the Allied Supreme Commander, General Eisenhower, needed a general who would not falter under an overwhelming task, he chose Patton. He led his army in the dead of winter against an army that had dug in and created formidable defenses. Patton's mark in history was playing a major part in the Battle of the Bulge. His army's role was to rescue the 101st Airborne Division, which was hopelessly surrounded by the German Army and refused to surrender.

Another question that a soldier might ask about Alma's victory is what made the difference in these battles. Was this Nephite victory determined by skill or by faith? I will raise this question many times as we review the experiences of Book of Mormon warriors. In this case, it is skill and faith. Man is given opportunities on this earth to change lives and to impact key situations, such as war. Do great leaders make an amazing impact on history without preparation? Never! Alma knew his role. He was the temporal and spiritual leader, and he was physically prepared to fight Amlici. However, Alma recognized that his greatest power was not founded on his proficiency with the sword—it was founded on his faith.

The people of Alma recognized the danger the Amlicites brought to their democracy, and they attempted to destroy their potential by pursuing them into the wilderness and continuing the battle. So many died that Alma said the bodies could not be numbered and were tossed into the River Sidon to be carried to the sea (see Alma 2:35–37; 3:1).

This battle was also not the end to the war,

which lasted a whole year. Yet another Lamanite army entered Nephite lands and was defeated by a Nephite army sent by Alma. This time, however, Alma did not contend with them. He was injured and could not go (Alma 3:20–26).

## An Important Lesson from Alma: Acknowledge the Hand of the Lord

The way this story is written emphasizes the key role of preparation and faith in the success of man. Alma wrote this history and explained how the Nephites prepared, but more important, he always gave credit to the Lord for his personal success and for his nation's victory. This is so important! In latter-day scripture, the Lord revealed to Joseph Smith His feelings regarding this significant principle.

*And it pleaseth God that he hath given all these things unto man; for unto this end were they made to be used, with judgment, not to excess, neither by extortion.* **And in nothing doth man offend God, or against none is his wrath kindled, save those who confess not his hand in all things, and obey not his commandments.** *Behold, this is according to the law and the prophets; wherefore, trouble me no more concerning this matter. (Doctrine*

*and Covenants 59:20–22; emphasis added)*

The authors of the Book of Mormon clearly point out that Alma was unquestionably grateful and willing to acknowledge the hand of the Lord in his personal triumph and in the success of his people temporally and in war. He admonished his people to "remember" their blessings, "always returning thanks to God" (Alma 7:23).

## Alma's Spiritual Message to the Church and to Us

Alma was a sensitive man who saw his people turning away from the Lord. He described the behavior of the Church after this remarkable war with the Amlicites and Lamanites. The people were humbled because of their huge losses, but in a short time, only six years, they drifted away from the Lord. Inequality, pride, and costly apparel were the marks of this unfortunate change.

*And it came to pass in the eighth year of the reign of the judges, that the people of the church began to wax proud, because of their exceeding riches, and their fine silks, and their fine-twined linen, and because of their many flocks and herds, and their gold and their silver, and all manner of precious things, which they had obtained by their industry; and in all these things were they lifted up in the pride of their eyes, for they began to wear very costly apparel.*

*Now this was the cause of much affliction to Alma, yea, and to many of the people whom Alma had consecrated to be teachers, and priests, and elders over the church. . . .*

**There began to be great contentions among the people of the church; yea, there were envyings, and strife, and malice, and persecutions, and pride, even to exceed the pride of those who did not belong to the church of God.** *And thus ended the eighth year of the reign of the judges; and the wickedness of the church was a great stumbling-block to those who did not belong to the church; and thus the church began to fail in its progress. . . .*

*Yea, he [Alma] saw great inequality among the people, some lifting themselves up with their pride, despising others, turning their backs upon the needy. . . . . . Now this was a great cause for lamentations among the people. (Alma 4:6–7, 9–10, 12–13; emphasis added)*

This turn of events and change of behavior was of such concern to Alma that he resigned as the chief judge and tuned the judgeship over to Nephihah. Alma then concentrated on his role as the prophet and high priest over the church.

**And this he [Alma] did that he himself might go forth among his people, or among the people of Nephi, that he might preach the Word of God unto them, to stir them up in remembrance of their duty,** *and that he might pull down, by the word of God, all the pride and craftiness and all the contentions which were among his people, seeing no way that he might reclaim them save it were in bearing down in pure testimony against them. (Alma 4:19; emphasis added)*

In great sorrow, Alma turned to the power of the word and preached to his people who were headed for moral decay. They had known the promptings of the Spirit and needed to return to righteousness. Alma started his mission in the capital city of Zarahemla. He taught the people who had been converted by his father, Alma. These people were at one time enslaved by the Lamanites. Alma gave one of the most uniquely beautiful sermons recorded in scripture. Alma wanted them to return to their devotion of the past. Here are the important words to watch for in some of the key verses of his sermon that follow—"remembrance" and "change of heart."

*And now behold, I say unto you, my brethren, you that belong to this church, have you sufficiently retained in **remembrance** the captivity of your fathers? Yea, and have you sufficiently retained in **remembrance** his mercy and long-suffering toward them? And moreover, have ye sufficiently retained in **remembrance** that he has delivered their souls from hell? Behold, he **changed their hearts;** yea, he awakened them out of a deep sleep, and they awoke unto God. (Alma 5:6–7; emphasis added)*

It is evident that Alma was much more than a great warrior. Now we see him as a prophet and a teacher of great wisdom. His remarkable perception is reflected in his poetic language. Alma used a new instructional technique not used previously in the Book of Mormon. Questions and inquiries were inserted in his sermon to stimulate their thoughts. Note how his questions caused his people to reflect on their past. The questions then brought the people to recognize the need to be spiritually born of God and demonstrate their conviction through a change in behavior. These church members knew better—but they needed to "remember" how blessed they had been and then have a mighty change of heart. The following questions appear in his discourse in the book of Alma, chapter five.

- *And now behold, I ask of you, my brethren of the church, have ye spiritually been born of God?*
- *Have ye received his image in your countenances?*
- *Have ye experienced this mighty change in your hearts?*
- *Do ye exercise faith in the redemption of him who created you?*
- *Do you look forward with an eye of faith, and view this mortal body raised in immortality, and this corruption raised in incorruption, to stand before God to be judged according to the deeds which have been done in the mortal body?*
- *I say unto you, can you imagine to yourselves that ye hear the voice of the Lord, saying unto you, in that day: Come unto me ye blessed, for behold, your works have been the works of righteousness upon the face of the earth?*
- *Or do ye imagine to yourselves that ye can lie unto the Lord in that day,*

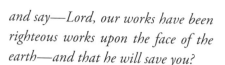 

and say—Lord, our works have been righteous works upon the face of the earth—and that he will save you?

- Or otherwise, can ye imagine yourselves brought before the tribunal of God with your souls filled with guilt and remorse, having a remembrance of all your guilt, yea, a perfect remembrance of all your wickedness, yea, a remembrance that ye have set at defiance the commandments of God?

- I say unto you, can ye look up to God at that day with a pure heart and clean hands?

- I say unto you, can you look up, having the image of God engraven upon your countenances?

- I say unto you, can ye think of being saved when you have yielded yourselves to become subjects to the devil?

- And now I ask of you, my brethren, how will any of you feel, if ye shall stand before the bar of God, having your garments stained with blood and all manner of filthiness? . . .

- And now behold, I say unto you, my brethren, if ye have experienced a change of heart, and if ye have felt to sing the song of redeeming love, I would ask, can ye feel so now?

- Have ye walked, keeping yourselves

blameless before God?

- Behold, are ye stripped of pride?

- And again I say unto you, is there one among you that doth make a mock of his brother, or that heapeth upon him persecutions?

**[Alma makes his final conclusions with a number of verses. Below are several.]**

- And this is not all. Do ye not suppose that I know of these things myself? Behold, I testify unto you that I do know that these things whereof I have spoken are true. And how do ye suppose that I know of their surety?

- Behold, I say unto you they are made known unto me by the Holy Spirit of God. Behold, I have fasted and prayed many days that I might know these things of myself. And now I do know of myself that they are true; for the Lord God hath made them manifest unto me by his Holy Spirit; and this is the spirit of revelation which is in me. (Alma 5:14–22, 26–30, 45–46; emphasis and bullets)

Did Alma touch the hearts of his father's former converts? Can a speaker be more eloquent? Can the message be delivered with more clarity? Can we recognize that he is also speaking to us? Is it possible that Alma's struggles as a wayward youth, his conversion, and his battlefield experience provided him with the context to form these penetrating questions? Is this a timeless message from which we can all benefit? Alma concludes this sermon with his testimony of Christ.

*And now, my brethren, I would that ye should hear me, for I speak in the energy of my soul; for behold, I have spoken unto you plainly that ye cannot err, or have spoken according to the commandments of God. For I am called to speak after this manner, according to the holy order of God, which is in Christ Jesus; yea, I am commanded to stand and testify unto this people the things which have been spoken by our fathers concerning the things which are to come. . . . I* **say unto you, that I know that Jesus Christ shall come, yea, the Son, the Only Begotten of the Father, full of grace, and mercy, and truth. And behold, it is he that cometh to take away the sins of the world, yea, the sins of every man who steadfastly believeth on his name.** *(Alma 5:43–44, 48; emphasis added)*

Alma the Younger's message to his father's converts is clear: "remember" Christ and move forward with a mighty change of heart.

## Alma's Timeless Message on Faith

Alma continued his mission to change the hearts of the people. He traveled to the land of the Zoramites. They were characterized by a wealthy group of people that worshipped and prayed from a platform called the Rameumptom. Alma described the Zoramites to the Lord as he prayed for help before going into their city.

*Behold, O my God, their costly apparel, and their ringlets, and their bracelets, and their ornaments of gold, and all their precious things which they are ornamented with; and behold, their hearts are set upon them, and yet they cry unto thee and say—We thank thee, O God, for we are a chosen people unto thee, while others shall perish. Yea, and they say that thou hast made it known unto them that there shall be no Christ. (Alma 31:28–29)*

The Zoramites, who were consumed by wealth and pride, were not teachable, but the poor, who were kept from the synagogues, were anxious to learn, so Alma taught them first. This

is perhaps one of the most poignant sermons on faith in all of scripture. Alma used the growth of a seed as a metaphor to teach these humble and deprived people.

> *And now as I said concerning faith—faith is not to have a perfect knowledge of things; therefore if ye have faith ye hope for things which are not seen, which are true. . . .*
>
> *But behold, if ye will awake and arouse your faculties, even to an experiment upon my words, and exercise a particle of faith, yea, even if ye can no more than desire to believe, let this desire work in you, even until ye believe in a manner that ye can give place for a portion of my words.*
>
> ***Now, we will compare the word unto a seed. Now, if ye give place, that a seed may be planted in your heart, behold, if it be a true seed, or a good seed, if ye do not cast it out by your unbelief, that ye will resist the Spirit of the Lord, behold, it will begin to swell within your breasts; and when you feel these swelling motions, ye will begin to say within yourselves—*** *It must needs be that this is a good seed, or that the word is good, for it beginneth to enlarge my soul; yea, it beginneth*
>
> *to enlighten my understanding, yea, it beginneth to be delicious to me.*
>
> *But behold, as the seed swelleth, and sprouteth, and beginneth to grow, then you must needs say that the seed is good; for behold it swelleth, and sprouteth, and beginneth to grow. And now, behold, will not this strengthen your faith? (Alma 32:21, 27–28, 30; emphasis added)*

This is certainly a beautiful narrative on faith. To Alma, faith is miraculous and truly "delicious." Alma went on to illustrate how wonderful the blessings of faith can be.

> *But if ye will nourish the word, yea, nourish the tree as it beginneth to grow, by your faith with great diligence, and with patience, looking forward to the fruit thereof, it shall take root; and behold it shall be a tree springing up unto everlasting life.*
>
> *And because of your diligence and your faith and your patience with the word in nourishing it, that it may take root in you, behold, **by and by ye shall pluck the fruit thereof, which is most precious, which is sweet above all that is sweet, and which is white above all that is white, yea, and pure above all that is pure;** and ye shall feast upon this fruit even until ye are filled, that ye*

*hunger not, neither shall ye thirst. (Alma 32:41–42; emphasis added)*

Alma's alliterations are some of the most beautiful in all of scripture. When he talks about the fruit of the gospel, he is truly articulate. Alma describes the fruit or blessings of the gospel eloquently. He said it is "sweet above all that is sweet, and which is white above all that is white, yea, and pure above all that is pure" (Alma 32:42). This lesson on faith is particularly applicable to those who are at the beginning of their journey.

There is so much more to be said about Alma. His missionary journeys with his dear friend Amulek, his teachings to each of his sons, and his conversion are examples of his tremendous ability to adjust to life and live by faith. In Mosiah 27 and Alma 36, he tells his conversion story. He explains his youthful wayward behavior and the visit of an angel who spoke with a "voice of thunder." Alma was struck dumb—unable to speak—for three days, during which he was "racked with eternal torment." He remembers his father's teachings and turns to Christ and is forgiven. In his words, "And oh, what joy and what marvelous light I did behold; yea, my soul was filled with joy as exceeding as was my pain!" (Alma 36:20).

Alma exemplifies greatness throughout his life. It is important to read the books of Mosiah and Alma to get a full picture. This short commentary, shows that Alma was a thoughtful father, a fearless warrior, a powerful leader, an inspiring missionary, and a man of faith. I will end with Alma's direction on how we should live.

*And now I would that ye should be humble, and be submissive and gentle; easy to be entreated; full of patience and long-suffering; being temperate in all things; being diligent in keeping the commandments of God at all times; asking for whatsoever things ye stand in need, both spiritual and temporal; always returning thanks unto God for whatsoever things ye do receive. (Alma 7:23)*

Take note—*"always returning thanks unto God for whatsoever things ye do receive."* Alma did this, and he invites all of us to do the same.

# Three

# AMMON, VALIANT SERVANT MISSIONARY

*Surely there has not been any servant among all
my servants that has been so faithful as this man [Ammon]; for even
he doth remember all my commandments to execute them."*
KING LAMONI IN ALMA 18:10

Ammon was a son of King Mosiah, leader of the Nephites in the land of Zarahemla. He had been rebellious as a youth and a close friend of Alma, the son of Alma, the Nephite prophet. Ammon's defining moment and the key to the beginning of his story is the appearance of the angel to Alma, Ammon's disobedient friend. Ammon and the other sons of Mosiah were with Alma and, consequently, their lives were permanently altered. Following this dramatic event, Ammon and the other sons of Mosiah repented and tried to make amends for their sins, which had been to convince the believers to rebel against the church of Christ. The repentance of the sons of Mosiah was explained in the book of Mosiah.

*And four of them were the sons of Mosiah; and their names were Ammon, and Aaron, and Omner, and Himni; these were the names of the sons of Mosiah. And they traveled throughout all the land of Zarahemla, and among all the people who were under the reign of king Mosiah, zealously striving to repair all the injuries which they had done to the church, confessing all their sins, and publishing all the things which they had seen, and explaining the prophecies and the scriptures to all who desired to hear them.*

*And thus they were instruments in the hands of God in bringing many to the knowledge of the truth, yea, to the knowledge of their Redeemer. And how blessed are they! For they did publish peace; they did publish good tidings of good; and they did declare unto the people that the Lord reigneth. (Mosiah 27:34–37)*

The sons of Mosiah made every effort to repair the damage they had inflicted on the church. The sincerity and the depth of their conviction were illustrated by the fact that none of them accepted the offer to become king of the Nephites. Their desire, on the other hand, was to go on a mission to the Lamanites (see Mosiah 28).

## The Setting—Two Alienated Nations

The historical account of Ammon takes place before the resignation of King Mosiah and during the reign of Alma, the chief judge, between 95 and 88 BC. The Nephite nation started a democracy and elected judges because the sons of Mosiah refused to be appointed king. Ammon and his brothers went to their father, the king, and asked permission to go the land of the Lamanites on a mission to spread the knowledge of Christ. This was a time of war and not long after the Nephite battles with the Amlicites and the Lamanite armies. A mission to the Lamanites would be extremely dangerous because tremendous animosity existed between the Nephites and the Lamanites. In addition, Ammon and his brothers were princes of the Nephites. If they were discovered, they would certainly be murdered. As princes, they were also trained military warriors and military commanders. A point of interest in this story is that Ammon used his training to demonstrate his loyalty to the Lamanites.

First, it is important to understand the perilous nature of this mission. Zeniff, a great leader who lived about ninety years before King Mosiah, explained the hatred in detail.

*Now, the Lamanites knew nothing concerning the Lord, nor the strength of the Lord, therefore they depended upon their own strength. Yet they were a strong people, as to the strength of men. They were a wild, and ferocious, and a bloodthirsty people, believing in the traditions of their fathers, which is this—*

- *Believing that they were driven out of the land of Jerusalem because of the*

*iniquities of their fathers, and that*

- *they were wronged in the wilderness by their brethren, and*
- *they were also wronged while crossing the sea; and again, that*
- *they were wronged while in the land of their first inheritance . . .*
- *they said that he [Nephi] had taken the ruling of the people out of their hands . . .*
- *they were wroth because he [Nephi] departed into the wilderness as the Lord had commanded him, and took the records which were engraven on the plates of brass, for they said that he robbed them.*

*And thus they have taught their children that they should hate them [the Nephites], and that they should murder them, and that they should rob and plunder them, and do all they could to destroy them; therefore they have an eternal hatred toward the children of Nephi.* (Mosiah 10:11–17; emphasis and bullets points added)

King Mosiah wrote an account of the conversation with his sons shortly after they had made every effort to repent and repair the damage they had done to the church in their youth.

*Now it came to pass that after the sons of Mosiah had done all these things, they . . . returned to their father, the king, and desired of him that he would grant unto them that they might, with these whom they had selected, go up to the land of Nephi that they might preach the things which they had heard, and that they might impart the word of God to their brethren, the Lamanites—*

*That perhaps they might bring them to the knowledge of the Lord their God, and convince them of the iniquity of their fathers; and that perhaps they might cure them of their hatred toward the Nephites, that they might also be brought to rejoice in the Lord their God, that they might become friendly to one another, and that there should be no more contentions in all the land which the Lord their God had given them.*

***Now they were desirous that salvation should be declared to every creature, for they could not bear that any human soul should perish; yea, even the very thoughts that any soul should endure endless torment did cause them to quake and tremble. . . .***

*And it came to pass that they did plead with their father many days that they might go up to the land of Nephi.*

*And king Mosiah went and inquired of the Lord if he should let his sons go up among the Lamanites to preach the word. And the Lord said unto Mosiah: Let them go up, for many shall believe on their words, and they shall have eternal life; and I will deliver thy sons out of the hands of the Lamanites. And it came to pass that Mosiah granted that they might go and do according to their request. (Mosiah 28:1–3, 5–8; emphasis added)*

With their father's blessing, the brothers began their fourteen year saga when they left Zarahemla and "journeyed into the wilderness." In approximately 90 BC, the young band of missionaries traveled somewhere between 150 and 200 miles to the Land of First Inheritance, where most Lamanites lived. The following map illustrates how they traveled southward. Often the account says they went up to the land of Nephi (Land of First Inheritance). The descriptive word "up" is used by the writers because the journey included a difficult trip up and over a mountainous wilderness.

The group of missionaries is described as humble and teachable. The current and future missionaries of the LDS faith should take note of the character and behavior of these young missionaries.

*And it came to pass that they journeyed many days in the wilderness, and they fasted much that the Lord would grant unto them a portion of his spirit . . . that they might be an instrument in the hands of God to bring . . . their brethren, the Lamanites, to the knowledge of the truth . . .*

*The Lord did visit them with his Spirit and said unto them: Be comforted . . . Go forth unto the Lamanites . . . be patient in long-suffering and afflictions. . . . [And] show forth good examples unto them. (Alma 17:10–11; emphasis)*

What a marvelous list of missionary attributes: (1) fasting to receive the Spirit, (2) being patient in the work, (3) expecting long-suffering and afflictions, and (4) showing forth good examples to the people. As this story proceeds, we will see that the sons of Mosiah were amazing examples to the Lamanites and very patient in their harsh afflictions. Moreover, they have been worthy examples for countless Mormon missionaries of the latter days who have read the Book of Mormon and marveled at their missionary adventure.

When the sons of Mosiah reached the borders of the Lamanite nation, the brothers split up. Aaron went to the city called Jerusalem, and

Mission of the Sons of Mosiah to the Lamanites

Ammon went to the Land of Ishmael, which was named after Ishmael who traveled to the promised land with Lehi. Ishmael's sons followed Laman, a rebellious son of Lehi, and eventually became Lamanites. The mission of Ammon among the Lamanites is well documented in the historical accounts in the book of Alma. Our purpose in this commentary is to focus on the missionary activities of Ammon.

### Ammon's Demonstration of Humility

Ammon entered the land of Ishmael alone and in great danger. The author described the dangerous risk of Ammon by explaining he was immediately bound and brought before the Lamanite king. The words are clear and show that the king had the power of life and death: "Thus it was left to the pleasure of the king to slay [him] or to retain [him] in captivity, or to cast [him] into prison, or to cast [him] out of his land . . ." (Alma 17:20).

The next few passages are some of the most humble and poignant in all of scripture. Faced with the peril of his life, Ammon responded with humility and a display of incredible loyalty. The king, whose name was Lamoni, asked if Ammon wanted to "dwell in the land among the Lamanites" (Alma 17:22). Ammon replied with such sincerity that the king was totally astonished. Ammon replied, "Yea, I desire to dwell among this people for a time; yea, and perhaps until the day I die" (Alma 17:23). The king was so taken with Ammon that he offered him one of his daughters as a wife. We only have a small part of the conversation, but it should be noted that this is a Lamanite king with ultimate power and that Ammon is an unknown Nephite, a member of the nation that has been hated and despised by the Lamanites for centuries. This was much more than a simple gesture of friendship. He was inviting this "Nephite" into the king's family and court. I'm sure the members of the king's court who heard this implausible offer were about to collapse in disbelief.

Ammon replied, "Nay, but I will be thy servant" (Alma 17:25), another statement illustrating exceptional humility. If Ammon married a member of the king's family, he would have been royalty and lived in affluence. However, luxury was not Ammon's purpose; he would rather be a humble servant. Keep in mind that Ammon had already refused to be king of the Nephites in favor of a mission. The Lamanite king was probably taken aback by this request and assigned Ammon to be a simple herder of the king's flocks. Don't forget that Ammon was a Nephite prince—to take this job as a servant was a serious downgrade in social standing. It

probably was one of the least important servant jobs in the Lamanite kingdom.

## Ammon's Courageous Opportunity

After three days of working, Ammon and his fellow servants were attacked by a gang of renegades, who scattered the King's flocks for personal gain. Ammon's fellow servants were struck with fear and cried, "Now the king will slay us, as he has our brethren because their flocks were scattered by the wickedness of these men. And they began to weep exceedingly" (Alma 17:28).

In modern terms, I am sure Ammon thought that this was a rather ineffective management practice. However, the text tells us that Ammon immediately saw this as an opportunity to please the king. He quickly calmed the servants and helped them gather up the flocks to await the renegades' return. The scriptures describe Ammon's thoughts. "Now when Ammon saw this his heart was swollen within him with joy; for said he, . . . I may win the hearts of these my fellow-servants that I may lead them to believe in my words" (Alma 17:29). He told the servants to encircle the flocks and keep them from scattering, saying he "will contend" with these men.

Ammon was now ready to use one of the many skills he brought with him. As a Nephite prince, he was undoubtedly trained in sword combat. Had he remained in his own land, in time of war, he would have been a chief captain (general), and most likely would have gone into battle at the front of his army. As a skilled soldier, Ammon was an expert with the sword. The text explains that he attacked the men with a sling to drive them away.

*But Ammon stood forth and began to cast stones at them with his sling; yea, with mighty power he did sling stones amongst them; and thus he slew a certain number of them insomuch that they began to be astonished at his power; nevertheless they were angry because of the slain of their brethren, and they were determined that he should fall; therefore, seeing that they could not hit him with their stones, they came forth with clubs to slay him.*

*But behold, every man that lifted his club to smite Ammon, he smote off their arms with his sword; for he did withstand their blows by smiting their arms with the edge of his sword, insomuch that they began to be astonished, and began to flee before him; yea, and they were not few in number; and he caused them to flee by the strength of his arm.*

*Now six of them had fallen by the sling, but he slew none save it were their leader with his sword; and he smote off as many of their arms as were lifted against him, and they were not a few. (Alma 17:36–38)*

Ammon was so effective that the attackers were quickly disoriented and driven back by Ammon's sling. Then he engaged them in combat with his sword, killing the leader and severing the arms of those who angrily attacked him. Their anger led them to an awful consequence. Anger in battle often leads men into poor decisions. This was obviously the case with these untrained thieves. It is important to understand that this took courage for Ammon because he was critically outnumbered. It is also essential to note that the Lord had promised Mosiah that He would protect his sons. In addition, it is vital to note that Ammon was a superbly trained and prepared warrior. When a soldier says that someone is a well-trained warrior, it is a compliment. Training is the indispensable trade of a soldier. Through training, the competent soldier becomes aware of what will likely happen and what will be expected in battle. And then, the warrior must practice until his response to the enemy is instinctive and instantaneous. Without timely and precise responses, the warrior may fall in battle. I

picture Ammon as a well-defined, strong, and mighty man, capable of standing shoulder to shoulder among the great warriors of all time.

## Ammon's Inspired Instruction

This story now continued into the courts of King Lamoni. The fellow herdsmen of Ammon were so impressed with his deed that they gathered up the arms of the slain robbers and took them to the king.

*And when they had all testified to the things which they had seen, and he had learned of the faithfulness of Ammon in preserving his flocks, and also of his great power in contending against those who sought to slay him, he [King Lamoni] was astonished exceedingly, and said: Surely, this is more than a man. Behold, is not this the Great Spirit who doth send such great punishments upon this people, because of their murders?*

*And they answered the king, and said: Whether he be the Great Spirit or a man, we know not; but this much we do know, that he cannot be slain by the enemies of the king; neither can they scatter the king's flocks when he is with us, because of his expertness and great strength; therefore, we know that he is a friend to the king.*

*And now, O king, we do not believe that a man has such great power, for we know he cannot be slain. (Alma 18:2–3)*

We are told that the traditions of the Lamanites included a legend of a "Great Spirit" that would come and judge them. Ammon used this belief and turned into it into an opportunity. The story continued:

*Now this was the tradition of Lamoni, which he had received from his father, that there was a Great Spirit. Notwithstanding they believed in a Great Spirit, they supposed the whatsoever they did was right; nevertheless, Lamoni began to fear exceedingly, with fear lest he had done wrong in slaying his servants; for he had slain many of them because their brethren had scattered their flocks at the place of water; and thus, because they had had their flocks scattered they were slain. (Alma 18:5–6)*

The stage was now set for Ammon to speak with the king. The king was terrified that the Great Spirit had come to earth bringing retribution for King Lamoni's ruthless leadership. On the other hand, this apprehension turned to amazement when the king asked the herdsmen where Ammon had gone. Ammon was preparing the king's horses for a trip—fulfilling an earlier assignment. Ammon's service had made an exceptional impression on the king.

*Now when king Lamoni heard that Ammon was preparing his horses and his chariots he was more astonished, because of the faithfulness of Ammon, saying: **Surely there has not been any servant among all my servants that has been so faithful as this man; for even he doth remember all my commandments to execute them.** Now I surely know that this is the Great Spirit, and I would desire him that he come in unto me, but I durst not. (Alma 18:10–11; emphasis added)*

Ammon was a marvelous example of accountability. How many of us would have desired the praise of men and gone to the king's court with the other servants to receive his accolades? However, Ammon's purpose was to be a remarkable servant for the king, and he refused to be distracted from his assignments. He had been told by the Spirit to be an excellent example and that is exactly what he did.

When his responsibilities were complete, Ammon returned to the king to report that the horses were ready and was stunned because "the countenance of the king was changed" (Alma 18:12). Ammon, being respectful, turned to leave when a servant called to him and said that the king wanted him to stay. Ammon turned back to the king and respectfully said, "What wilt thou that I should do for thee, O king? And the king answered him not for the space of an hour. . . . And it came to pass that Ammon said unto him again: What desirest thou of me? But the king answered him not" (Alma 18:14–15). Ammon was an obedient missionary. Remember before embarking on their mission the Sons of Mosiah had fasted and asked for guidance. "**The Lord did visit them with his Spirit and said unto them: Be comforted** . . . Go forth unto the Lamanites . . . **be patient** in long-suffering and afflictions . . . [And] **show forth good examples** unto them" (Alma 17:10–11). Ammon had indeed demonstrated obedience to this guidance. Not only was he a superb example to the king, his patience was exceptional. Ammon waited for the king to speak for over an hour. Then the Spirit told Ammon that Lamoni was afraid Ammon was the Great Spirit and had come to punish him. Ammon spoke these words to calm the king, who marveled in silence.

*Is it because thou hast heard that I defended thy servants and thy flocks, and slew seven of their brethren with the sling and with the sword, and smote off the arms of others, in order to defend thy flocks and thy servants; behold, is it this that causeth thy marvelings? I say unto you, what is it, that thy marvelings are so great? **Behold, I am a man, and am thy servant;** therefore, whatsoever thou desirest which is right, that will I do.*

*Now when the king had heard these words, he marveled again, for he beheld that Ammon could discern his thoughts; but notwithstanding this, king Lamoni did open his mouth, and said unto him: **Who art thou? Art thou that Great Spirit, who knows all things?** (Alma 18:16–18; emphasis added)*

Ammon was blessed with discernment of the king's thoughts. King Lamoni was so amazed that he really didn't hear Ammon's first statement about being only a man. This reaction is common among all of us. When a person is filled with fear and amazement, he fails to listen to the people speaking to him. I have seen this several times in my work in military intelligence. Fear can be helpful in gaining information, but it can also hinder communication. This conversation between Ammon and the king is another small but clear witness to the authenticity of the Book of Mormon because the conversation is so realistic. Ammon had told Lamoni that he was a man and remained Lamoni's servant, but the king could only respond with questions that showed that his fear and amazement were stopping him from clear communication. He repeated his question.

> *Who art thou? Art thou the Great spirit, who knows all things? Ammon answered and said unto him: I am not. And the king said: How knowest thou the thoughts of my heart? Thou mayest speak boldly, and tell me concerning these things; and also tell me by what power ye slew and smote off the arms of my brethren that scattered my flocks.* (Alma 18:18–20)

Note how the two address each other. It is indicative of the times and the power of the king in his court. Ammon is quietly respectful, and the king gives him the right to speak "boldly." This is a reminder of the etiquette required in the king's court. Look at it this way: Lamoni (the great king with the power of life and death) giving Ammon (a visiting Nephite servant) permission to appraise the king or maybe even speak with disapproval. The conversation is very fascinating. The members of the king's court must have been watching in total disbelief. They had just witnessed a Nephite servant being given the right to criticize their Lamanite king. Lamoni began by granting Ammon anything he desired, but Ammon only wanted the king to hear his message.

> *And now if thou wilt tell me concerning these things, whatsoever thou desirest I will give unto thee;* and if it were needed, I would guard thee with my armies; but I know that thou art more powerful than all they; nevertheless, whatsoever thou desirest of me I will grant it unto thee.
> Now Ammon being wise, yet harmless, he said unto Lamoni: **Wilt thou hearken unto my words, if I tell thee by what power I do these things?** And this is the thing that I desire of thee. And the king answered him, and said: **Yea, I will believe all thy words.** And thus he was caught with guile. And Ammon began to speak unto him with boldness, and said unto him: Believest thou that there is a God? And he answered, and said unto him: I do not know what that meaneth. And then Ammon said: Believest thou that there is a Great Spirit? (Alma 18:21–26; emphasis added)

Ammon's teachings are so simple, yet so powerful. The writer does not give us all of his words but does gives us Ammon's central message to a man who had literally no knowledge of the one true God.

*And Ammon said unto him: The heavens is a place where God dwells and all his holy angels. And king Lamoni said: Is it above the earth? And Ammon said:* **Yea, and he looketh down upon all the children of men; and he knows all the thoughts and intents of the heart;** *for by his hand were they all created from the beginning. And king Lamoni said: I believe all these things which thou hast spoken. Art thou sent from God?*

*Ammon said unto him:* **I am a man. . . . And a portion of that Spirit dwelleth in me, which giveth me knowledge, and also power according to my faith and desires which are in God.**

*Now when Ammon had said these words, he began at the creation of the world, and also the creation of Adam, and told him all the things concerning the fall of man, and rehearsed and laid before him the records and the holy scriptures of the people, which had been spoken by the prophets, even down to the time that their father, Lehi, left Jerusalem. (Alma 18:30–36; emphasis added)*

Ammon is an ideal model of the humble missionary. Not seeking any self-aggrandizement—he teaches and gives credit to the Lord.

Ammon didn't realize that his straightforward act of courage, loyalty, and humility would affect the Lamanite and the Nephite nations for centuries to come.

After being taught very basic doctrines and becoming converted, King Lamoni collapsed and was unconscious for two days (Alma 18:42–43). The people thought he was dead and his wife, sons, and daughters mourned. This seemingly unique experience was not new to Ammon because he had seen his friend Alma faint after being confronted by an angel. He knew the Lord was working with Lamoni on his repentance. After the king fainted, Ammon was called to visit the queen and told her Lamoni was "not dead but he sleepeth in God" (Alma 19:8). She believed at once and Ammon made a revealing comment. "Behold, I say unto thee, woman [the queen] that there has not been such great faith among all the people of the Nephites" (Alma 19:10). What an amazing act of childlike faith. Each of us has seen this type of faith at some point in our lives. It might have been on our missions, in our wards, or in our families. It is a gift of God to have this simple and lasting faith, and it is also a gift from God to see it happen.

The group then returned to Lamoni, who had been prepared for burial. The king then awakened and immediately praised the Lord.

*For as sure as thou livest, behold, I have seen my Redeemer; and he shall come forth, and be born of a woman, and he shall redeem all mankind who believe on his name. Now, when he had said these words, his heart was swollen within him, and he sunk again with joy; and the queen also sunk down, being overpowered by the Spirit. (Alma 19:13)*

There was so much faith among these new converts, and the Spirit was so strong that they all collapsed. What an incredible demonstration of faith! These people were moving from a corrupt and unrighteous environment to near exaltation in a matter of hours. They included Lamoni, his wife, Ammon, and all of the servants, save one—a Lamanite woman named Abish, who was a convert to the Lord through a vision of her father. Apparently she had been living as a Christian but not able to speak about her beliefs in the Lamanite culture. She went among the people telling of the wonderful experience, and a multitude gathered in the court of the king (Alma 19:13–20). At this point, a Lamanite man whose brother had been slain by Ammon came forward to kill Ammon with a sword but was struck dead by the Lord. The author's comment is profound.

*Now we see that Ammon could not be slain, for the Lord had said unto Mosiah, his father: I will spare him, and it shall be unto him according to thy faith—therefore, Mosiah trusted him unto the Lord. (Alma 19:23)*

The role of Abish in this story is charming. The Lord is always several steps ahead of us. He had prepared this faithful woman for a wonderful role, and she waited patiently for the Lord to use her faith among her fellow Lamanites. Abish was brought to tears when the multitude began to argue and contend. Some thought Ammon was the "Great Spirit," while others thought he was a "monster sent by the Nephites" (Alma 19:26). Abish went to the Queen and touched her hand. She awakened and declared her faith, very much like Lamoni (Alma 19:24–28).

*And it came to pass that she went and took the queen by the hand, that perhaps she might raise her from the ground; and as soon as she touched her hand she arose and stood upon her feet, and cried with a loud voice, saying: O blessed Jesus, who has saved me from an awful hell! O blessed God, have mercy on this people! (Alma 19:29)*

Then the queen touched the king, and he rose a second time to quell the emotions of a confused and disoriented group of people.

*And he, immediately, seeing the contention among his people, went forth and began to rebuke them, and to teach them the words which he had heard from the mouth of Ammon; and as many as heard his words believed, and were converted unto the Lord. . . .*

*And it came to pass that when Ammon arose he also administered unto them, and also did all the servants of Lamoni; and they did all declare unto the people the selfsame thing—that their hearts had been changed; that they had no more desire to do evil. And behold, many did declare unto the people that they had seen angels and had conversed with them. . . .*

*And it came to pass that there were many that did believe in their words; and as many as did believe were baptized; and they became a righteous people, and they did establish a church among them. **And thus the work of the Lord did commence among the Lamanites; thus the Lord did begin to pour out his Spirit upon them; and we see that his arm is extended to all people who will repent and believe on his name.** (Alma 19:31, 33, 35–36; emphasis added)*

Please pay attention to the final commentary on this marvelous conversion story. The author, presumably, Alma or possibly even Mormon, points out that the Lord did "**pour out his spirit upon them**" (Alma 19:36). The conversion of the Lamanites had been in the prayers of the Nephite prophets for centuries and their prayers were finally answered (see 2 Nephi 33:3; Enos 1:11; Words of Mormon 1:8).

## Ammon's Confrontation with Lamoni's Father

The story continues with a trip to Middoni, which is contained in Alma chapter 20. Lamoni wanted to take Ammon to his father in the land of Nephi, but the voice of the Lord came to Ammon and told him to go to Middoni to rescue his brothers, who were suffering in prison. Lamoni told Ammon he would go and plead for their freedom, so the two traveled together. While underway, they came across Lamoni's father, the king over all the Lamanite lands. Lamoni's father was angry with him because Lamoni did not attend a feast the father had planned to celebrate with his sons and his kingdom. The father inquired as to why the son had not come and was immediately angry. He said, "Whither art thou going with this Nephite, who is one of the children of a liar" (Alma 20:10). Lamoni told him about Ammon

and the conversions. Lamoni's father became even more enraged:

> *And now when Lamoni had rehearsed unto him all these things, behold, to his astonishment, his father was angry with him, and said: Lamoni, thou art going to deliver these Nephites, who are sons of a liar. Behold, he robbed our fathers; and now his children are also come amongst us that they may, by their cunning and their lyings, deceive us, that they again may rob us of our property.*
>
> ***Now the father of Lamoni commanded him that he should slay Ammon with the sword.*** *And he also commanded him that he should not go to the land of Middoni, but that he should return with him to the land of Ishmael. But Lamoni said unto him: I will not slay Ammon, neither will I return to the land of Ishmael, but I go to the land of Middoni that I may release the brethren of Ammon, for I know that they are just men and holy prophets of the true God. Now when his father had heard these words, he was angry with him, and he drew his sword that he might smite him to the earth. (Alma 20:13–16; emphasis added)*

When Lamoni would not slay Ammon, the king became so furious that he drew his sword

with the intention to kill his own son. This certainly bespeaks the vicious nature of their culture and the depth of the hatred the Lamanites had for the Nephites. However, Ammon, with his expert swordsmanship, protected Lamoni and contended with the great king. Remember that kings were among the most expert in hand-to-hand combat of all the ancient warriors. They were first in battle and the most formidable among the soldiers with the instruments of war. It is difficult to illustrate how profound this confrontation was. This was a display of hand-to-hand combat between two of the ancient world's best swordsmen. For Ammon to be victorious would be an accomplishment of incredible magnitude. A young Nephite would have defeated the senior Lamanite king with the sword. The account is explained in the following passages.

> *But Ammon stood forth and said unto him: Behold, thou shalt not slay thy son; nevertheless, it were better that he should fall than thee, for behold, he has repented of his sins; but if thou shouldst fall at this time, in thine anger, thy soul could not be saved. . . .*
>
> *And he [the king] stretched forth his hand to slay Ammon. But Ammon withstood his blows, and also smote his arm that he could not use it. Now when the*

*king saw that Ammon could slay him, he began to plead with Ammon that he would spare his life. But Ammon raised his sword, and said unto him: Behold, I will smite thee except thou wilt grant unto me that my brethren may be cast out of prison.*

*Now the king, fearing he should lose his life, said: If thou wilt spare me I will grant unto thee whatsoever thou wilt ask, even to half of the kingdom.*

*Now when Ammon saw that he had wrought upon the old king according to his desire, he said unto him: If thou wilt grant that my brethren may be cast out of prison, and also that Lamoni may retain his kingdom, and that ye be not displeased with him, but grant that he may do according to his own desires in whatsoever thing he thinketh, then will I spare thee; otherwise I will smite thee to the earth.*

*Now when Ammon had said these words, the king began to rejoice because of his life. And when he saw that Ammon had no desire to destroy him, and when he also saw the great love he had for his son Lamoni, he was astonished exceedingly, and said: Because this is all that thou hast desired, that I would release thy brethren, and suffer that my son Lamoni should retain his kingdom, behold, I will*

*grant unto you that my son may retain his kingdom from this time and forever; and I will govern him no more. (Alma 20:17, 20–26)*

Again, it is important to notice that the Lord was using the skills of Ammon to achieve His purposes. Ammon, the master swordsman, was using his skill to save his friend and bring the knowledge of Christ to his mortal enemy. What a stunning turn of events—missionary work was now open to the Lamanites.

This illustration of Ammon's skill is profound and important for us in the latter days. For example, if the Lord used Ammon's swordsmanship to help on his mission, what skills can we develop for Him to use in our latter-day missions? The Lord could use a missionary today that knows his scriptures well, has a knowledge of great literature, is well versed in the cultures of the world, can write effectively in his or her native tongue, has learned to study hard so that a new language can be easily mastered, has learned to listen and communicate with others in a personable way, has practiced and learned to teach effective lessons, has a healthy and strong body capable of living and being active in all climates, has learned to be humble and unselfish, has developed a respect for all people regardless of their social standing, has learned to manage his or her money, has learned to purchase and prepare healthy food, has learned to follow and obey direction from leaders, and, most important, can listen to and follow the Spirit. Ammon was most definitely prepared for his time; and, consequently, the Lord used his skills to bring about conversions.

Following the confrontation with the great king, Lamoni and Ammon went to the prison and freed his brothers. The brothers had suffered terribly. They were bound with cords and had been treated poorly.

> *And it came to pass that Ammon and Lamoni proceeded on their journey toward the land of Middoni. And Lamoni found favor in the eyes of the king of the land; therefore the brethren of Ammon were brought forth out of prison.*
>
> *And when Ammon did meet them he was exceedingly sorrowful, for behold they were naked, and their skins were worn exceedingly because of being bound with strong cords. And they also had suffered hunger, thirst, and all kinds of afflictions; nevertheless they were patient in all their sufferings.*
>
> *And, as it happened, it was their lot to have fallen into the hands of a more hardened and a more stiffnecked people; therefore they would not hearken unto their words, and they had cast them out, and had smitten them, and had driven them from house to house, and from place to place, even until they had arrived in the land of Middoni; and there they were taken and cast into prison. (Alma 20:28–30)*

These comments are so remarkable—I love the unique use of words: "it was their lot to have fallen into the hands of a more stiffnecked people." All missionaries should take note. All will have some degree of sacrifice on their missions—maybe not prison—but most certainly a harsh climate, strange food, heartless people, or limited success. Remember, the sons of Mosiah were told when they began this amazing saga that they should "be patient in long-suffering and afflictions . . . [and] show forth good examples unto them" (Alma 17:11).

There is no difference in missionary work today; many will suffer various afflictions and may even come home with maladies that take many years to heal. However, the blessings will greatly overpower the suffering. Any missionary will testify to this truth. When one sacrifices for the Lord, wonderful blessings are forthcoming.

NARROW NECK OF LAND

RIVER SIDON

WILDERNESS

WILDERNESS

Shemlon

Lemuel

Ishmael

Nephi

Middoni

**Mission**
of the Sons of Mosiah -
**Cities Converted**
**Success in the Cities
and in the Wilderness**

### Lamanite Conversion and Covenants

We are told that thousands were converted. Not only Lamoni's kingdom but also the greater part of the Lamanite nation were opened for religious freedom. This liberty happened after Ammon's brother Aaron taught the great king, Lamoni's father. The king sent a proclamation throughout the Lamanite nation to not harm the missionaries (Alma 22:27). The author, in Alma 22–23, takes the time to tell us how this missionary miracle unfolded. Most of the Lamanite nation was involved. It is explained that the Nephite lands were nearly surrounded by Lamanite lands and notes that the missionaries could go from sea to sea in all the land southward. We were informed that many Lamanites lived in tents in the adjacent wilderness, and we were given the names of major cities were many where converted—Nephi, Lemuel, Shemlon, and Middoni. The map on page 78 gives some perspective of the immense area that was opened to the missionaries. Lamanites lived mostly south of Nephite city of Manti but lived in tents in the wilderness that surrounded the Sidon river valley, where the Nephite cities of Zarahemla and Bountiful were found.

The narrative about the mass conversion of the Lamanites is impressive. The labor lasted thirteen years and was an incredible missionary effort.

*And now it came to pass that when the king had sent forth this proclamation, that Aaron and his brethren went forth from city to city, and from one house of worship to another, establishing churches . . . and thus they began to have great success.*

*And thousands were brought to the knowledge of the Lord, yea, thousands were brought to believe in the traditions of the Nephites; and they were taught the records and prophecies which were handed down even to the present time. . . . **yea, I say unto you, as the Lord liveth, as many of the Lamanites as believed in their preaching, and were converted unto the Lord, never did fall away.*** (Alma 23:4–6; emphasis added)

This statement "never did fall away" is an announcement by the author, probably Mormon. He knew the history from start to finish. The strength of this Lamanite conversion is remarkable. It is founded in an earlier prophecy by Lehi to his rebellious sons, Laman and Lemuel. Remember, Lehi had seen a vision of the tree of life and knew his older sons would fall away from their faith (see 1 Nephi 8). In light of this knowledge, it is noteworthy that Lehi made this statement in a blessing to his rebellious child. This blessing was given shortly before the death of Lehi.

> *Wherefore, after my father . . . called the children of Laman, his sons, and his daughters, and said unto them: Behold, my sons, and my daughters, who are the sons and the daughters of my first-born, I would that ye should give ear unto my words.*
>
> *For the Lord God hath said that: Inasmuch as ye shall keep my commandments ye shall prosper in the land; and inasmuch as ye will not keep my commandments ye shall be cut off from my presence.*
>
> *But behold, my sons and my daughters, I cannot go down to my grave save I should leave a blessing upon you; for behold,* **I [Lehi] know that if ye are brought up in the way ye should go ye will not depart from it.** *(2 Nephi 4:3–5; emphasis added)*

We can now see how visionary this blessing was. He knew that at some time in the future the descendants of Laman and Lemuel would get an opportunity to demonstrate their faith. Many of the great Nephite prophets prayed for them and for their time to come (2 Nephi 33:3; Enos 1:11; Title Page). When the Savior visited this great remnant of the house of Jacob, He stated three times that the remnant of the house of Israel (the Lamanites) will be among the Gentiles and will "rise as a lion" (3 Nephi 20:12). The Savior was speaking of the latter days. It is clear the opportunity to teach the Lamanites rests upon this generation in these latter days. Our sons and daughters will be the new "sons of Mosiah" to help the remnant of the Lamanites, who are in the western hemisphere, to accept the gospel and truly rise as a lion and be a powerful force for good.

### The Ultimate Spiritual Warriors: The Anti-Nephi-Lehies

The converts of the sons of Mosiah became known as the Anti-Nephi-Lehies. The name comes from the son of the great king of the Lamanites. We know that he had two sons. One son was Lamoni, and the other was given the name Anti-Nephi-Lehi when he was anointed as the successor to the great king. Hence, the Lamanite converts of the sons of Mosiah were called the Anti-Nephi-Lehies. The strength of their conversion is indicated by the subsequent oaths and covenants that they made.

> *For they became a righteous people; they did lay down the weapons of their rebellion, that they did not fight against*

*God any more, neither against any of their brethren.*

*And it came to pass that they called their names Anti-Nephi-Lehies; and they were called by this name and were no more called Lamanites.*

*And they began to be a very industrious people; yea, and they were friendly with the Nephites; therefore, they did open a correspondence with them, and the curse of God did no more follow them. (Alma 23:7, 17–18)*

The blessings of Lehi and the Lord's covenant for the Land of Promise were fulfilled. When the people keep the commandments, they are blessed. These converts were so focused on repentance that they made a covenant to never use their weapons of war. They wanted to earn the forgiveness that had been extended to them. They met in council with Ammon, their spiritual leader, and the Great Lamanite King was their spokesperson.

*Oh, how merciful is our God! And now behold, since it has been as much as we could do to get our stains taken away from us, and our swords are made bright, let us hide them away that they may be kept bright, as a testimony to our God at the last day, or at the day that we*

*shall be brought to stand before him to be judged. . . .*

*And now, my brethren, if our brethren seek to destroy us, behold, we will hide away our swords, yea, even we will bury them deep in the earth, that they may be kept bright, as a testimony that we have never used them, at the last day; and if our brethren destroy us, behold, we shall go to our God and shall be saved.*

*And this they did, it being in their view a testimony to God, and also to men, that they never would use weapons again for the shedding of man's blood; and this they did, vouching and covenanting with God, that rather than shed the blood of their brethren they would give up their own lives. . . .*

***And thus we see that, when these Lamanites were brought to believe and to know the truth, they were firm, and would suffer even unto death rather than commit sin;*** *and thus we see that they buried their weapons of peace, or they buried the weapons of war, for peace. (Alma 24:15–16, 18–19; emphasis added)*

When the phrase "thus we see" is used, it is the author speaking in reflection. This phrase is generally thought to be the words of Mormon, the compiler and editor of the Book of Mormon. Moreover, it is a very direct statement to latter-day readers. The author might as well be saying, "Please pay attention! There is a moral to this story." He wants us to see the astounding nature of this statement of faith. This peace-loving covenant did not remain untested. A short time later, the surrounding Lamanites who hated the Anti-Nephi-Lehies gathered armies to attack them, and the details were recorded in the following verses.

> *And it came to pass that their brethren, the Lamanites, made preparations for war, and came up to the land of Nephi for the purpose of destroying the king, and to place another in his stead, and also of destroying the people of Anti-Nephi-Lehi out of the land.*
>
> *Now when the people saw that they were coming against them they went out to meet them, and prostrated themselves before them to the earth, and began to call on the name of the Lord; and thus they were in this attitude when the Lamanites began to fall upon them, and began to slay them with the sword.*
>
> *And thus without meeting any resistance, they did slay a thousand and five of them; and we know that they are blessed, for they have gone to dwell with their God.*
>
> **Now when the Lamanites saw that their brethren would not flee from the sword, neither would they turn aside to the right hand or to the left, but that they would lie down and perish. . . .**
>
> **When the Lamanites saw this they did forbear from slaying them. . . .** *And it came to pass that they threw down their weapons of war, and they would not take them again, for they were stung for the murders which they had committed. . . .*
>
> **And it came to pass that the people of God were joined that day by more than the number who had been slain;** *and those who had been slain were righteous people, therefore we have no reason to doubt but what they were saved. And there was not a wicked man slain among them; but there were more than a thousand brought to the knowledge of the truth;* **thus we see that the Lord worketh in many ways to the salvation of his people.** *(Alma 24:20–27; emphasis added)*

It is difficult to imagine this horrendous slaughter by the sword. The carnage must have been monumental. However, this turned out to be a marvelous illustration of faith and commitment. The Lamanites who slaughtered the people of Ammon were so touched that more Lamanite soldiers were converted to the faith than were slain by the sword. Again, we hear the author saying, "thus we see." He is saying again to pay attention. Be aware that in spite of the carnage, their deaths were not in vain. Their deaths were not without purpose. This epic example of faith and commitment to a covenant touched the hearts of some of the most hardened bloodthirsty soldiers ever to live. The writer illustrated one more point.

> *Now the greatest number of those of the Lamanites who slew so many of their brethren were Amalekites and Amulonites, the greatest number of whom were after the order of the Nehors. Now, among those who joined the people of the Lord, there were none who were Amalekites or Amulonites, or who were of the order of Nehor, but they were actual descendants of Laman and Lemuel.*
>
> ***And thus we can plainly discern,*** *that after a people have been once enlightened by the Spirit of God, and have had great knowledge of things pertaining to righteousness, and then have fallen away into sin and transgression, they become more hardened, and thus their state becomes worse than though they had never*

*known these things. (Alma 24:28–30; emphasis added)*

These people (the Amalekites and Amulonites) were former Nephites who had transgressed and left the faith. They joined the Lamanites and added their brand of hatred. Mormon, once again, wants us to understand that Satan has a greater influence over those who have fallen from grace into transgression. We were told earlier that among the thousands of Lamanite converts in all the Lamanite lands, there were no Amulonites and only one Amalekite. What a truly sad commentary.

One of my experiences during the war in Iraq has reinforced the true nature of this tremendous Lamanite conversion. With some minor comparisons, I can see this type of conversion story happening in our day. In Iraq, I had the opportunity to talk with tribal leaders. They were great men with high values and tremendous influence. The tribes of the Middle East are very much like the tribes of the Lamanites, and the size of the tribes ranges from thousands to millions of family-oriented people who could easily be influenced by the Lord—much like the Lamanites were influenced by the Lord and the sons of Mosiah.

My friendship with some of these Iraqi tribal

leaders became very strong in a short time. Our greetings often turned from handshakes into bear hugs. They sensed our desire to help them and their people. Our military mission was a joint effort to rebuild their country and bring safety to their families. We were not allowed to talk about our faith, but I am convinced that a time will come when, just like Ammon and Lamoni, a close relationship and a single conversion of a tribal leader could open the minds and hearts of tens of thousands, perhaps millions, of true descendants of Abraham through the line of Ishmael.

## The Message of this Amazing Story: Faith, Courage, Sacrifice, and Joy

After the success and many conversions throughout the land, the missionaries and the leaders of the Lamanites met twice. They met to plan for the safety of the converts because the Lamanite armies were planning a major campaign to destroy the converts. They also met on the trip back to the Land of the Zarahemla (see Alma 26–27). Each time they reflected on the success they had experienced.

The courage, faith, and sacrifice in this story are illustrated by the missionaries and the converts. The sons of Mosiah entered the land of a bloodthirsty enemy. Their faith and patience was shown by their undaunted trek into the heart of the Lamanite lands. They walked right into the courts of the kings and were even thrown into prison. Ammon made the following comment at the end of their mission, thirteen years after leaving Zarahemla. He referred to the fact that before the sons of Mosiah left on their mission, the Nephite people thought they were foolish.

*Now do ye remember, my brethren, that we said unto our brethren in the land of Zarahemla, we go up to the land of Nephi, to preach unto our brethren, the Lamanites, and they laughed us to scorn?*

*For they said unto us: Do ye suppose that ye can bring the Lamanites to the knowledge of the truth? Do ye suppose that ye can convince the Lamanites of the incorrectness of the traditions of their fathers, as stiffnecked a people as they are; whose hearts delight in the shedding of blood; whose days have been spent in the grossest iniquity; whose ways have been the ways of a transgressor from the beginning? Now my brethren, ye remember that this was their language. . . .*

*Now when our hearts were depressed, and we were about to turn back, behold, the Lord comforted us, and said: Go amongst thy brethren, the Lamanites, and bear with patience thine* *afflictions, and I will give unto you success. And now behold, we have come, and been forth amongst them; and we have been patient in our sufferings, and **we have suffered every privation; yea, we have traveled from house to house, relying upon the mercies of the world—not upon the mercies of the world alone but upon the mercies of God.***

*And we have entered into their houses and taught them, and we have taught them in their streets; yea, and we have taught them upon their hills; and we have also entered into their temples and their synagogues and taught them; and we have been cast out, and mocked, and spit upon, and smote upon our cheeks; and we have been stoned, and taken and bound with strong cords, and cast into prison; and through the power and wisdom of God we have been delivered again.*

***And we have suffered all manner of afflictions, and all this, that perhaps we might be the means of saving some soul; and we supposed that our joy would be full if perhaps we could be the means of saving some.*** *(Alma 26:23–24, 27–30; emphasis added)*

Ammon aptly described the joy they had experienced. His energy and excitement is further illustrated when he spoke to his fellow missionaries about the wonderful blessings of missionary work.

*And now, these are the words of Ammon to his brethren, which say thus: My brothers and my brethren, behold I say unto you, how great reason have we to rejoice; for could we have supposed when we started from the land of Zarahemla that God would have granted unto us such great blessings? And now, I ask, what great blessings has he bestowed upon us? Can ye tell?*

*Behold, I answer for you; for our brethren, the Lamanites, were in darkness, yea, even in the darkest abyss, but behold, how many of them are brought to behold the marvelous light of God! **And this is the blessing which hath been bestowed upon us, that we have been made instruments in the hands of God to bring about this great work.** Behold, thousands of them do rejoice, and have been brought into the fold of God. . . .*

***Blessed be the name of our God; let us sing to his praise, yea, let us give thanks to his holy name, for he doth work righteousness forever.*** *For if we had not come up out of the land*

of Zarahemla, these our dearly beloved
brethren, who have so dearly beloved us,
would still have been racked with hatred
against us, yea, and they would also have
been strangers to God. (Alma 26:1–4, 8;
emphasis added)

It is easy to see the happiness in the words
spoken by Ammon. However, his brother
brought him back to reality as brothers often
do. The Book of Mormon is true, and the con-
versations within are evidence of that. The following comment brings reality to the statements
and illustrates the personal nature of their
discussion.

> And it came to pass that when
> Ammon had said these words, his brother
> Aaron rebuked him, saying: Ammon, I
> fear that thy joy doth carry thee away unto
> boasting.
>
> **But Ammon said unto him: I do
> not boast in my own strength, nor in
> my own wisdom; but behold, my joy
> is full, yea, my heart is brim with joy,
> and I will rejoice in my God.**
>
> Yea, I know that I am nothing; as to
> my strength I am weak; therefore I will
> not boast of myself, but I will boast of
> my God, for in his strength I can do all
> things; yea, behold, many mighty miracles

we have wrought in this land, for which
we will praise his name forever. (Alma
26:10–12)

Ammon was not finished and spoke more
of his joy. Near the end of his dialogue, he came
back to the same point he had made earlier.

> Now behold, we can look forth and
> see the fruits of our labors; and are they
> few? I say unto you, Nay, they are many;
> yea, and we can witness of their sincerity,
> because of their love toward their brethren
> and also toward us.
>
> For behold, they had rather sacrifice
> their lives than even to take the life of
> their enemy; and they have buried their
> weapons of war deep in the earth, because
> of their love toward their brethren. **And
> now behold I say unto you, has there
> been so great love in all the land?
> Behold, I say unto you, Nay, there has
> not, even among the Nephites. . . .**
>
> **Now have we not reason to rejoice?
> Yea, I say unto you, there never were
> men that had so great reason to
> rejoice as we, since the world began;
> yea, and my joy is carried away, even
> unto boasting in my God;** for he has all
> power, all wisdom, and all understand-
> ing; he comprehendeth all things, and he
> is a merciful Being, even unto salvation,

*to those who will repent and believe on his name.*

*Now if this is boasting, even so will I boast; for this is my life and my light, my joy and my salvation, and my redemption from everlasting wo.* **Yea, blessed is the name of my God, who has been mindful of this people, who are a branch of the tree of Israel, and has been lost from its body in a strange land; yea, I say, blessed be the name of my God, who has been mindful of us, wanderers in a strange land.** *(Alma 26:31–33, 35–36; emphasis added)*

Burying their weapons, making an oath, and sacrificing their lives demonstrated the strength of the Anti-Nephi-Lehies' conversion. An additional act that illustrates the depth of their conversion is when they were willing to live under the protection of the Nephites and be their slaves (Alma 27:7–9). Ammon told them that the Nephites would forgive them and would not allow slavery. These converts demonstrated humility and a willingness to sacrifice that are uniquely rare among men.

Later, Ammon and the missionaries met with Alma on the trail back to Zarahemla and collapsed from his joy and excitement. There is no question that Ammon was a man of honor, humility, and emotion. He brought this remarkable story of conversion to a great conclusion with this statement.

*Now my brethren, we see that God is mindful of every people, whatsoever land they may be in; yea, he numbereth his people, and his bowels of mercy are over all the earth. Now this is my joy, and my great thanksgiving; yea, and I will give thanks unto my God forever. Amen. (Alma 26:37)*

The authors of the Book of Mormon have purposely placed before us the example of a humble, courageous, faithful missionary. The example matures into a story of a monumental covenant to never take up weapons again. Among the many stories found in scripture, this stands as an illustration of the power of faith and the support that God gives to those who trust in Him by making and keeping covenants.

# Four

# THE STRIPLING WARRIORS

*Now they had never fought yet they did not fear death;*
*and they did think more upon the liberty of their fathers*
*than they did upon their lives.*
CAPTAIN HELAMAN IN ALMA 56:47

The tale of the stripling warriors is one of the greatest stories of youthful courage ever recorded. The stage was set when the Lamanite Christian converts of the sons of Mosiah were attacked in their own land by their own people. These converts had taken an oath to never use weapons of war and had buried their weapons in the earth. This chapter will chronicle the events that followed this courageous act and miraculous conversion.

The time was approximately 77 BC. Many thousands of Lamanite converts were in grave danger. The hate-filled Lamanite armies considered them to be traitors to the traditions of the Lamanites. To prevent further slaughter, Ammon and his brothers suggested that the converts go to the land of the Nephites where they could be protected. The king of the Lamanite converts, Anti-Nephi-Lehi, however, thought the Nephites would kill them because of their previous wickedness. When they were assured this would not happen, they illustrated their repentance and humility by stating that they were willing to become slaves to the Nephites. Of course, Ammon and the Nephites gave no serious thought to this suggestion because slavery was against Nephite law (Alma 27:4–9).

## The Setting

Under the direction of Alma, the chief judge, the Anti-Nephi-Lehies were given the land of Jershon and became known as the people of Ammon. This was the fifteenth year of the judges (approximately 76 BC). The people of Ammon settled in this Nephite-protected area, and Ammon was appointed their high priest. At this point, the Lamanite armies came into the northern Nephite lands, and there was a huge battle.

*And thus there was a tremendous battle; yea, even such an one as never had been known among all the people in the land from the time Lehi left Jerusalem; yea, and tens of thousands of the Lamanites were slain and scattered abroad.*

*Yea, and also there was a tremendous slaughter among the people of Nephi; nevertheless, the Lamanites were driven and scattered, and the people of Nephi returned again to their land.*

*And now this was a time that there was a great mourning and lamentation heard throughout all the land, among all the people of Nephi—*

*Yea, the cry of widows mourning for their husbands, and also of fathers mourning for their sons, and the daughter for the brother, yea, the brother for the father; and thus the cry of mourning was heard among all of them, mourning for their kindred who had been slain.*

*And now surely this was a sorrowful day; yea, a time of solemnity, and a time of much fasting and prayer. (Alma 28:2–6)*

It is apparent that the writer (probably Alma the Younger) was a soldier who felt deep sorrow at this dreadful time in history and the sacrifice of war. He described the mourning of not just a nation, but of individual fathers, mothers, sisters, and brothers. This was a very personal, heartfelt description regarding the grief and devastation of war.

These events must have been very difficult for the people of Ammon because they could see so much suffering around them. After all, the slaughter was caused by an attack from their people, the Lamanites. Moreover, their new friends and Christian brothers were dying in the terrible wars. Not only did they feel like it was their fault, they felt guilty because they were not supporting the Nephites in combat. This state of war continued for nearly ten years—until the twenty-sixth year of the reign of judges (66 BC). At this time, the suffering was so heartfelt that the people of Ammon gave serious thought to breaking their oath against war and returning to the battlefield (Alma 53:10–15).

## Helaman—An Inspiring Leader

Helaman was the son of Alma the Younger and had been given leadership of the church and responsibility for recording the Nephite history. During this time, Helaman and others were working feverishly as high priests to teach the Nephites and bring them to repentance. They knew that victory in the wars required a righteous Nephite nation and had gone among the people to inspire them to change. In the middle of this mission, the Lamanite converts of Ammon decided that it was time to break their oath not to shed blood by war. Helaman persuaded them not to break their oath. However, they did have sons who had not taken the oath. Helaman explained the situation.

> But behold, it came to pass they had many sons, who had not entered into a covenant that they would not take their weapons of war to defend themselves against their enemies; therefore they did assemble themselves together at this time, as many as were able to take up arms, and they called themselves Nephites.
>
> And they entered into a covenant to fight for the liberty of the Nephites, yea, to protect the land unto the laying down of their lives; yea, even they covenanted that they never would give up their liberty, but they would fight in all cases to protect the Nephites and themselves from bondage. (Alma 53:16–17)

As noted earlier, the Book of Mormon is a story of covenants and this is an excellent illustration. The Ammonites at this point were persuaded not to break their oath. Breaking their oath was so serious that Helaman felt they would "lose their souls." It is clear that the Nephite people and their leaders understood the importance of making and keeping covenants.

Helaman reported that the sons of the Ammonites came forward with a desire to join in the war and requested that Helaman become their military commander (Alma 53:17–18; 56:6–8). They had not been old enough to make the oath against war and were not under the obligation of that covenant. Most of these young men were just teenagers. As they came forward, they made a new covenant of their own: "they covenanted that they never would give up their liberty, but they would fight in all cases to protect the Nephites and themselves from bondage" (Alma 53:17).

Helaman's father, Alma the Younger, was the first elected Nephite chief judge. As the son of a Nephite judge, Helaman had most certainly been trained as a military leader. Helaman was also the probable author of the war chapters in the Book of Mormon (Alma 45–62). An insight into the character of Helaman is given in the teachings of his father to him at a young age.

> *And now, O my son Helaman, behold, thou art in thy youth, and therefore, I beseech of thee that thou wilt hear my words and learn of me; for I do know that whosoever shall put their trust in God shall be supported in their trials, and their troubles, and their afflictions, and shall be lifted up at the last day. (Alma 36:3)*

Alma taught Helaman that those who "trust in God shall be supported in their trials and troubles and afflictions" (Alma 36:3). As you will see in the story of the stripling warriors, Helaman taught the same principle to the young soldiers whom he eventually called his sons.

## The Stripling Warriors: An Impressive Group of Young Men

These two thousand men of faith and commitment were very young. Accordingly, they were called the "stripling warriors." This story begins a little more than ten years after the first Ammonite oath not to shed blood. The Ammonites under oath probably would have been all Ammonite men down to and including teenagers. This group of teenagers must have been very young children when their fathers took the oath. Moreover, they were raised by the Ammonites, who were against the shedding of blood. Consequently, they wouldn't be trained in the art of war. They would have little knowledge or skill with the weapons of hand-to-hand combat. Knowing this background makes it very clear that their commander, Helaman, took charge of some awfully young and inexperienced teenagers. They had, nevertheless, been raised by parents who taught them the value of making a commitment.

It is likely that many of their fathers were among the one thousand Ammonites who willingly gave their lives rather than break an oath to not fight. With the same strength and dedication as their fathers, these young men took an oath to obey every order of Helaman and fight for the freedom of their people.

The unfolding of this heartwarming story

of youthful courage and valor was told in a letter from Chief Captain Helaman to the higher-ranking Chief Nephite Captain Moroni. These two great captains were in the midst of the greatest war in the history of the people of Nephi up to this time. They were fighting the Lamanites on opposite ends of the land. The letter from Helaman in many ways was a progress report to Captain Moroni. The letter also gave us an understanding of the depth of honor and love Captain Helaman had for Captain Moroni.

*And these are the words which he wrote, saying: My dearly beloved brother, Moroni, as well in the Lord as in the tribulations of our warfare; behold, my beloved brother, I have somewhat to tell you concerning our warfare in this part of the land. (Alma 56:2)*

Helaman explained to Moroni that the war in his region had been difficult and that he had assigned the two thousand young men to assist the army of Antipus. Helaman also showed his love for the stripling warriors by calling them his sons.

*But behold, here is one thing in which we may have great joy. For behold, in the twenty and sixth year, I, Helaman, did march at the head of these two thousand young men to the city of Judea, to assist Antipus, whom ye had appointed a leader over the people of that part of the land.*

*And I did join my two thousand sons, (for they are worthy to be called sons) to the army of Antipus . . . for behold, his army had been reduced by the Lamanites because their forces had slain a vast number of our men, for which cause we have to mourn. . . .*

*And the Lamanites had also retained many prisoners, all of whom are chief captains, for none other have they spared alive. And we suppose that they are now at this time in the land of Nephi; it is so if they are not slain. (Alma 56:9–10, 12)*

Reflecting on this report we can see that the war had been difficult and that the army of Antipus had been severely weakened by casualties. Hence, the addition of two thousand men was very welcome. The enormous danger these young soldiers faced is illustrated in verse 12. Helaman explained that the Lamanites were killing all the prisoners taken in battle except the chief captains.

As a soldier, this small piece of information gives me insight into the horrid nature of this war. The Lamanites only kept the high-ranking prisoners alive. The captains had more strategic intelligence (information) and were more valuable to be exchanged for other prisoners. Moreover, prisoners are a battle-field problem—an army must take part of the fighters to keep track of the imprisoned captives. The Lamanites were a long way from their home territory and wanted to keep only a small number of prisoners. While it is not stated specifically, it is evident that these two thousand young soldiers were in grave danger if they were used in combat. The Nephites would need decisive victories in every battle because the youths would certainly be killed if captured because of the Lamanite hatred for the Ammonites. The Lamanite army policy to kill prisoners of war, given by their leader Ammoron, is a distant departure from the policy of Captain Moroni, the leader of the Nephite armies. His policy was to show mercy and preserve life where possible. Captain Moroni had set precedence in an earlier battle at Manti by allowing captured Lamanites to go free if they would take an oath to no longer make war and not return to Nephite lands (see Alma 43 and 44).

From a military standpoint, the Lamanite decision to not take prisoners and kill all enemy soldiers on a victorious battlefield is venge-ful and unproductive. First, the army could not collect battlefield intelligence from a large number of frightened prisoners. Second, the knowledge that surrender meant certain death would make every Nephite fight with increased intensity. When there is no chance of survival as a prisoner, every soldier fights to the death. Just imagine the terror and violence of the battlefield under these conditions.

## The Successful Strategy of Antipus and Helaman

The status of the war in the southern part of the Nephite lands was grim. Helaman explained that the Lamanites had captured four major cities and that the morale of his army was poor (Alma 56:14–16)

Because of the addition of the stripling warriors, the Lamanites did not attack Judea. The new young soldiers also brought supplies from the people of Ammon, who were con-cerned about their children. The older people of Ammon did not take up the sword, but they did all they could to support the Nephite armies with supplies. The size of the Nephite army in Judea had grown to ten thousand and was again refreshed and strengthened. The four strong-hold cities captured by the Lamanites were too fortified to attack, so the Nephite captains Antipus and Helaman were in search of a "strat-agem" to lure the Lamanites out of the strong-holds. Additionally, the Nephites kept spies out to make sure that the Lamanite armies could not pass by the city of Judea on their way to the north (Alma 56:17–27).

The stage was set for the use of a decoy to lure the Lamanites out into the open. The use of decoys was a very successful strategy because the Lamanites' hatred was so intense that an apparent opportunity to destroy a small unit of Nephites could not be passed up. It was decided that the stripling warriors would be the decoy. They were young and inexperienced, and the Nephites intended to use them only as a decoy and not in combat.

The plan was to march the youthful warriors past the city of Antiparah, which was the base of the largest and most powerful of the Lamanite armies. This would lure the Lamanites into the open, and then the Nephite army led by Antipus would attack the Lamanites from the rear. The plan worked but brought many complications. The first was that the Lamanites did not stop to fight Antipus. They sped up to catch Helaman and his small unit. Antipus was very frightened for the young unit and set his men at a speed march to catch up with the Lamanite army (Alma 56:28–38).

Night came and the young decoy unit rested and then moved toward the wilderness. Helaman reported the following.

*Now they durst not turn to the right*

*nor to the left lest they should be surrounded; neither would I turn to the right nor to the left lest they should overtake me, and we could not stand against them, but be slain, and they would make their escape; and thus we did flee all that day into the wilderness, even until it was dark. (Alma 56:40)*

After two full days of marching, Helaman's young unit awoke with the Lamanites almost upon them. "And it came to pass that again, when the light of the morning came we saw the Lamanites upon us, and we did flee before them" (Alma 56:41). For some reason the Lamanites stopped chasing the decoy and turned to engage the Nephite army. At this point in the story, a critical moment of decision occurred. Note the words of Helaman.

*And now, whether they were overtaken by Antipus we knew not, but I said unto my men: Behold, we know not but they have halted for the purpose that we should come against them, that they might catch us in their snare; Therefore what say ye, my sons, will ye go against them to battle?*

*And now I say unto you, my beloved brother Moroni, that never had I seen so great courage, nay, not amongst all the*

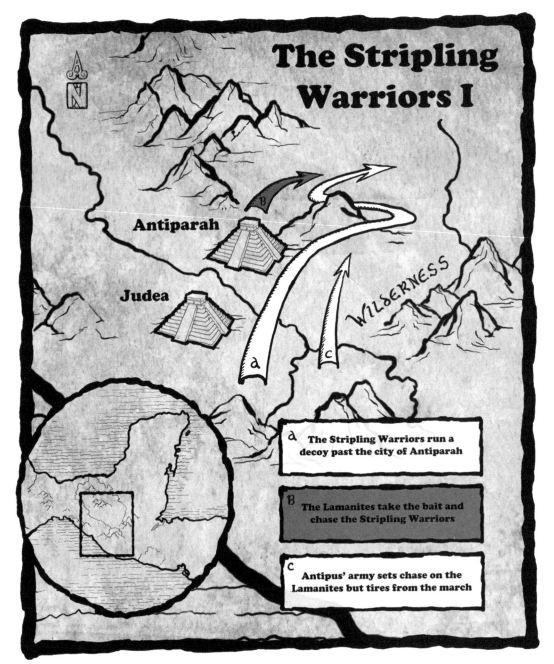

# The Stripling Warriors I

Antiparah

Judea

WILDERNESS

**a** The Stripling Warriors run a decoy past the city of Antiparah

**B** The Lamanites take the bait and chase the Stripling Warriors

**c** Antipus' army sets chase on the Lamanites but tires from the march

*Nephites. For as I had ever called them my sons (for they were all of them very young) even so they said unto me: Father, behold our God is with us, and he will not suffer that we should fall; then let us go forth; we would not slay our brethren if they would let us alone; therefore let us go, lest they should overpower the army of Antipus.*

*Now they never had fought, yet they did not fear death; and they did think more upon the liberty of their fathers than they did upon their lives; yea, they had been taught by their mothers, that if they did not doubt, God would deliver them. And they rehearsed unto me the words of their mothers, saying: We do not doubt our mothers knew it.*

*And it came to pass that I did return with my two thousand against these Lamanites who had pursued us. And now behold, the armies of Antipus had over-taken them, and a terrible battle had commenced. (Alma 56:43–49)*

This brief dialogue between Helaman and his "sons" is remarkable. We all should note that at many times in life, critical moments come upon us quickly and test our commitment to principle. Captain Helaman spoke to his young men: "What say ye my sons, will you go against

them to battle?" (Alma 56:44) Our challenge may not come in war, but it will come. Will we be up to the challenge when we are asked, "What say ye?" Will our leader reflect on our character as Helaman reflected on his warriors'? "And now I say unto you, Moroni, that never had I seen so great courage, nay, not amongst all the Nephites" (Alma 56:45)

Helaman explained the important parts of their youthful and courageous response:

**First**, they expressed their faith in their God. "Father, behold our God is with us and he will not suffer that we should fall: then let us go forth."

**Second**, they were fearless in their support of liberty. "Now they had never fought yet they did not fear death; and they did think more upon the liberty of their fathers than they did upon their lives."

**Third**, they remembered the teachings of their mothers. "We do not doubt our mothers knew it" (Alma 56:47–48)

One may ask why they talked about their mothers at this moment. Remember the thousand Lamanite Christian men who were slaughtered by the Lamanites because they would not take up the sword? It is very likely that many of these young stripling warriors were sons of those men. They had been raised by faithful single mothers, who loved their new faith

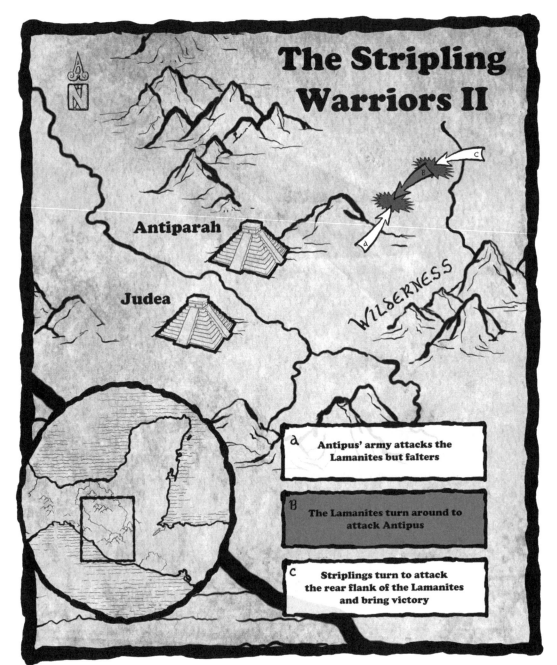

# The Stripling Warriors II

**Antiparah**

**Judea**

WILDERNESS

a — Antipus' army attacks the Lamanites but falters

B — The Lamanites turn around to attack Antipus

C — Striplings turn to attack the rear flank of the Lamanites and bring victory

and knew how to teach their sons to be faithful and valiant to their oaths, just like their fathers, who had given up their lives rather than break an oath. This is perhaps the greatest tribute in all of scripture to motherhood and the impact that righteous mothers have on the lives of young children. This heartfelt compliment to mothers brings tears to many readers who have a mother that played a central role in the development of their character. If many of these young Lamanites were raised without fathers, it explains why they revered Helaman and desired to call him father.

Helaman explained battle and the plight of the Nephite army of their captain, Antipus.

*And it came to pass that I did return with my two thousand against these Lamanites who had pursued us. And now behold, the armies of Antipus had overtaken them, and a terrible battle had commenced. The army of Antipus being weary, because of their long march in so short a space of time, were about to fall into the hands of the Lamanites; and had I not returned with my two thousand they would have obtained their purpose. (Alma 56:49–50)*

Having lost Antipus and being weak from the speed march, the Nephite army was about to collapse when Helaman and his two thousand attacked the Lamanites from the rear. Helaman explained the situation.

*And it came to pass that the Lamanites took courage, and began to pursue them; and thus were the Lamanites pursuing them with great vigor when Helaman came upon their rear with his two thousand, and began to slay them exceedingly, insomuch that the whole army of the Lamanites halted and turned upon Helaman. Now when the people of Antipus saw that the Lamanites had turned them about, they gathered together their men and came again upon the rear of the Lamanites.*

*And now it came to pass that we, the people of Nephi, the people of Antipus, and I with my two thousand, did surround the Lamanites, and did slay them; yea, insomuch that they were compelled to deliver up their weapons of war and also themselves as prisoners of war. (Alma 56:52–54)*

After this tremendously emotional battle, Helaman took a moment to reflect on the valor and character of his wonderful young warriors and the role they had played in winning the battle.

*And now it came to pass that when they had surrendered themselves up unto us, behold, I numbered those young men who had fought with me, fearing lest there were many of them slain.*

***But behold, to my great joy, there had not one soul of them fallen to the earth; yea, and they had fought as if with the strength of God; yea, never were men known to have fought with such miraculous strength;*** *and with such mighty power did they fall upon the Lamanites, that they did frighten them; and for this cause did the Lamanites deliver themselves up as prisoners of war.* (Alma 56:55–56; emphasis added)

The Lamanite army became confused when surrounded. Note that there was a formal surrender and that the Lamanites became prisoners: a real departure from the practice of the Lamanite army who killed all of the captives save the chief captains.

It is important, speaking as a soldier, to make a final comment on the remarkable nature of this battle. These young men, probably twelve to fifteen years old, were inexperienced and had never fought before. They went into fierce face-to-face combat with experienced battle hardened Lamanites. They were filled with hatred for these young Lamanite Christians who had turned away from their Lamanite traditions. The performance by this youthful unit of soldiers without a single death was more than remarkable—it was a military miracle. Helaman's comments are certainly fitting: "They had fought as if with the strength of God; yea, never were men known to have fought with such miraculous strength" (Alma 56:56).

## The Battle of Cumeni: An Example of Battlefield Perfection

After the successful battle with the army of Antipus, Helaman and his army returned to the city of Antiparah. The Lamanites fled from Antiparah to other cities out of fear. Helaman then surrounded the city of Cumeni. The siege caused them to surrender when supplies could not reach the city. The Nephites, on the other hand, were able to get supplies from the north, including an additional sixty stripling warriors come to fight with their young brothers (Alma 57:1–12).

The next part of this saga adds depth to the truth of the historical account. The truth is that it was very difficult to manage and transport prisoners of war. With the Nephite victories in Antiparah and the surrender of Cumeni, there were large numbers of hostile Lamanite prisoners of war. The Nephites made an effort to return the prisoners north to Zarahemla, but the prisoners rebelled and escaped. It is extremely difficult to control, constrain, and transport a large number of prisoners. Guards are often outnumbered ten or more to one. Consequently, it would only take a small rebellion to free some prisoners, who then would begin to fight with stones and clubs to set others free. The sheer numbers would make the transportation almost impossible.

Helaman, the writer, thought this rebellion was providential because the guards returned to help Helaman and his army in a decisive battle against the Lamanites. Ammoron, the Lamanite leader, had sent a large army to the city of Cumeni, and Helaman was under attack and about to fall when the guards returned and changed the tide of the battle (Alma 57:13–17).

Helaman's army along with his stripling warriors were in a fierce battle to save the city of Cumeni from this refreshed Lamanite army sent by Ammoron. Helaman describes with wonder the performance of his young soldiers.

> *But behold, my little band of two thousand and sixty fought most desperately; yea, they were firm before the Lamanites, and did administer death unto all those who opposed them. And as the remainder of our army were about to give way before the Lamanites, behold, those two thousand and sixty were firm and undaunted.*
>
> **Yea, and they did obey and observe to perform every word of command with exactness; yea, and even according to their faith it was done unto them; and I did remember the words which they said unto me that their mothers had taught them.**
>
> *And now behold, it was these my sons, and those men who had been selected to convey the prisoners, to whom we owe this great victory; for it was they who did beat the Lamanites.* (Alma 57:19–22; emphasis added)

Please observe the illustrative words used by Helaman to describe the marvelous military performance of his sons, the 2,060 young warriors.

First, they were an inspiration to the more seasoned Nephite soldiers: "As the remainder of our army was about to give way . . . those two thousand and sixty were firm and undaunted" (v. 20).

Second, their obedience was exceptional: "they did obey and observe to perform every word of command with exactness" (v. 21).

Third, their faith carried them through: "yea, and even according to their faith it was done unto them; and I did remember the words which they said unto me that their mothers had taught them" (v. 21).

This description of the young warriors is exactly what any military commander would want in his soldiers: (1) Men of commitment, "undaunted," (2) men that would obey without question, "perform every word of command," and (3) men of great faith, "according to their faith." Writing as a former army officer, my feelings are even more heartfelt. I have no doubt that other officers would agree—commanding young soldiers is a challenge. My son is a navy officer and a commander in need of young sailors who would be examples of youthful excellence. Having dedicated and obedient young men is a commander's blessing.

Following the battle of Cumeni, Helaman feared that many of his young warriors were slain.

*And it came to pass that after the Lamanites had fled, I immediately gave orders that my men who had been wounded should be taken from among the dead, and caused that their wounds should be dressed. And it came to pass that there were two hundred, out of my two thousand and sixty, who had fainted because of the loss of blood; nevertheless, according to the goodness of God, and to our great astonishment, and also the joy*

*of our whole army, there was not one soul of them who did perish; yea, and neither was there one soul among them who had not received many wounds.*

***And now, their preservation was astonishing to our whole army, yea, that they should be spared while there was a thousand of our brethren who were slain.*** *And we do justly ascribe it to the miraculous power of God, because of their exceeding faith in that which they had been taught to believe—that there was a just God, and whosoever did not doubt, that they should be preserved by his marvelous power.* (Alma 57:24–26; emphasis added)

The description of this additional miracle of war is astounding: (1) two hundred fainted from loss of blood, (2) not one soul perished, and (3) not one had escaped this battle without being wounded. The miracle was widely praised because the whole army was astonished. Helaman's statement about his Stripling Warriors is worth repeating. *"And we do justly ascribe it to the miraculous power of God, because of their exceeding faith"* (Helaman 57:26). Helaman's final tribute in his letter to Moroni describes the greatness of the sons of Helaman, *"they are young, and their minds are firm, and they do put their trust in God continually"* (Alma 57:27).

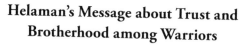 

## Helaman's Message about Trust and Brotherhood among Warriors

Earlier in this chapter, we learned of the great story about mothers and how they affected the behavior of their marvelous stripling warrior sons. We also saw the father-son relationship that developed between Helaman and his young warriors. There is, however, another relationship that can't be overlooked: the brotherhood of these great young men.

Soldiers form very strong bonds of friendship. They train together and learn their physical weaknesses. They live together and learn their emotional and personal frailties. They play together and learn to enjoy wildlife, games, and the beauties of life. Moreover, the more they learn the more they develop leaders from within their ranks.

In addition, the strongest bond comes from participation in battle. Imagine the horrors of ancient battle. Swords, spears, and other close quarter weapons were frighteningly vicious. The greatest fear of these battles would be to be attacked from behind or from a blind side. Trusting your fellow soldiers to cover the most vulnerable side creates a strong brotherhood. Your brother not only carries out his role in battle, he makes sure you are not taken from behind. Battle lines, semicircles, and full circles become necessary to protect each other from being blindly attacked. Being in this type of battle engendered much more that simple gratitude. It developed an appreciation that your life had literally been protected or saved because of the courage, bravery, and expertise of your brother in battle. This form of brotherhood and bravery is clearly exemplified by the stripling warriors. Remember when Helaman took his young army into battle for the first time? The army of Antipus was under assault by the Lamanites and about to fall. Helaman attacked the Lamanites from the rear. Note how the attitude and momentum of battle changed when an attack from the rear took place.

*The army of Antipus being weary, because of their long march in so short a space of time, were about to fall into the hands of the Lamanites; and had I not returned with my two thousand they would have obtained their purpose.*

*And it came to pass that the Lamanites took courage, and began to pursue them; and thus were the Lamanites pursuing them with great vigor when Helaman* **came upon their rear with his two thousand, and began to slay them exceedingly, insomuch that the whole army of the Lamanites halted and turned upon Helaman. Now when the people of Antipus saw**

*that the Lamanites had turned them about, they gathered together their men and came again upon the rear of the Lamanites.*

*And now it came to pass that we, the people of Nephi, the people of Antipus, and I with my two thousand, did surround the Lamanites, and did slay them; yea, insomuch that they were compelled to deliver up their weapons of war and also themselves as prisoners of war. (Alma 56:50, 52–54; emphasis added)*

As discussed earlier, these young soldiers had great faith, were well trained, and were obedient to the letter. In addition, the bond of brotherhood multiplied their ability to trust each other in battle and made them an incredible, unbeatable force. Christ understood this kind of love when he stated, "Greater love hath no man than this, that a man lay down his life for his friends" (John 15:13). Indeed, the friendship among the stripling warriors was exceptional. The God in whom these young men had so much faith was pleased with the action, trust, and faith demonstrated that day. There is no doubt their Savior supported and protected them in their battle for freedom.

## Helaman's Final Message: The Journey of Life

Remember that Mormon wrote that he could only include a one-hundredth part of the history of the people of Lehi. It is easy to see why he was so impressed with this tale of miraculous courage. I'm sure he read the plates, which were engraved by the prophet Helaman, and knew from the Spirit that this story was needed as an example to today's youth.

Our latter-day problems are very much like those of the Nephites. To make a lasting impact on this world fraught with corruption and sin, we need youth who will make an oath to the Lord and show their faith to the world. We need young people who will follow the lead of great men and not waver in their obedience to correct principles. Moreover, we need young people who will not be afraid to honor their parents. As a person who had an angel for a mother, it brings tears to my eyes when I read that these stripling warriors faced death on the battlefield and performed with absolute perfection because their mothers taught them obedience and faith.

A parallel to life's journey exists in this wonderful story. Each of us has come to earth to learn correct principles and be tested to see if we can do battle against sin and the challenges of earth. The only guarantee is that the Lord will be with us and redeem us because we were unable to be perfect.

Look at the parallel with the stripling warriors. They found the Savior and made a commitment to their faith. They went on a terribly difficult journey, which brought them into enormous danger. Not a single warrior escaped the weapons of the enemy. Two hundred of them fainted from their wounds and all were wounded many times, but they were saved by their faith and were able to return to their families.

Our earthly journey will be similar. All who come to earth will be injured by the trappings of Satan and the ruggedness of life. If we are faithful to the Savior and follow his direction, we will be rewarded just like the stripling warriors. All will be wounded, some of us will faint; but if we are true, the Savior will atone for our weakness and heal us so we can return to our eternal family.

# Five

# CAPTAIN MORONI, DEFENDER OF FREEDOM

*Yea, and he [Captain Moroni] was a man who was firm in the faith of Christ,*
*and he had sworn with an oath to defend his people, his rights,*
*and his country, and his religion, even to the loss of his blood.*
MORMON IN ALMA 48:13

Moroni, commonly called Captain Moroni, was an extraordinary military leader of the Nephite nation. The rank of "captain" is equivalent to "general" in the Nephite military rank structure. Moroni was the "chief captain" of the Nephites or, in modern language, the commanding general of all the armies. Captain Moroni was a contemporary of Alma the Younger when Alma was the Nephite prophet. He took over Nephite military leadership after Alma resigned his judgeship to call his nation to repentance. Speaking as a soldier and military officer, I am amazed by the leadership and military acumen demonstrated by Moroni. This chapter will introduce you to one of the most outstanding Nephite leaders and one of the greatest military leaders of all time.

## The Setting

In the fifteenth year of the reign of the judges (76 BC), a tremendous battle was fought between the Nephites and the Lamanites. It was the largest battle in Nephite history, involving tens of thousands of soldiers. The Lamanites invaded the land of Zarahemla with a huge army. The Nephites finally drove the Lamanites out of the land, and Alma records the terrible consequence.

*And thus there was a tremendous battle; yea, even such an one as never had been known among all the people in the land from the time Lehi left Jerusalem; yea, and tens of thousands of the Lamanites were slain and scattered abroad. Yea, and also there was a tremendous slaughter among the people of Nephi; nevertheless, the Lamanites were driven and scattered, and the people of Nephi returned again to their land.*

*And now this was a time that there was a great mourning and lamentation heard throughout all the land, among all the people of Nephi—Yea, the cry of widows mourning for their husbands, and also of fathers mourning for their sons, and the daughter for the brother, yea, the brother for the father; and thus the cry of mourning was heard among all of them, mourning for their kindred who had been slain. (Alma 28:2–5; emphasis added)*

We are told in no uncertain terms about the tragic nature of war. It brings terrible mourning into the lives of families, which have lost fathers and sons. Sometimes we must read carefully to see why a story is placed into the Book of Mormon (see Alma 28). However, it is very clear why this brief chapter was included. The editor, Mormon, makes a poignant comment at the end of the chapter. Mormon's comments on this battle and the tragedy of war are highlighted by his often-used reflective phrase: "And thus we see."

*While many thousands of others truly mourn for the loss of their kindred, yet they rejoice and exult in the hope, and even know, according to the promises of the Lord, that they are raised to dwell at the right hand of God, in a state of never-ending happiness.*

*And thus we see how great the inequality of man is because of sin and transgression, and the power of the devil, which comes by the cunning plans which he hath devised to ensnare the hearts of men.*

*And thus we see the great call of diligence of men to labor in the vineyards of the Lord; and thus we see the great reason of sorrow, and also of rejoicing—sorrow because of death and destruction among men, and joy because of the light of Christ unto life.*
*(Alma 28:12–14; emphasis added)*

This dreadful time of sorrow sets the stage for the historical account of Captain Moroni. It begins several years after this battle, when Nephihah is the chief judge (elected political leader) and Alma is the prophet. Alma had left his judgeship to go on a spiritual mission to correct the iniquity that had overcome his people. While Alma was on his mission, the Lamanites gathered for another battle, and a very young twenty-five-year-old Nephite soldier, Moroni, was appointed as chief captain (commanding general) of all the Nephite armies.

*Now, the leader of the Nephites, or the man who had been appointed to be the chief captain over the Nephites—now the chief captain took the command of all the armies of the Nephites—and his name was Moroni. And Moroni took all the command, and the government of their wars. And he was only twenty and five years old when he was appointed chief captain over the armies of the Nephites. (Alma 43:16–17)*

Remember that Mormon, the editor of the Book of Mormon, said numerous times he couldn't include even a "hundredth part" of the history, yet he includes a detailed account of Moroni's military campaigns. A possible answer may be found in Mormon's reflections regarding Moroni. Mormon was so impressed that he couldn't hold back his feelings about perhaps the greatest of all Nephite generals. Mormon wrote the following comment on Captain Moroni some 350 years later while he was transferring an edited history from one set of metal plates to another.

*Yea, verily, verily I say unto you, if all men had been, and were, and ever would be, like unto Moroni, behold, the very powers of hell would have been shaken forever; yea, the devil would never have power over the hearts of the children of men. (Alma 48:17)*

It is evident that Mormon is giving the people of the latter days a role model to follow. He respected Moroni so much that he said if men were like Captain Moroni, the powers of hell would be eliminated. Remember, if he could include only a hundredth part of the Nephite history, what he does include must be significant. Another indication of Mormon's respect for this great warrior is that he named his son Moroni.

The story of Captain Moroni is so impressive that it will be necessary to break it into several parts to accurately cover the key elements. First, we will examine the history of Moroni's early military campaigns and his military leadership.

Second, we will contrast Moroni's character to that of the wicked leader Amalickiah. Third, we will discuss the peaceful times among the Nephites under Captain Moroni. Fourth, we will demonstrate evidence of Moroni's honorable character by comparing Moroni to the evil men of his time.

## The Battle for Manti: A Story of Masterful Strategy

The Lamanites lived and were concentrated in the lands to the south of the Nephites—in the land of first inheritance usually called the Land of Nephi. After the great missionary efforts of the sons of Mosiah, thousands of Lamanite converts to Christianity were moved several hundred miles north, where they could be protected by the Nephites. These people were now called Ammonites, named after the missionary who was chiefly responsible for the conversion of the first Lamanite king, Lamoni. To be protected from Lamanite threats, they were moved far to the north in a land called Jershon (see illustration). The Lamanite people considered the Ammonites traitors to their traditions because of their conversion, and there was much animosity. Consequently, in 73 BC the Lamanites sent a large army to attack the Ammonites in Jershon.

The defense of the land was up to the chief captain, Moroni. One of first successful actions of the captain was to design body armor for his soldiers. Zerahemnah, the Lamanite army commander, planned his first attack on the Ammonites in Jershon; however, he retreated when he compared the armor of Moroni's army to the unarmored sparse clothing of his Lamanite soldiers.

*And when the armies of the Lamanites saw that the people of Nephi, or that Moroni, had prepared his people with breastplates and with arm-shields, yea, and also shields to defend their heads, and also they were dressed with thick clothing—*

*Now the army of Zerahemnah was not prepared with any such thing; they had only their swords and their cimeters, their bows and their arrows, their stones and their slings; and they were naked, save it were a skin which was girded about their loins; yea, all were naked, save it were the Zoramites and the Amalekites. (Alma 43:19–20)*

As shown on page 111, Zerahemnah and his Lamanite army retreated from Jershon into the wilderness as a deception. They were preparing for a covert attack on a less-fortified city in the

**THE BATTLE OF MANTI**

**Phase I**

*Zerahemnah Turns Away from Fortified Jershon*

*Moroni and Lehi Prepare for the Attack*

south, called Manti. Captain Moroni needed information on the enemy. In modern military language, the collection of information about the enemy is called "military intelligence." Moroni knew the importance of military intelligence and made two important moves: (1) he sent messengers to ask the prophet Alma to ask the Lord where the Lamanite armies were going, and (2) he sent spies to watch the movements of Zerahemnah's army. Alma sent a message back to Moroni that the attack would be on the southernmost city of Manti. Moroni's spies continued to track the enemy through the wilderness, while Moroni traveled to Manti to prepare for a battle and to motivate the people of Manti to build an army to merge with his and protect the city (see Alma 43:23–29).

Moroni set the trap by concealing his armies from Zerahemnah. He sent Captain Lehi to the south and the west of the hill Riplah, a large and convenient place to conceal his armies from the sight and movement of the Lamanite army. The spies were told to track Zerahemnah and warn Lehi of the enemy movement.

Moroni continued to track the Lamanite army while concealing Captain Lehi's army behind the hill Riplah. Zerahemnah fell into Moroni's trap by coming out of the wilderness on the north side of the hill. Captain Lehi was concealed and waiting to attack from the high ground and from behind (see Alma 43:30–37).

Zerahemnah planned to attack the city of Manti clandestinely. He had moved through the wilderness toward the southern Nephite city. However, after passing the hill Riplah on the way to the River Sidon, his army was surprised by an attack from the rear. Lehi attacked Zerahemnah from higher ground. Historically, it has always been a strategic advantage to attack from higher ground. The army on the higher ground has a clear view of enemy movement and can move rapidly into position. Moreover, the individual soldiers have the advantage in combat because they can shoot arrows down on the enemy below, and, when attacking, they can force the enemy onto the heels of their feet and knock them down with swift movements going downhill. Captain Lehi must have planned an excellent strategy because a fierce battle ensued, and Zerahemnah, who had two times the number of soldiers, finally retreated to the River Sidon. As he retreated, he encountered the army of Moroni. The consequence was a military battle disaster for the Lamanite army. Zerahemnah retreated toward the river and saw Moroni's army on the other shore. He couldn't go up or down the river and was trapped with no possibility of escape. The strategies of Moroni and Lehi had worked perfectly (see Alma 43:48–54).

From a military analyst's point of view, it is

interesting to take note of Moroni's successful strategy, especially when his army was outnumbered two to one (Alma 43).

First, Moroni created armor to protect his men in hand-to-hand combat.

Second, he contacted Alma the prophet for guidance about enemy movement.

Third, he used a network of spies to track and report the movement of the Lamanites.

Fourth, he designed an element of surprise and set up an ambush by hiding the army of Lehi behind the hill Riplah and his army in the city of Manti.

Fifth, he directed Captain Lehi to attack from the rear and from the high ground behind the hill Riplah, giving Lehi's army a distinct advantage.

Sixth, he surrounded the enemy by placing his armies at the river, making a Lamanite retreat impossible.

## The Battle for Manti: A Contrast in Motivation

The strategy of the battle for Manti is fascinating, but there are exact verses that I must quote to illustrate the contrast in leadership and motivation. First, Zerahemnah motivated his army by hate and anger. Alma tells us how he used former Nephites as his leaders. The

Amalekites and the Zoramites were former Nephite dissenters who hated the Christian church and the Nephites.

*And it came to pass that the Lamanites came with their thousands; . . . and a man by the name of Zerahemnah was their leader. And now, as the Amalekites were of a more wicked and murderous disposition than the Lamanites were, in and of themselves, therefore, Zerahemnah appointed chief captains over the Lamanites, and they were all Amalekites and Zoramites.*

*Now this he did that he might preserve their hatred towards the Nephites, that he might bring them into subjection to the accomplishment of his designs. For behold, his designs were to stir up the Lamanites to anger against the Nephites; this he did that he might usurp great power over them, and also that he might gain power over the Nephites by bringing them into bondage. (Alma 43:5–8)*

Moreover, Zerahemnah, leader of the Lamanite armies, sought to enslave the Nephites by defeating them in war. He had motivated his army through greed—promising his soldiers the spoils of war and the profit from slavery. After a victory, his Lamanite army could create

## THE BATTLE OF MANTI

### Phase III

*Zerahemnah Moves toward Manti*

**THE BATTLE OF MANTI**

Phase IV

*Zerahemnah Caught in Moroni's Trap*

incredible wealth by enslaving of the conquered Nephites. He had chosen leaders who were the most "wicked and murderous." Finally, Zerahemnah's overpowering desire to defeat his enemy made him totally irrational.

By comparison, the Nephites under the leadership of Captain Moroni had completely different motivations. Their motivations were based on righteousness, love of family, and liberty.

> *And now the design of the Nephites was to support their lands, and their houses, and their wives, and their children, that they might preserve them from the hands of their enemies; and also that they might preserve their rights and their privileges, yea, and also their liberty, that they might worship God according to their desires.*
>
> *For they knew that if they should fall into the hands of the Lamanites, that whosoever should worship God in spirit and in truth, the true and the living God, the Lamanites would destroy. (Alma 43:9–10)*

Alma, the author, and Mormon, the editor, in their wisdom have given us a great illustration of contrasting leadership. Moroni loved his people and wanted freedom, while Zerahemnah was driven by hatred and a desire for power, bondage, and wealth. There is also a comparison of the individual soldiers. The Lamanites had left their families far behind and taken a twisted and horrible risk based on hate. The Nephites, on the other hand, were motivated by the preservation of their families, the desire for freedom, and a longing to worship God. These pages of the Book of Mormon clearly illustrate the contrast between love and hatred. (Alma 43:44–49)

## The Battle for Manti: A Display of Fierce Combat and a Unique Surrender

The great battle commenced when Lehi descended from the hill Riplah and attacked Zerahemnah from behind. The Lamanites were no match for the Nephites because of the protective Nephite body armor.

> *And it came to pass that the Lamanites, when they saw the Nephites coming upon them in their rear, turned them about and began to contend with the army of Lehi.*
>
> *And the work of death commenced on both sides, but it was more dreadful on the part of the Lamanites, for their nakedness was exposed to the heavy blows of the Nephites with their swords and their cimeters, which brought death almost at every stroke.*

*While on the other hand, there was now and then a man fell among the Nephites, by their swords and the loss of blood, they being shielded from the more vital parts of the body, or the more vital parts of the body being shielded from the strokes of the Lamanites, by their breast-plates, and their arm shields, and their head-plates; and thus the Nephites did carry on the work of death among the Lamanites.*

*And it came to pass that the Laman-ites became frightened, because of the great destruction among them, even until they began to flee toward the river Sidon. And they were pursued by Lehi and his men; and they were driven by Lehi into the waters of Sidon, and they crossed the waters of Sidon. And Lehi retained his armies upon the bank of the river Sidon that they should not cross. (Alma 43:36–40)*

The Lamanite army was hopelessly trapped in the planned ambush. It is true with animals as well as armies—when they are trapped they become more vicious and fight harder. The Lamanite entrapment was an unbearable dilemma for Zerahemnah's army. They were exhausted from battle and retreating through the river. At this point, they were confronted by Moroni's fresh army that had been waiting and

preparing for this battle. Even in this difficult situation, the Lamanites fought like "dragons."

*And it came to pass that Moroni and his army met the Lamanites in the valley, on the other side of the river Sidon, and began to fall upon them and to slay them. And the Lamanites did flee again before them, towards the land of Manti; and they were met again by the armies of Moroni.*

*Now in this case the Lamanites did fight exceedingly; yea, never had the Lamanites been known to fight with such exceedingly great strength and courage, no, not even from the beginning.* ***And they were inspired by the Zoramites and the Amalekites, who were their chief captains and leaders, and by Zera-hemnah, who was their chief captain, or their chief leader and commander; yea, they did fight like dragons,*** *and many of the Nephites were slain by their hands, yea, for they did smite in two many of their head-plates, and they did pierce many of their breastplates, and they did smite off many of their arms; and thus the Lamanites did smite in their fierce anger. (Alma 43:41–44; emphasis added).*

The Lamanites were highly motivated by their leaders filled with animosity and a desire to enslave their enemy while the Nephites were motivated by Moroni who reminded them of their families and freedom.

> *Nevertheless, the Nephites were inspired by a better cause, for they were not fighting for monarchy nor power but they were fighting for their homes and their liberties, their wives and their children, and their all, yea, for their rites of worship and their church.* (Alma 43:45)

The leadership of Moroni prevailed in this battle. When he saw that his men might falter at the fierceness of the Lamanite army, he reminded them of their noble purpose—to defend their land and their families from bondage. Moreover, he appealed to them, asking that they would turn to the Lord for help.

> *And it came to pass that when the men of Moroni saw the fierceness and the anger of the Lamanites, they were about to shrink and flee from them.* **And Moroni, perceiving their intent, sent forth and inspired their hearts with these thoughts—yea, the thoughts of their lands, their liberty, yea, their freedom from bondage.**
>
> **And it came to pass that they turned upon the Lamanites, and they cried with one voice unto the Lord their God, for their liberty and their freedom from bondage.** *And they began to stand against the Lamanites with power; and in that selfsame hour that they cried unto the Lord for their freedom, the Lamanites began to flee before them; and they fled even to the waters of Sidon.*
>
> *Now, the Lamanites were more numerous, yea, by more than double the number of the Nephites; nevertheless, they were driven insomuch that they were gathered together in one body in the valley, upon the bank by the river Sidon.* (Alma 43:48–51; emphasis added)

Perhaps the most noble of Moroni's character traits is demonstrated here. Seeing the terror in his enemy and the loss of life, Moroni showed mercy to his enemy and halted the attack.

> *Therefore the armies of Moroni encircled them about, yea, even on both sides of the river, for behold, on the east were the men of Lehi. Therefore when Zerahemnah saw the men of Lehi on the east of the river Sidon, and the armies of Moroni on the west of the river Sidon, that they were encircled about by the Nephites, they were struck with terror.* **Now Moroni, when he saw their terror, commanded his men that they should stop shedding their blood.** (Alma 43:52–54; emphasis added)

### The Battle's Conclusion Demonstrates the Nature of Pride and the Purpose of Oaths

The end of this battle and the surrender of the Lamanites illustrate the compassion of Moroni and the unyielding nature of Zerahemnah. The battle was stopped in anticipation of surrender and Moroni started the process with a statement regarding the battle and the role of God in the battle. This is typical of the great Nephite commanders. They gave credit to the Lord for their success

> *And it came to pass that they did stop and withdrew a pace from them. And Moroni said unto Zerahemnah: Behold, Zerahemnah that we do not desire to be men of blood. Ye know that ye are in our hands, yet we do not desire to slay you. . . . But now, ye behold that the Lord is with us; and ye behold that he has delivered you into our hands. . . .*
>
> *Now ye see that this is the true faith of God; yea, ye see that God will support, and keep, and preserve us, so long as we are faithful unto him, and unto our faith, and our religion; and never will the Lord suffer that we shall be destroyed except we should fall into transgression and deny our faith. (Alma 44:1, 3–4)*

Moroni then demanded that Zerahemnah and his men give up their weapons and make an oath to never return. This seems to be a sensible demand for a reasonable person; however, Zerahemnah was absurdly irrational and rejected the offer.

> *And now, Zerahemnah, I command you, in the name of that all-powerful God, who has strengthened our arms that we have gained power over you. . . .*
>
> *Yea, and this is not all; I command you by all the desires which ye have for life, that ye deliver up your weapons of war unto us, and we will seek not your blood, but we will spare your lives, if ye will go your way and come not again to war against us.*
>
> *And now it came to pass that when Zerahemnah had heard these sayings he came forth and delivered up his sword and his cimeter, and his bow into the hands of Moroni, and said unto him: Behold, here are our weapons of war; we will deliver them up unto you, but we will not suffer ourselves to take an oath unto you, which we know that we shall break, and also our children; but take our weapons of war, and suffer that we may depart into the wilderness; otherwise we will retain our swords, and we will perish or conquer.*
>
> *Behold, we are not of your faith; we*

*do not believe that it is God that has delivered us into your hands; but we believe that it is your cunning that has preserved you from our swords. Behold, it is your breastplates and your shields that have preserved you.*

*And now when Zerahemnah had made an end of speaking these words, Moroni returned the sword and the weapons of war, which he had received, unto Zerahemnah, saying: Behold, we will end the conflict. . . . And now when Moroni had said these words, Zerahemnah retained his sword, and he was angry with Moroni, and he rushed forward that he might slay Moroni; but as he raised his sword, behold, one of Moroni's soldiers smote it even to the earth, and it broke by the hilt; and he also smote Zerahemnah that he took off his scalp and it fell to the earth. And Zerahemnah withdrew from before them into the midst of his soldiers. (Alma 44:5–6, 8–10, 12)*

Zerahemnah refused the oath and attempted to kill Moroni. Zerahemnah was so beset with pride, anger, and stubbornness that he made a foolish decision. Consequently, the battle resumed and the Nephites took control of it again. The conclusion and the surrender is described in the following passages.

*Now Zerahemnah, when he saw that they were all about to be destroyed, cried mightily unto Moroni, promising that he would covenant and also his people with them, if they would spare the remainder of their lives, that they never would come to war again against them.*

*And it came to pass that Moroni caused that the work of death should cease again among the people. And he took the weapons of war from the Lamanites; and after they had entered into a covenant with him of peace they were suffered to depart into the wilderness. (Alma 44:19–20)*

Take note of how the Nephites celebrated the victory—they gave credit to their God and then fasted and prayed. They were clearly following the leadership of their chief captain and primary example—Moroni.

*Behold, now it came to pass that the people of Nephi were exceedingly rejoiced, because the Lord had again delivered them out of the hands of their enemies; therefore they gave thanks unto the Lord their God; yea, and they did fast much and pray much, and they did worship God with exceedingly great joy. (Alma 45:1; emphasis added).*

## Amalickiah—
## A Cunning and Deceitful Nephite

Following this difficult war with the Lamanites led by Zerahemnah, the Nephite nation rejoiced, and Alma ordained his son Helaman to be the prophet and head of the church. Helaman moved into the cities to establish the church and cry repentance. There was, however, a dissension among the people led by a cunning and deceitful leader named Amalickiah. He wanted the Nephites to discontinue their democracy and declare him king. He convinced many elected lower judges to support him as king. This is the equivalent of a modern-day leader convincing city, state, and regional leaders to turn from the national leaders and terminate the voice of the voters.

*Now the leader of those who were wroth against their brethren was a large and a strong man; and his name was Amalickiah. And Amalickiah was desirous to be a king; and those people who were wroth were also desirous that he should be their king; and they were the greater part of them the lower judges of the land, and they were seeking for power. (Alma 46:3–4)*

The wicked leaders in the Book of Mormon were often large, powerful, and very cunning.

The treachery of these wicked men was clear. Amalickiah was an especially evil and ruthless man who deceived the people to get power and subverted the success of the church. This was very personal to Helaman, and it can be seen in the descriptive phrases that follow.

*And they had been led by the flatteries of Amalickiah, that if they would support him and establish him to be their king that he would make them rulers over the people. Thus they were led away by Amalickiah to dissensions, notwithstanding the preaching of Helaman and his brethren, yea, notwithstanding their exceedingly great care over the church, for they were high priests over the church.*

*And there were many in the church who believed in the flattering words of Amalickiah, therefore they dissented even from the church; and thus were the affairs of the people of Nephi exceedingly precarious and dangerous, notwithstanding their great victory which they had had over the Lamanites, and their great rejoicings which they had had because of their deliverance by the hand of the Lord. (Alma 46:5–7)*

The discussion of Amalickiah continues with a comment probably from Mormon.

Remember, Mormon often makes editorial comments and begins with the phrase: "Thus we see . . ." In these passages, Mormon refers to the people as being quick to forget the Lord, and how one wicked man can influence an entire nation.

> *Thus we see how quick the children of men do forget the Lord their God, yea, how quick to do iniquity, and to be led away by the evil one.* **Yea, and we also see the great wickedness one very wicked man can cause to take place among the children of men.**
>
> **Yea, we see that Amalickiah, because he was a man of cunning device and a man of many flattering words, that he led away the hearts of many people to do wickedly;** *yea, and to seek to destroy the church of God, and to destroy the foundation of liberty which God had granted unto them, or which blessing God had sent upon the face of the land for the righteous' sake. (Alma 46:8–10; emphasis added)*

A few years earlier, we saw the rise of Amlici and his followers, who were defeated by Alma. Less than a generation later, another cunning leader came forth. Remember, the Book of Mormon was written for our day—to help us compare the wickedness of their day and that of ours. It is obvious that the authors are giving us a significant warning—*watch out for wicked men who will deceive the people and take control of your nations by cunning deceit and corruption!* A brief look at the twentieth century illustrates how many wicked, cunning men have risen to powerful positions and virtually destroyed their nations because of a desire for control. Adolf Hitler (Germany), Joseph Stalin (Russia), Benito Mussolini (Italy), Mao Tse-tung (China), Pol Pot (Cambodia), Slobodan Milošević (Yugoslavia), Saddam Hussein (Iraq), and Fidel Castro (Cuba) are just a few recent wicked leaders who have stripped their nations of freedom and established dictatorships.

Perhaps the most notable of these wicked leaders was German Chancellor Adolf Hitler. He rose to power in 1933 by deceptive means, and by 1940 he had pulled most of the developed nations into World War II. His greatest atrocities do not include the millions of soldiers, sailors, and airmen who lost their lives fighting his armies. His evil character is demonstrated by his systematic execution of between eleven and fourteen million people. The United States Holocaust Museum reports the following about his campaigns to destroy innocent people that he determined were undesirable. They report that the Jewish population in Europe was reduced to three million by the systematic murder of six million Jews during World War II.[2]

Historians also note that two hundred thousand Gypsies and at least two hundred thousand mentally or physically disabled patients died.[2]

Another unbelievably wicked dictator was Joseph Stalin of Soviet Russia. He ruled the Union of Soviet Socialist Republics between 1922 and 1953. He was a ruthless leader during the war against Hitler's Germany. He stopped the advance of the German armies in Russia and then pursued the German army in its retreat. His desire to reach Germany before the other allies caused the death of millions. He was ruthless and had little or no concern for the unnecessary deaths in his army. Military historian David Glantz estimates that the armies of Stalin sustained approximately 35 million casualties and 14.7 million deaths in his march to Germany.[3]

The worst of Stalin's carnage did not happen during war but following the war against his own people. He purged the people he considered unwanted and others whom he thought were political opponents. Stalin's crimes against humanity amount to the murder of nine to ten million of his own people to maintain political control of his people and his army.[4]

Another horrific leader of the modern era was the Chairman of the Peoples Republic of China, Mao Tse-tung. He ruled as a supreme leader from 1949 until his death in 1976. His policies were extremely inhumane. Historians report that Mao's political purges caused the death of approximately twenty million of his own citizens. His failed agricultural policies caused the starvation of tens of millions. As noted below, when compared to other murderous villains of the modern era, Mao is often considered the worst.

The mass murders committed by Mao Tse-tung surpassed any human in history. The Holocaust is estimated to have caused the murder of six million Jews and six million Christians. Estimates of Stalin's victims hover around twenty million. Mao exterminated more than Hitler and Stalin combined. Professor Rummel, the world's leading expert in such grisly studies, accepts the figure of around thirty-eight million people killed by Mao. That is a number beyond our power to truly grasp.[5]

It seems certain that Mormon placed these stories of wicked men like Amalickiah to help us see that comparable wicked leaders would be among us in the latter-days. Are there more in the future? How vigilant should we be in confronting their advance? Remember Mormon's warning, set apart by his familiar phrase—"thus we see."

*Thus we see how quick the children of men do forget the Lord their God, yea, how quick to do iniquity, and to be led away by the evil one. Yea, and we also see the great wickedness one very wicked man can cause to take place among the children of men. (Alma 46:8–9)*

## Moroni and the Title of Liberty

Captain Moroni is perhaps the greatest example of an authentic patriot in all of scripture. He loved his country and liberty with all his being. The depth of the great captain's feeling is demonstrated by his reaction to Amalickiah when he attempted to destroy the fledgling Nephite democracy and become king. This well-known scripture describes how Moroni ripped apart his coat and created the "title of liberty" to take among the people and motivate them to action.

*And now it came to pass that when Moroni, who was the chief commander of the armies of the Nephites, had heard of these dissensions, he was angry with Amalickiah. And it came to pass that he rent his coat; and he took a piece thereof, and wrote upon it—**In memory of our God, our religion, and freedom, and our peace, our wives, and our children—***

*and he fastened it upon the end of a pole.*

***And he fastened on his head-plate, and his breastplate, and his shields, and girded on his armor about his loins;** and he took the pole, which had on the end thereof his rent coat, (and he called it the title of liberty) and **he bowed himself to the earth, and he prayed mightily unto his God for the blessings of liberty to rest upon his brethren,** so long as there should be a band of Christians remain to possess the land—For thus were all the true believers of Christ. . . .*

*And therefore, at this time, Moroni prayed that the cause of the Christians, and the freedom of the land might be favored. And it came to pass that when he had poured out his soul to God, **he named all the land which was south of the land Desolation, yea, and in fine, all the land, both on the north and on the south—A chosen land, and the land of liberty.** (Alma 46:11–14, 16–17; emphasis added)*

This is one of the most delightful of all passages in the Book of Mormon. As a patriot, soldier, and Christian, my heart is touched profoundly by this wonderful display of patriotic love. Wouldn't it be breathtaking to have modern-day leaders speak with such sincere clarity? Wouldn't it be astonishing to see latter-day leaders remind us of our Christian heritage and invoke the blessings of God on our nation? The cowardly ideology of political correctness has robbed us of the ability to speak with such honest transparency.

There are four key elements to this stirring event. The first is the wording on the title of liberty. Moroni tore his coat into pieces allowing him to make a banner. On this standard he wrote, "In memory of our God, our religion, and freedom, and our peace, our wives, and our children" (Alma 46:12). As a soldier, I see this event as exceptionally insightful. Moroni needed people to take up arms. The country had probably sent the armies home after winning the battle of Manti and now faced an insurrection within the Nephite nation: a group under unscrupulous leadership wanted to destroy new democracy. The Nephites (and the freedom-loving people of the world) never fight war for selfish reasons. They fight for principle—for freedom. Additionally they fight to protect their homes, wives, and children. Having been to war, I know where my heart was every single day—with my family. I saw beautiful, sweet children everywhere in Iraq. They seemed to materialize out of nowhere, no matter where we stopped. We were in full body armor and carrying weapons: yet they came forward and just

wanted to touch us. From this experience, I had an epiphany that has not gone away: we do not fight wars for ourselves—we fight wars for the children. Their future must be protected at any cost. Their freedom is the overriding motivation to be found in the minds and hearts of soldiers. Moroni's title of liberty was absolutely right! I stand as his witness!

The second key element of this event was what Moroni did immediately after rending his coat and writing on it: he put on his armor. This action in front of the people illustrated that he was ready for battle and was willing to give his life for the principles written on his garment. He was totally committed. The tearing of his garment and creating the title of liberty represented an ancient Jewish custom used as an oath. Putting on his armor demonstrated his readiness to carry out that oath.

The third element of this great event was that Moroni knelt in prayer: "He bowed himself to the earth, and he prayed mightily unto his God for the blessings of liberty to rest upon his brethren, so long as there should be a band of Christians remain to possess the land—For thus were all the true believers of Christ, who belonged to the church of God called" (Alma 46:13–14). Moroni had read his scriptures, and he knew of the founding charge given by Father Lehi when he first arrived in the promised land.

*Wherefore, I, Lehi, have obtained a promise, that inasmuch as those whom the Lord God shall bring out of the land of Jerusalem shall keep his commandments, they shall prosper upon the face of this land; and they shall be kept from all other nations, that they may possess this land unto themselves. (2 Nephi 1:9)*

Moroni knew the key to any victory was the righteousness of the people and the help of the Lord. The Lord had made a covenant to protect his people, and Moroni was refreshing the memory of this covenant among his people through prayer. This is an admirable example of Moroni's knowledge of history and his spiritual strength.

The fourth element of this event was to give the land a new name. This was a brilliant act of a master patriot. Moroni wanted the people to develop their patriotism. Renaming the land "Liberty" was his way of placing his founding principle for war in front of the people. They were now "citizens of Liberty."

*Moroni prayed that the cause of the Christians and the freedom of the land might be favored. And it came to pass that when he had poured out his soul to God, he named all the land which was south of the land Desolation, yea, and in fine, all*

*the land, both on the north and on the south—A chosen land, and the land of liberty. (Alma 46:16–17)*

Moroni finished this wonderful testament to liberty by inviting the people to join him in a covenant. Note how they responded to him: they rend their garments to show their conviction to the covenant. This ancient Jewish custom adds depth and validity to this wonderful story.

*And he said: Surely God shall not suffer that we, who are despised because we take upon us the name of Christ, shall be trodden down and destroyed, until we bring it upon us by our own transgressions. And when Moroni had said these words, he went forth among the people, waving the rent part of his garment in the air, that all might see the writing which he had written upon the rent part, and crying with a loud voice, saying:*

**Behold, whosoever will maintain this title upon the land, let them come forth in the strength of the Lord, and enter into a covenant** *that they will maintain their rights, and their religion, that the Lord God may bless them.*

*And it came to pass that when Moroni had proclaimed these words, behold,* **the people came running together with** *their armor girded about their loins, rending their garments in token, or as a covenant, that they would not forsake the Lord their God; or, in other words, if they should transgress the commandments of God, or fall into transgression, and be ashamed to take upon them the name of Christ, the Lord should rend them even as they had rent their garments. (Alma 46:18–21; emphasis added)*

Taking an oath to commit to the defense of liberty is also an American custom. The practice of taking an oath began in 1775 with the Continental Army. Printed below is the oath of the United States Army National Guard soldier, an oath that I took when I entered as an enlisted soldier. The second oath printed below is the oath I took when I was appointed a warrant officer in the United States Army.

I, (insert name), do solemnly swear (or affirm) that I will support and defend the Constitution of the United States and the State of (STATE NAME) against all enemies, foreign and domestic; that I will bear true faith and allegiance to the same; and that I will obey the orders of the President of the United States and the Governor of (STATE NAME) and the orders of the officers appointed over me, according to law and regulations. So help me God.

I (insert name), having been appointed a (insert rank) in the U.S. Army under the conditions indicated in this document, do accept such appointment and do solemnly swear (or affirm) that I will support and defend the Constitution of the United States against all enemies, foreign and domestic, that I will bear true faith and allegiance to the same; that I take this obligation freely, without any mental reservation or purpose of evasion; and that I will well and faithfully discharge the duties of the office on which I am about to enter, so help me God.

The solemnity of these oaths illustrate how entering United States military service is an honor that carries with it a sacred obligation. Having been an American soldier and having taken an oath of military service, I have a better understanding of the oath that Moroni required of his army.

Captain Moroni subsequently went through the major Nephite cities with the title of liberty and brought many into the covenant. He explained the indispensable nature of the covenant with this comment.

*Moroni said unto them: Behold, we are a remnant of the seed of Jacob; yea, we are a remnant of the seed of Joseph, whose coat was rent by his brethren into many pieces; yea, and now behold, let us remember to keep the commandments of God, or our garments shall be rent by our brethren, and we be cast into prison, or be sold, or be slain.*

*Yea, let us preserve our liberty as a remnant of Joseph; yea, let us remember the words of Jacob, before his death, for behold, he saw that a part of the remnant of the coat of Joseph was preserved and had not decayed. And he said—Even as this remnant of garment of my son hath been preserved, so shall a remnant of the seed of my son be preserved by the hand of God, and be taken unto himself, while the remainder of the seed of Joseph shall perish, even as the remnant of his garment. (Alma 46:23–24.)*

Moroni was reminding the people of the Lord's covenant with the Jewish patriarchs. Remember, the rending of the garment to illustrate an oath was a custom the Nephites brought with them from Jerusalem. The Nephites had not forgotten their traditions and blessings as descendants of Abraham. The same is true of an American soldier who swears allegiance to the tradition set by the laws of freedom defined in the Constitution, a document that defines the covenants of the American people.

Moroni's motivation turned the people against Amalickiah, stopping his insurrection and causing him to flee from the land of Liberty.

*And it came to pass that when Amalickiah saw that the people of Moroni were more numerous than the Amalickiahites—and he also saw that his people were doubtful concerning the justice of the cause in which they had undertaken—therefore, fearing that he should not gain the point, he took those of his people who would and departed into the land of Nephi.*

*Now Moroni thought it was not expedient that the Lamanites should have any more strength; therefore he thought to cut off the people of Amalickiah, or to take them and bring them back, and put Amalickiah to death; yea, for he knew that he would stir up the Lamanites to anger against them, and cause them to come to battle against them; and this he knew that Amalickiah would do that he might obtain his purposes. (Alma 46:29–30.)*

Moroni gained control of the Nephite lands through motivation and without a battle. His influence caused Amalickiah to leave the country. Moroni pursued them with his army, but Amalickiah escaped into the Lamanite territories. Notice that Moroni returned with captives. Moroni was given authority to hold a military court and try these captives for treason. I suspect these prisoners were tried in the courts as traitors, much like the military tribunals of the modern era. Military traitors who aid the enemy in modern times can also be sentenced to death. The Nephite chief judges had given authority to Moroni to deal with these traitors. Again, we see the importance of following the laws of the land and value of an oath in the Nephite culture.

*Now, Moroni being a man who was appointed by the chief judges and the voice of the people, therefore he had power according to his will with the armies of the Nephites, to establish and to exercise authority over them.*

*And it came to pass that whomsoever of the Amalickiahites that would not enter into a covenant to support the cause of freedom, that they might maintain a free government, he caused to be put to death; and there were but few who denied the covenant of freedom. (Alma 46:34–35)*

These men were traitors to the Nephite cause and a threat to the liberty of the land. Their choice was simple—make an oath to the cause of freedom and be set free or die for the cause of a murderous wicked man. How can hate be so all encompassing that someone would choose death over freedom? It is so hard to justify and

cannot be understood with rational minds alone. It is satanic. Understanding the power and influence of Satan is the only way to get a grasp on such behavior.

Today, we can see the evidence of how Satan can command the minds of men even to death. The Kamikaze pilots of the Japanese air force crashed their planes in suicide missions. Muslim terrorists strap bombs to their bodies and go to certain death to kill innocent people, create terror, and influence the policy of nations.

By influencing his nation to join the cause of freedom and cleansing his nation of evil, Captain Moroni brought peace to the land. The title of liberty had been used effectively to influence the people throughout the land which Moroni had subsequently named "Liberty."

*And it came to pass also, that he caused the title of liberty to be hoisted upon every tower which was in all the land, which was possessed by the Nephites; and thus Moroni planted the standard of liberty among the Nephites. And they began to have peace again in the land; and thus they did maintain peace in the land until nearly the end of the nineteenth year of the reign of the judges. (Alma 46:36–37)*

The Nephites under Captain Moroni knew what they stood for; they saw heaven's help in fighting to preserve those gifts bestowed upon them by their Heavenly Father. In staying true to those righteous values, they found a large measure of peace in otherwise uncertain times.

## Amalickiah Deceived the Lamanites with Satanic Behavior

Helaman, the author of these chapters in the Book of Mormon, gives the reader an understanding of Amalickiah's evil nature by explaining what he did after escaping the Nephites and living among the Lamanites. It takes him only one verse.

> *Now behold, this was the desire of Amalickiah; for he being a very subtle man to do evil therefore he laid the plan in his heart to dethrone the king of the Lamanites. (Alma 47:4)*

The story of Amalickiah's rise to power through abhorrent malice and deceptive behavior is recorded in Alma 47. While prophets often serve as types of Christ, men like Amalickiah were clearly examples, or types, of Satan. To understand the satanic nature of Amalickiah, I will give you a brief review of his story. First, Amalickiah fled to the Lamanites and incited the anger of the Lamanites against the Nephites. He influenced the Lamanite king,

who ordered his people to raise armies to go against the Nephites. However, a majority of the Lamanites didn't want war. Consequently, the Lamanite king gave power to Amalickiah to take command of a small army and force the larger Lamanite army to consent to war.

The larger army of the Lamanites was commanded by a man named Lehonti. He had steadfastly promised his army that they would not go to war. He took his army to the top of mount Antipas, and Amalickiah followed him. Amalickiah sent messengers three times to get Lehonti to meet him in the valley, but Lehonti would not come. Finally Amalickiah went up the mountain and asked a fourth time, and Lehonti agreed. Amalickiah suggested that Lehonti take charge of both armies by coming down and surrounding Amalickiah's army, which slept in the valley below the mountain, and have them surrender. The treachery in this arrangement was that Amalickiah would then become second in command. The custom of the Lamanites was to promote the second in command to the highest position if the main commander died. The premeditated evil plan was to kill Lehonti so Amalickiah could become the senior commander.

Lehonti agreed with Amalickiah's plan to go down the mountain and surround Amalickiah's army. Consequently, the small army was surrounded and surrendered. Amalickiah then became second in command. Subsequently he had a servant poison Lehonti slowly. Through his deception and murder of Lehonti, Amalickiah took command of all the Lamanite armies.

Amalickiah then returned this army to the land of the Lamanites and the capital city of Nephi. When the Lamanite king came to greet them, Amalickiah directed one of his servants to bow before the king and then stab the king to death. The servants of Amalickiah then blamed the king's guards, who fled but in the process looked guilty.

The next step in this wicked plan was chasing the guards into Nephite lands, making them look like traitors. Amalickiah proceeded to convince the Lamanite queen to become his wife, making him the king of the Lamanites. This plan was filled with dishonesty, deception, and murder. Amalickiah had charted a course that gave him power over the Lamanites and the ability to manipulate their wicked emotions. He could then pursue his hate-filled desire to enslave the Nephites and to destroy their freedom.

Amalickiah was a former Nephite and a descendant of Zoram. Special note was made of his evil nature early in the story. When Amalickiah was first introduced in Alma 46, this was the comment of the editor, Mormon.

*Thus we see how quick the children of men do forget the Lord their God, yea, how quick to do iniquity, and to be led away by the evil one. Yea, and we also see the great wickedness one very wicked man can cause to take place among the children of men. (Alma 46:8–9)*

After recounting the story of Amalickiah's treachery in Alma 47, the author commented on the attitude and purpose of the Nephite dissenters who were surrounding Amalickiah and inflaming the Lamanite hatred.

*Now these dissenters, having the same instruction and the same information of the Nephites, yea, having been instructed in the same knowledge of the Lord, nevertheless, it is strange to relate, **not long after their dissensions they became more hardened and impenitent, and more wild, wicked and ferocious than the Lamanites**—drinking in with the traditions of the Lamanites; giving way to indolence, and all manner of lasciviousness; yea, entirely forgetting the Lord their God. (Alma 47:36; emphasis added)*

*And thus he did inspire their hearts against the Nephites, insomuch that in the latter end of the nineteenth year of the reign of the judges, he having accomplished his designs thus far, yea, having been made king over the Lamanites, he sought also to reign over all the land, yea, and all the people who were in the land, the Nephites as well as the Lamanites.* **Therefore he had accomplished his design, for he had hardened the hearts of the Lamanites and blinded their minds, and stirred them up to anger,** *insomuch that he had gathered together a numerous host to go to battle against the Nephites. (Alma 48:2–3; emphasis added)*

The Lamanites under Amalickiah were influenced to follow his wicked designs for power over the Lamanites and the Nephites. It is interesting to observe the contrast in what Captain Moroni was doing during this same time frame.

*Now it came to pass that while Amalickiah had thus been obtaining power by fraud and deceit,* **Moroni, on the other hand, had been preparing the minds of the people to be faithful unto the Lord their God.**

*Yea, he had been strengthening the armies of the Nephites, and erecting small forts, or places of resort; throwing up banks of earth round about to enclose his armies, and also building walls of stone to encircle them about, round about their cities and the borders of their lands; yea, all round about the land. And in their weakest fortifications he did place the greater number of men; and thus he did fortify and strengthen the land which was possessed by the Nephites.*

**And thus he was preparing to support their liberty, their lands, their wives, and their children, and their peace, and that they might live unto the Lord their God,** *and that they might maintain that which was called by their enemies the cause of Christians. (Alma 48:7–10; emphasis added)*

Earlier we learned how Moroni had designed body armor to protect his men, and now we learn how he created fortifications to protect his cities. These incredible fortifications are still visible in the ruins of Mesoamerica. In addition to the fortifications, Moroni's military strategy included placing the largest number of men at the least fortified places.

At this point in chapter 48, there is a commentary on the great captain. I believe the comment is from Mormon. As he read from the plates of Nephi and prepared to transfer the story to the golden plates of Mormon, he saw this stark contrast between these two prominent leaders, Amalickiah and Moroni. Mormon's feelings were so strong that he had to stop writing the story and make some personal observations. Remember how Mormon had said he could only include a hundredth part of the history of the Nephites? It is obvious why he included this account. In the latter days, we need to understand the necessity to stand against the wicked leaders of our generations and support those leaders of strong character like Moroni. Mormon's comments regarding Moroni are a quintessential compliment. Outside of his writings concerning the Savior Jesus Christ, these comments are as heartfelt and strong as any in scripture. Mormon praises the great captain in the following passages.

> *And Moroni was a strong and a mighty man; he was a man of a perfect understanding;* yea, a man that did not delight in bloodshed; a man whose soul did joy in the liberty and the freedom of his country, and his brethren from bondage and slavery; Yea, a man whose heart did swell with thanksgiving to his God, for the many privileges and blessings which he bestowed upon his people; a man who did labor exceedingly for the welfare and safety of his people.
>
> *Yea, and he was a man who was firm in the faith of Christ,* and he had sworn with an oath to defend his people, his rights, and his country, and his religion, even to the loss of his blood. . . .
>
> *Yea, verily, verily I say unto you, if all men had been, and were, and ever would be, like unto Moroni, behold, the very powers of hell would have been shaken forever; yea, the devil would never have power over the hearts of the children of men.*
> (Alma 48: 11–13, 17; emphasis added)

At the same time Moroni was fortifying the cities and motivating his people, the prophet Helaman was preparing the people spiritually. Their mutual success was portrayed in this way by the continued comments from Mormon.

> Now behold, Helaman and his brethren were no less serviceable unto the people than was Moroni; for they did preach the word of God, and they did baptize unto repentance all men whosoever would hearken unto their words.
>
> And thus they went forth, and the people did humble themselves because of their words, insomuch that they were highly favored of the Lord, and thus they were free from wars and contentions

*among themselves, yea, even for the space of four years.*

*But, as I have said, in the latter end of the nineteenth year, yea, notwithstanding their peace amongst themselves, they were compelled reluctantly to contend with their brethren, the Lamanites.* (Alma 48:19–21)

## Moroni Confounds Lamanite Armies by Using Defensive Fortification around Every City

Based on his animosity for the Nephites, it was only a matter of time before Amalickiah attacked the Nephites with his armies. Within two years, Amalickiah had solidified his control of the Lamanites and was ready to invade the Nephites. He made dissenting former Nephites the chief captains of his armies and, with a plan to attack Ammonihah, sent them into the western part of the Nephite lands. It is interesting and unusual that he did not personally come with his armies. This may indicate that either he needed to stay in the capital because he was afraid of being overthrown by a Lamanite insurrection or that he was cowardly and wanted to weaken Moroni's foothold before coming with his personal army. It may

also show his lack of leadership for the culture of his time. Remember, the kings led their armies to battle to illustrate their commitment to the war. Contrast this with Moroni: he creatively fortified his cities, designed body armor, and motivated every city with the Title of Liberty. Whatever the reason, Amalickiah did not come and the initial Lamanite effort to take Nephite cities failed miserably. Here is the report of their attempt.

*Behold, I said that the city of Ammonihah had been rebuilt. I say unto you, yea, that it was in part rebuilt; and because the Lamanites had destroyed it once because of the iniquity of the people, they supposed that it would again become an easy prey for them.*

*But behold, how great was their disappointment; for behold, **the Nephites had dug up a ridge of earth round about them, which was so high that the Lamanites could not cast their stones and their arrows at them that they might take effect,** neither could they come upon them save it was by their place of entrance.*

***Now at this time the chief captains of the Lamanites were astonished exceedingly, because of the wisdom of the Nephites in preparing***

*their places of security. Now the leaders of the Lamanites had supposed, because of the greatness of their numbers . . . and they had also prepared themselves with shields, and with breastplates; and they had also prepared themselves with garments of skins, yea, very thick garments to cover their nakedness. And being thus prepared they supposed that they should easily overpower and subject their brethren to the yoke of bondage, or slay and massacre them according to their pleasure.*

***But behold, to their uttermost astonishment, they [the Nephites] were prepared for them, in a manner which never had been known among the children of Lehi.*** *Now they were prepared for the Lamanites, to battle after the manner of the instructions of Moroni. . . .*

*Now, if king Amalickiah had come down out of the land of Nephi, at the head of his army, perhaps he would have caused the Lamanites to have attacked the Nephites at the city of Ammonihah; for behold, he did care not for the blood of his people. (Alma 49:3–8, 10; emphasis added)*

The preparations and fortifications for war "astonished" the Lamanites. Moroni had again gained an advantage through his brilliant military strategies. These mounds of earth around the cities were probably like an empty moat—very deep and very steep. They were most likely as much as fifty feet deep and one hundred feet across with a high mound of dirt on the inside. Consequently, the attacking army would need to go into a deep ditch and climb a hill in their attack. The only feasible method to assault a fortified city was through the entrances or gates. The author also points out that had Amalickiah come with them, they probably would have attempted a foolish attack because he, Amalickiah, had no regard for the lives of his army.

The Lamanite chief captains moved away from Ammonihah and went to the city of Noah, thinking that an attack there would be easier. This scriptural account points out something that's almost dumbfounding from a military perspective. The chief captains of the Lamanites were mostly apostate Nephites motivated by incredible anger and hatred for their former countrymen. They knew that King Amalickiah would be terribly angry with them for not attacking Ammonihah, so they took an oath before they arrived at the city of Noah, an oath to destroy the city. They didn't know that Moroni had fortified Noah even more than Ammonihah. Nevertheless, they foolishly attacked this extremely fortified city.

*But behold, to their astonishment, the city of Noah, which had hitherto been a weak place, had now, by the means of Moroni, become strong, yea, even to exceed the strength of the city Ammonihah.*

**And now, behold, this was wisdom in Moroni; for he had supposed that they would be frightened at the city Ammonihah; and as the city of Noah had hitherto been the weakest part of the land. . . .** *And behold, Moroni had appointed Lehi to be chief captain over the men of that city; and it was that same Lehi who fought with the Lamanites in the valley on the east of the river Sidon.*

*And now behold it came to pass, that when the Lamanites had found that Lehi commanded the city they were again disappointed, for they feared Lehi exceedingly; nevertheless their chief captains had sworn with an oath to attack the city; therefore, they brought up their armies.* (Alma 49:14–17)

What an irrational attack! Before it began, it was doomed to fail. Not only was the city well fortified, but it also had an outstanding military commander, Captain Lehi. The Lamanite military leaders knew Lehi was one of the best Nephite captains. Moroni had placed him there knowing the city would be prepared with fortifications and have the advantage of exceptional leadership.

In our modern armies, the study of key enemy leaders is called a study of personalities. An excellent army knows the characteristics of the enemy commanders, specifically, their tendencies in battle. Entering the battlefield, a modern general knows if his enemy's leaders are aggressive or passive; moreover, he knows the enemy commander's past preparations, successes, and strategies. In this ancient battle for the city of Noah, we see that the Lamanites knew Lehi was an aggressive and formidable opponent. Without question, the city of Noah was a well-prepared city, defended by Moroni's most excellent chief captain, Lehi. Knowing this information makes this attempt by the prideful and foolish Lamanite chief captains even more irrational.

*Now behold, the Lamanites could not get into their forts of security by any other way save by the entrance, because of the highness of the bank which had been thrown up, and the depth of the ditch which had been dug round about, save it were by the entrance.*

*And thus were the Nephites prepared to destroy all such as should attempt to climb up to enter the fort by any other way, by casting over stones and arrows at them. Thus they were prepared, yea, a*

**Amalickiah's Failed Attack Through His Captains**

- Captain Lehi Victorious at Noah -

MOVEMENT OF AmalicKiah's Captains

*body of their strongest men. . . .*

*And it came to pass that the captains of the Lamanites brought up their armies before the place of entrance, and began to contend with the Nephites, to get into their place of security; but behold, they were driven back from time to time, insomuch that they were slain with an immense slaughter.*

*Now when they found that they could not obtain power over the Nephites by the pass, they began to dig down their banks of earth that they might obtain a pass to their armies, that they might have an equal chance to fight; but behold, in these attempts they were swept off by the stones and arrows . . . **and thus the Lamanites did attempt to destroy the Nephites until their chief captains were all slain; yea, and more than a thousand of the Lamanites were slain; while, on the other hand, there was not a single soul of the Nephites which was slain.***

*(Alma 49:18–23; emphasis added)*

All of the Lamanite chief captains were slain because of their foolish pride, which caused them to attempt an impossible military mission. There was virtually no chance for success, but because of their irrational oath they attacked and were destroyed along with the heart of their army. This is so illogical and satanic. Satan himself has sworn to take the souls of our Heavenly Father's children, and his defeat is certain; yet he continues to ruin the lives of his followers. He persuades them through pride and hate to make unwise and absurd decisions. This attack on the city of Noah was an incredible abuse of military leadership—the lives of the soldiers were sacrificed because of their leaders' foolish decisions.

Many modern wars have also been dominated by pride. For example, Saddam Hussein went to war with Iran in the 1980s. Although he slaughtered hundreds of thousands of Iranians and lost a similar number of his own men, he gained virtually no territory or advantage. In 1992 he was driven from Kuwait and was soundly defeated by the American army, but he told his people he had won the war and driven them back to America—a preposterous lie. He built a huge palace to honor his victory. This gaudy eyesore was called the "Victory Over America Palace." Saddam wasted the lives of his army with virtually no chance of success and then lied to his people. In one of my interviews, one of his senior generals told me that he had told Saddam that a victory was not possible against the superior United States Army. After hearing this honest evaluation, Saddam put the general in jail and said he had no faith in God. When I was stationed in Iraq, I lived in the summer palace of Saddam's son. The complex had seven man-made lakes and thirty-four palaces decorated with Italian marble, crystal chandeliers, and Persian rugs. While his people starved, Saddam lived in luxury and built palaces for his cruel and inhumane friends. His actions proved he was driven by satanic pride and selfishness, with no concern for his people. These glimpses of Iraqi history were given to me personally by Iraqi generals during Operation Iraqi Freedom in 2003.

The authors of the Book of Mormon were very clear. They want us to read about the wicked ways of ancient leaders and be wise enough to know the wickedness when we see it in the latter days.

## The Blood Oath of Amalickiah

After their defeat in the battle for Noah, the devastated armies of the Lamanites retreated home to be confronted by an extremely angry King Amalickiah. He displayed his anger by making an oath regarding Moroni.

*And it came to pass that he [Amalickiah] was exceedingly angry with his people, because he had not obtained his desire over the Nephites; he had not subjected them to the yoke of bondage. Yea,*

*he was exceedingly wroth, and **he did curse God, and also Moroni, swearing with an oath that he would drink his blood;** and this because Moroni had kept the commandments of God in preparing for the safety of his people.*

*And it came to pass, that on the other hand, the people of Nephi did thank the Lord their God, because of his matchless power in delivering them from the hands of their enemies. (Alma 49:26–28; emphasis added)*

Isn't this behavior almost unbelievable? The horrible defeat of his Lamanite armies brought no coherent analysis of failure or even sadness from the loss of life. On the contrary, it engendered intense rage from the former Nephite, who was now the Lamanite king. The oath to drink the blood of Moroni was born from deep-seeded wrath. Even so, Amalickiah and the Lamanites were unable to mount an effective attack for over four years. Regardless of the threats and hate, Moroni continued to prepare for the future. He continued to fortify his nation—ordering all cities to dig the great ditches and build walls of timber with pickets on the top. Moreover, he built towers on the walls to protect the guards.

*And now it came to pass that Moroni did not stop making preparations for war, or to defend his people against the Lamanites; for he caused that his armies should commence in the commencement of the twentieth year of the reign of the judges, that they should commence in digging up heaps of earth round about all the cities, throughout all the land which was possessed by the Nephites.*

*And upon the top of these ridges of earth he caused that there should be timbers, yea, works of timbers built up to the height of a man, round about the cities. And he caused that upon those works of timbers there should be a frame of pickets built upon the timbers round about; and they were strong and high.*

*And he caused towers to be erected that overlooked those works of pickets, and he caused places of security to be built upon those towers, that the stones and the arrows of the Lamanites could not hurt them.*

*And they were prepared that they could cast stones from the top thereof, according to their pleasure and their strength, and slay him who should attempt to approach near the walls of the city. Thus Moroni did prepare strongholds against the coming of their enemies, round about every city in all the land. (Alma 50:1–6)*

## Four Years of Peace and Freedom— "Never Was There a Happier Time"

The defeat of the Lamanite armies brought peace and prosperity to the Nephite nation. Under the leadership of Captain Moroni, their lands were safe and well protected. The following statements are editorial comments written by Mormon. Not only does he use his familiar phrase, "thus we see," but he also takes time to illustrate how the prophecy of Lehi was fulfilled by the success of the Nephites under Chief Captain Moroni, Chief Judge Nephihah, and the prophet Helaman.

*And they [the Nephites] did prosper exceedingly, and they became exceedingly rich; yea, and they did multiply and wax strong in the land.*

***And thus we see how merciful and just are all the dealings of the Lord, to the fulfilling of all his words unto the children of men;*** *yea, we can behold that his words are verified, even at this time, which he spake unto Lehi, saying:*

*Blessed art thou and thy children; and they shall be blessed,* ***inasmuch as they shall keep my commandments they shall prosper in the land. But remember, inasmuch as they will not keep my commandments they shall be cut off from the presence of the Lord.***

*And we see that these promises have been verified to the people of Nephi; for it has been their quarrelings and their contentions, yea, their murderings, and their plunderings, their idolatry, their whoredoms, and their abominations, which were among themselves, which brought upon them their wars and their destructions.*

*And those who were faithful in keeping the commandments of the Lord were delivered at all times, whilst thousands of their wicked brethren have been consigned to bondage, or to perish by the sword, or to dwindle in unbelief, and mingle with the Lamanites.*

***But behold there never was a happier time among the people of Nephi, since the days of Nephi, than in the days of Moroni, yea, even at this time, in the twenty and first year of the reign of the judges.*** *(Alma 50:18–23; emphasis added)*

Mormon had the opportunity to review the entire history of the Nephite nation and select the most important accounts to present to future readers. As I have previously noted, he also made sure to give commentaries as a part of the record. In the midst of war and contentions, Mormon tells us: "Never was there a happier time among the people of Nephi." Why would this be? It was a brief period of time and definitely not free of problems. I suggest that the people were happy because they were in control of their own destiny. With the blessings of God and with an enormous amount of personal effort, the Nephites enjoyed liberty and safety. My mother gave the answer to me at a young age with this oft-repeated axiom—*the Lord helps those who help themselves.*

## The Rise of the King-Men— Moroni's Response

Within a very short time, there was a movement of dissension in the Nephite nation. A group of people calling themselves the "king-men" attempted to win the elections for the chief judge (president). Their purpose was to replace the judges with kings. Chief Judge Pahoran won the election with the help of his supporters who were called the "freemen." I really enjoy the wording of Helaman in this part of the story. He talks about the "voice of the people."

*And it came to pass that this matter of **their contention was settled by the voice of the people.** And it came to pass that the voice of the people came in favor of the freemen, and Pahoran retained the* *judgment-seat, which caused much rejoicing among the brethren of Pahoran and also many of the people of liberty, who also put the king-men to silence, that they durst not oppose but were obliged to maintain the cause of freedom.*

***Now those who were in favor of kings were those of high birth, and they sought to be kings; and they were supported by those who sought power and authority over the people.***

*But behold, this was a critical time for such contentions to be among the people of Nephi; for behold, Amalickiah had again stirred up the hearts of the people of the Lamanites against the people of the Nephites, and he was gathering together soldiers from all parts of his land, and arming them, and preparing for war with all diligence; for he had sworn to drink the blood of Moroni. (Alma 51:7–9; emphasis added)*

The king-men became a critical problem because Amalickiah was bringing a huge army into Nephite lands. The king-men refused to join the armies of the Nephites. Captain Moroni petitioned the chief judge for authority to move against them. Note how the democracy worked. Moroni realized that his authority came from the elected officials. A battle took place, in which

four thousand king-men were killed. The rest were captured and brought back to be tried for treason but instead were thrown in jail because there was not enough time to prosecute them. Moroni had to defend against the approaching armies of Amalickiah (see Alma 51:9–23).

## Amalickiah's Last Military Effort

Captain Moroni had constructed new cities along the southern border as a strategy to defend against the incursions of the Lamanites. Among these cities were Nephihah, Lehi, and Moroni. They had become the chief captains' first line of defense and were intensely fortified.

By sheer numbers, Amalickiah took control of a number of these cities. He first took control of the Land of Moroni, which was by the eastern sea. He then moved north, along the eastern border by the sea. He had moved almost to the Land Bountiful when he met one of the most colorful and powerful Nephite characters, Chief Captain Teancum. He and his Nephite army were described this way.

*But it came to pass that they were met by Teancum, who had slain Morianton and had headed his people in his flight. And it came to pass that he headed Amalickiah also, as he was marching forth with his numerous army that he might take possession of the land Bountiful, and also the land northward.*

***But behold he met with a disappointment by being repulsed by Teancum and his men, for they were great warriors; for every man of Teancum did exceed the Lamanites in their strength and in their skill of war, insomuch that they did gain advantage over the Lamanites.***

*And it came to pass that they did harass them, insomuch that they did slay them even until it was dark. And it came to pass that Teancum and his men did pitch their tents in the borders of the land Bountiful; and Amalickiah did pitch his tents in the borders on the beach by the seashore, and after this manner were they driven. (Alma 51:29–32; emphasis added)*

Captain Teancum was undoubtedly a magnificent warrior. As a soldier, I can only imagine that he was a tremendous physical specimen who had trained his men far beyond what was normally expected for his time. To give a modern-day illustration, his army was much like the Army Special Forces, the Marine Corps, the 101st Airborne Division, or even the Navy Seals. From the discussion of the battle

between the forces of Teancum and the forces of Amalickiah, it appears Teancum and his army were so superior that his men caused fear and trembling among the Lamanites. The Lamanite armies were driven south from Bountiful back to the southern border. This distance would probably be more than one hundred miles. This defeat of Amalickiah's army sets the stage for the demise of Amalickiah, as told by Helaman.

*And it came to pass that when the night had come, Teancum and his servant stole forth and went out by night, and went into the camp of Amalickiah; and behold, sleep had overpowered them because of their much fatigue, which was caused by the labors and heat of the day.*

***And it came to pass that Teancum stole privily into the tent of the king, and put a javelin to his heart; and he did cause the death of the king immediately that he did not awake his servants.*** *And he returned again privily to his own camp, and behold, his men were asleep, and he awoke them and told them all the things that he had done.*

*And he caused that his armies should stand in readiness, lest the Lamanites had awakened and should come upon them.*

***And thus endeth the twenty and fifth year of the reign of the judges***

*over the people of Nephi; and thus endeth the days of Amalickiah.* (Alma 51:33–37; emphasis added)

Isn't this a fantastic story of courage and daring? Can you imagine sneaking into the enemy's compound? Teancum needed to slip through the enemy lines and get past the sentries posted to guard the encampment. The army would be very large with as many as twenty to thirty thousand men surrounding the commander's compound. Working his way through the compound, Teancum would have to find the tent of the king and commander. After finding the tent, he would have to get past the king's personal guards and enter the king's tent. This was an astonishing feat of personal courage. In my view, Teancum could be referred to as the bravest of the brave and a hero's hero.

Amalickiah was defeated by a single Nephite captain—a warrior of enormous strength and valor. In the night, the Lamanite army's vile commander was slain through an act of incredible bravery. The final statement of this chapter is befitting the death of a man who was as wicked and satanic as any man who ever lived. "And thus endeth the days of Amalickiah" (Alma 51:37).

## The Battle of Mulek

The remainder of Amalickiah's army was frightened by the might of Teancum's army and the death of their king and commander. They retreated south to the fortified city of Mulek, which was one of the Nephite cities they had captured on the southern border. These cities were difficult for the Nephites to recapture because of their own fortifications. Teancum protected the eastern lands and waited for orders from Captain Moroni. After almost two years of preparation, Moroni met with his chief captains to plan the recapture of the southern cities.

*And it came to pass that Moroni did arrive with his army at the land of Bountiful, in the latter end of the twenty and seventh year of the reign of the judges over the people of Nephi.*

**And in the commencement of the twenty and eighth year, Moroni and Teancum and many of the chief captains held a council of war—what they should do to cause the Lamanites to come out against them to battle; or that they might by some means flatter them out of their strongholds, that they might gain advantage over them and take again the city of Mulek.**

*And it came to pass they sent embassies to the army of the Lamanites, which*

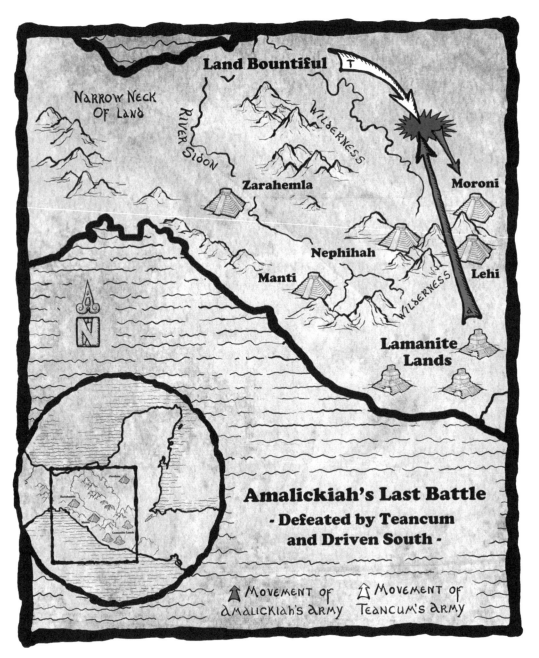

**Amalickiah's Last Battle**
**- Defeated by Teancum**
**and Driven South -**

MOVEMENT OF
AMALICKIAH'S ARMY

MOVEMENT OF
TEANCUM'S ARMY

*protected the city of Mulek, to their leader, whose name was Jacob, desiring him that he would come out with his armies to meet them upon the plains between the two cities. But behold, Jacob, who was a Zoramite, would not come out with his army to meet them upon the plains. (Alma 52:18–20; emphasis added)*

These verses reflect on Moroni's great leadership because he didn't act on his own. He held a council of war with his captains and devised a plan to bring Jacob and his army out of the strongholds. Meeting with his captains and getting their ideas united the leadership and strengthened their brotherhood. The plan set up a decoy using Teancum and his men. The Lamanites were so anxious to get revenge on Teancum that they made a foolish decision and took the bait.

*And it came to pass that Moroni, having no hopes of meeting them upon fair grounds, therefore, he resolved upon a plan that he might decoy the Lamanites out of their strongholds. Therefore he caused that Teancum should take a small number of men and march down near the seashore; and Moroni and his army, by night, marched in the wilderness, on the west of the city Mulek; and thus, on the morrow, when the guards of the Lamanites had discovered Teancum, they ran and told it unto Jacob, their leader.*

*And it came to pass that the armies of the Lamanites did march forth against Teancum, supposing by their numbers to overpower Teancum because of the smallness of his numbers. And as Teancum saw the armies of the Lamanites coming out against him he began to retreat down by the seashore, northward.*

*And it came to pass that when the Lamanites saw that he began to flee, they took courage and pursued them with vigor. And while Teancum was thus leading away the Lamanites who were pursuing them in vain, behold, Moroni commanded that a part of his army who were with him should march forth into the city, and take possession of it. (Alma 52:21–24)*

The strategy of using a decoy was amazingly effective. The Lamanite captains wanted to gain favor with their king by defeating the despised Nephite captain Teancum when he appeared to be undermanned and vulnerable. They just couldn't help themselves and left the city with their army and chased after Teancum. Of course, Teancum had taken his best athletes, making it almost impossible to overtake them. The city of Mulek was left vulnerable, and it was easily taken by Moroni's army and given to Lehi to defend. Mormon made an editorial comment concerning the friendship and brotherhood of Lehi and Moroni.

*And Moroni went to the city of Mulek with Lehi, and took command of the city and gave it unto Lehi. Now behold, this Lehi was a man who had been with Moroni in the more part of all his battles; and he was a man like unto Moroni, and they rejoiced in each other's safety; yea, they were beloved by each other, and also beloved by all the people of Nephi. (Alma 53:2)*

The bonds of brotherhood formed in war are very strong. It is clearly illustrated here. It is difficult for people who have not been to war to understand the bonds between soldiers, sailors, and airmen who serve together. One of my assignments in Iraq took me to an air base called Al Asad. We traveled there in two civilian vehicles to investigate reports that weapons of mass destruction had been stored on the complex. In my vehicle were two young army sergeants who were assigned as security guards. It was September, and the temperatures were well above one hundred degrees at midday. During our investigation, I interviewed people inside air-conditioned buildings. Sergeants Landon

and Huff stayed outside for hours as a protection detail—without a complaint! They were so loyal to our country and to their mission. Landon had a young family and desired to become a drill sergeant. Huff was a religious young man and looked like a middle linebacker on a college football team. I asked him one time if he participated in sports and he replied, "No, but I do read a lot." I will always be grateful to them for their service and sacrifice. They were brothers because their loyalty and dedication to the mission was never in question. When your fellow soldiers put their lives in danger for your protection they become part of your soul. These young men are the best of the best.

In the previous scripture, the writer—probably Mormon—gave Captain Lehi a remarkable compliment when he said, "He was a man like unto Moroni." This praise of Mormon regarding Captain Lehi is remarkable. Many awards and commendations are given to members of the military today, and they are often displayed by the ribbons worn on the dress uniform. The highest award of the American military is the Congressional Medal of Honor. Personally, I believe that Mormon's tribute to Lehi transcends all awards regardless of the war or the millennia. Moroni was one of the greatest military commanders in history. To be compared to him would be the ultimate commendation.

## Moroni's Response to an Exchange of Prisoners

In Alma 54, we read about an exchange of letters between Ammoron, the brother of Amalickiah, and Captain Moroni. Ammoron, who was appointed king after his brother was killed, wrote to Moroni and desired to exchange prisoners with the Nephites. This was positive to Moroni because he needed the provisions used for the prisoners to strengthen his own army. However, he was angry because he discovered that Ammoron had also taken soldiers' wives and children as prisoners. Ammoron wanted to trade Nephite wives and children for Lamanite soldiers. The account doesn't include the original letter, but it starts this way.

*And now it came to pass in the commencement of the twenty and ninth year of the judges, that Ammoron sent unto Moroni desiring that he would exchange prisoners.*

*And it came to pass that Moroni felt to rejoice exceedingly at this request, for he desired the provisions which were imparted for the support of the Lamanite prisoners for the support of his own people; and he also desired his own people for the strengthening of his army.*

*Now the Lamanites had taken many women and children, and there was not a woman nor a child among all the prisoners of Moroni, or the prisoners whom Moroni had taken; therefore Moroni resolved upon a stratagem to obtain as many prisoners of the Nephites from the Lamanites as it were possible. (Alma 54:1–3.)*

Moroni wrote back with a letter that reflects considerable annoyance. Here are some excerpts from his letter.

*Behold, Ammoron, I have written unto you somewhat concerning this war which ye have waged against my people, or rather which thy brother hath waged against them. . . .*

*Behold, I would tell you somewhat concerning the justice of God, and the sword of his almighty wrath, which doth hang over you except ye repent and withdraw your armies into your own lands. . . .*

*I would tell you concerning that awful hell that awaits to receive such murderers as thou and thy brother have been, except ye repent and withdraw your murderous purposes, and return with your armies to your own lands. . . .*

***But, as the Lord liveth, our armies shall come upon you except ye withdraw, and ye shall soon be visited***

*with death, for we will retain our cities and our lands; yea, and we will maintain our religion and the cause of our God.*

*But behold, it supposeth me that I talk to you concerning these things in vain; or it supposeth me that thou art a child of hell; therefore I will close my epistle by telling you that I will not exchange prisoners, save it be on conditions that ye will deliver up a man and his wife and his children, for one prisoner; if this be the case that ye will do it, I will exchange.*

*And behold, if ye do not this, I will come against you with my armies; yea, even I will arm my women and my children, and I will come against you, and I will follow you even into your own land, which is the land of our first inheritance; yea, and it shall be blood for blood, yea, life for life; and I will give you battle even until you are destroyed from off the face of the earth.*

*Behold, I am in my anger, and also my people; ye have sought to murder us, and we have only sought to defend ourselves. . . .*

*Now I close my epistle. I am Moroni; I am a leader of the people of the Nephites. Alma 54:5–7, 10–14; emphasis added)*

This letter illustrates the serious nature of the Nephite chief captain—Moroni was very clear. Saying, "as the Lord liveth," is the same as declaring an oath to God. Moroni's response to this enemy seems out of character for him, because he had shown mercy to other Lamanite armies by stopping the battles and letting them return home after they made an oath not to return.

Why did Moroni express so much anger? First, Ammoron was a former Nephite filled with incredible hate. Second, and most important, these Lamanite armies could not be trusted. They had grievously violated an important rule of war for their time. Lamanite armies took innocent women and children as hostages. Note that Moroni's armies had only taken soldiers and were obedient to this common law of decency. The reply from Ammoron agrees to the exchange and includes insights into his heart.

*I am Ammoron, the king of the Lamanites; I am the brother of Amalickiah whom ye have murdered. Behold, I will avenge his blood upon you, yea, and I will come upon you with my armies for I fear not your threatenings.*

*For behold, your fathers [Nephi] did wrong their brethren [Laman and Lemuel], insomuch that they did rob them* of their right to the government when it rightly belonged unto them.

*And now behold, if ye will lay down your arms, and subject yourselves to be governed by those to whom the government doth rightly belong, then will I cause that my people shall lay down their weapons and shall be at war no more. . . .*

*Nevertheless, I will grant to exchange prisoners according to your request, gladly, that I may preserve my food for my men of war; and we will wage a war which shall be eternal, either to the subjecting the Nephites to our authority or to their eternal extinction.*

*And as concerning that God whom ye say we have rejected, behold, we know not such a being; neither do ye; but if it so be that there is such a being, we know not but that he hath made us as well as you. And if it so be that there is a devil and a hell, behold will he not send you there to dwell with my brother whom ye have murdered, whom ye have hinted that he hath gone to such a place? But behold these things matter not.*

*I am Ammoron, and a descendant of Zoram, whom your fathers pressed and brought out of Jerusalem. And behold now, I am a bold Lamanite; behold, this war hath been waged to avenge their* *wrongs, and to maintain and to obtain their rights to the government; and I close my epistle to Moroni.* (Alma 54:16–24)

It is apparent this war had become personal and totally unreasonable. Ammoron had given Moroni only two options—never-ending war, or submitting to slavery. His rationalization for the war was taken from centuries of Lamanite hatred: (1) Nephi, son of Lehi, had stolen the right to govern from his older brother Laman, (2) the Lamanites wanted to enslave the Nephites for power and wealth, (3) they rejected a belief in God, and (4) they were enforcing an ancient law of vengeance. In the ancient deserts of the Middle East, the family's right for retribution was the basic rule of law. In other words, if your family hurts mine, I have a right to revenge. This old and crude law of civilization was only a small step above anarchy.

Moroni didn't exchange prisoners because he knew that the Lamanite king could not be trusted. Ammoron was too full of hatred and animosity. Apparently, Moroni had a strategy in mind. He was a master of military intelligence. His spies knew where the prisoners were kept, and he made a plan to deceive the Lamanites and set the prisoners free. They would trick the guards into drinking a lot of strong wine. He found a young Lamanite in his army named Laman to help carry it out. Laman and a few other Nephites took wine to the Lamanite guards of the city of Gid where the prisoners were kept. They said they had escaped imprisonment by the Nephites. The guards drank and fell asleep. While they were drunk, the Nephites entered the city and gave weapons to the prisoners. In the morning, the Lamanite army found itself surrounded by Nephites and at the mercy of the armed prisoners. The account that follows shows the merciful intent of Moroni: to free the prisoners without shedding blood.

*And now this was according to the design of Moroni. And Moroni had prepared his men with weapons of war; and he went to the city Gid, while the Lamanites were in a deep sleep and drunken, and cast in weapons of war unto the prisoners, insomuch that they were all armed;*

*Yea, even to their women, and all those of their children, as many as were able to use a weapon of war, when Moroni had armed all those prisoners; and all those things were done in a profound silence.*

**But had they awakened the Lamanites, behold they were drunken and the Nephites could have slain them. But behold, this was not the desire of Moroni; he did not delight in murder or bloodshed, but he delighted in the saving of his people from destruction; and for this cause he might not bring upon him injustice, he would not fall upon the Lamanites and destroy them in their drunkenness. . . .**

*Now behold this was done in the night-time, so that when the Lamanites awoke in the morning they beheld that they were surrounded by the Nephites without, and that their prisoners were armed within.*

*And thus they saw that the Nephites had power over them; and in these circumstances they found that it was not expedient that they should fight with the Nephites; therefore their chief captains demanded their weapons of war, and they brought them forth and cast them at the feet of the Nephites, pleading for mercy.*

*Now behold, this was the desire of Moroni. He took them prisoners of war, and took possession of the city, and caused that all the prisoners should be liberated, who were Nephites; and they did join the army of Moroni, and were a great strength to his army.*

*And it came to pass that he did cause the Lamanites, whom he had taken prisoners, that they should commence a labor in strengthening the fortifications round about the city Gid. (Alma 55:16–19, 22–25; emphasis added)*

This small story gives additional insight into the character of Captain Moroni. He took every action to avoid shedding blood. His desires were to free the prisoners and defend his cities. Moreover, the story displays his ingenious methods. He used excellent military intelligence or knowledge of the enemy and an artful deception to achieve his victory.

## Civil War—Pahoran and Moroni Demonstrate Their Love for Freedom

The next episode of this epic story takes place in the center of the Nephite homeland when it was overcome by tyranny of insurrection. Moroni learned of the Nephite civil war by an exchange of letters with Pahoran, chief judge of the Nephites. The armies of Helaman and Moroni were in great battles with the Lamanites when Moroni learned that Helaman had not received support from Pahoran and the city of Zarahemla. Moroni wrote two letters to ask for supplies and reinforcements. In the second letter, Moroni's anger was clearly displayed because his army and the armies of Helaman were in great danger. The letter is in Alma 60.

I will only give excerpts to give an idea of the expressed frustration.

*And it came to pass that he [Moroni] wrote again to the governor of the land, who was Pahoran, and these are the words which he wrote, saying: Behold, I direct mine epistle to Pahoran, in the city of Zarahemla, who is the chief judge and the governor over the land, and also to all those who have been chosen by this people to govern and manage the affairs of this war.*

*For behold, **I have somewhat to say unto them by the way of condemnation;** for behold, ye yourselves know that ye have been appointed to gather together men, and arm them. . . . And now behold, I say unto you that myself, and also my men, and also Helaman and his men, have suffered exceedingly great sufferings; yea, even hunger, thirst, and fatigue, and all manner of afflictions of every kind. But behold, were this all we had suffered we would not murmur nor complain.*

***But behold, great has been the slaughter among our people; yea, thousands have fallen by the sword, while it might have otherwise been if ye had rendered unto our armies***

*sufficient strength and succor for them. Yea, great has been your neglect toward us.* (Alma 60:1–5; emphasis added)

Moroni was obviously frustrated by the loss of life that resulted from his army not being supported with provisions and reinforcements. He went on to speak even more boldly.

*And now behold, we desire to know the cause of this exceedingly great neglect; yea, we desire to know the cause of your thoughtless state.* **Can you think to sit upon your thrones in a state of thoughtless stupor, while your enemies are spreading the work of death around you?** *Yea, while they are murdering thousands of your brethren. . . .*

*Yea, ye might have sent armies unto them, to have strengthened them, and have saved thousands of them from falling by the sword.*

*But behold, this is not all—ye have withheld your provisions from them, insomuch that many have fought and bled out their lives because of their great desires which they had for the welfare of this people; . . .*

*And now, my beloved brethren—for ye ought to be beloved; yea, **and ye ought to have stirred yourselves more***

*diligently for the welfare and the freedom of this people; but behold, ye have neglected them insomuch that the blood of thousands shall come upon your heads for vengeance; yea, for known unto God were all their cries, and all their sufferings.* (Alma 60:6–12; emphasis added)

These were some harsh words. While reading closely, one can feel Moroni's pain and his concern for his men—especially those who died or were taken captive along with their wives and children. Moroni was an action oriented leader. In the end of his letter he said he would take action against Pahoran if needed.

***Do ye suppose that God will look upon you as guiltless while ye sit still and behold these things? Behold I say unto you, Nay.*** *Now I would that ye should remember that God has said that the inward vessel shall be cleansed first, and then shall the outer vessel be cleansed also.*

*And now, except ye do repent of that which ye have done, and begin to be up and doing, and send forth food and men unto us, and also unto Helaman, that he may support those parts of our country which he has regained, and that we may* also recover the remainder of our possessions in these parts, behold it will be expedient that we contend no more with the Lamanites until we have first cleansed our inward vessel, yea, even the great head of our government.

And except ye grant mine epistle, and come out and show unto me a true spirit of freedom. . . . I will come unto you, and if there be any among you that has a desire for freedom, yea, if there be even a spark of freedom remaining, behold I will stir up insurrections among you, even until those who have desires to usurp power and authority shall become extinct.

Yea, behold I do not fear your power nor your authority, but it is my God whom I fear; and it is according to his commandments that I do take my sword to defend the cause of my country, and it is because of your iniquity that we have suffered so much loss.

Behold it is time, yea, the time is now at hand, that except ye do bestir yourselves in the defence of your country and your little ones, the sword of justice doth hang over you; yea, and it shall fall upon you and visit you even to your utter destruction. . . .

And now behold, **I, Moroni, am constrained, according to the covenant which I have made to keep the commandments of my God;** therefore I would that ye should adhere to the word of God, and send speedily unto me of your provisions and of your men, and also to Helaman. **And behold, if ye will not do this I come unto you speedily; for behold, God will not suffer that we should perish with hunger . . .**

**Behold, I am Moroni, your chief captain. I seek not for power, but to pull it down. I seek not for honor of the world, but for the glory of my God, and the freedom and welfare of my country. And thus I close mine epistle.** (Alma 60:23–25, 27–29, 34–36; emphasis added)

Can you imagine a more dedicated patriot? He does not seek power but seeks to establish freedom and bring prosperity to his people. If they would not help him fight for freedom, he would return to Zarahemla and bring liberty back to the people.

Pahoran responds to Moroni by explaining that the king-men had started a civil war and driven him from the capitol. He requested the help of Moroni to end the insurrection and explained that he had fled to Gideon. Through a proclamation, many were coming to help him. This is truly a story of two great men of honor.

Pahoran's letter reflects his honorable and humble status. Again, I give only excerpts to illustrate the magnitude of this admirable leader, Pahoran.

**And now, in your epistle you have censured me, but it mattereth not; I am not angry, but do rejoice in the greatness of your heart.** I, Pahoran, do not seek for power, save only to retain my judgment-seat that I may preserve the rights and the liberty of my people. **My soul standeth fast in that liberty in which God hath made us free.**

And now, behold, we will resist wickedness even unto bloodshed. We would not shed the blood of the Lamanites if they would stay in their own land. . . . We would subject ourselves to the yoke of bondage if it were requisite with the justice of God, or if he should command us so to do. . . .

Therefore, my beloved brother, Moroni, let us resist evil, and whatsoever evil we cannot resist with our words, yea, such as rebellions and dissensions, let us resist them with our swords, that we may retain our freedom, that we may rejoice in the great privilege of our church, and in the cause of our Redeemer and our God.

**Therefore, come unto me speedily with a few of your men, and leave the remainder in the charge of Lehi and Teancum; give unto them power to conduct the war in that part of the land, according to the Spirit of God, which is also the spirit of freedom which is in them.**

Behold I have sent a few provisions unto them, that they may not perish until ye can come unto me. Gather together whatsoever force ye can upon your march hither, and we will go speedily against those dissenters, in the strength of our God according to the faith which is in us. And we will take possession of the city of Zarahemla, that we may obtain more food to send forth unto Lehi and Teancum; yea, we will go forth against them in the strength of the Lord, and we will put an end to this great iniquity. . . .

**See that ye strengthen Lehi and Teancum in the Lord; tell them to fear not, for God will deliver them, yea, and also all those who stand fast in that liberty wherewith God hath made them free. And now I close mine epistle to my beloved brother, Moroni.** (Alma 61:9–10, 12, 14–18, 21; emphasis added)

This is such a great example of humble and honorable patriotism. Pahoran looks past the anger of Moroni and says: "And now, in your epistle you have censured me, but it mattereth not; I am not angry, but do rejoice in the greatness of your heart" (Alma 61:9). How many men could maintain control and patience in the face of Moroni's criticism? Pahoran is a gentleman's gentleman. His wisdom is revealed humbly and respectfully. Moreover, he closes his letter with a spiritual message to Lehi and Teancum: "Tell them to fear not, for God will deliver them, yea, and all those who stand fast in that liberty wherewith God hath made them free" (Alma 61:21). Pahoran's response is an example to all of us. Thank God that Mormon etched these two letters onto the golden plates. We are so fortunate to have these two pieces of literature.

After receiving the letter, Moroni did exactly as Pahoran suggested. He left the war in the hands of Lehi and Teancum and returned to help Pahoran. His return to the heartland was successful. They gathered strength and went back to Zarahemla to free the city from Pachus, leader of the king-men. A key to his success is reflected in a few short passages.

*And it came to pass that Moroni took a small number of men, according to the desire of Pahoran, and gave Lehi and Teancum command over the remainder of his army, and took his march toward the land of Gideon.*

*And he did raise the standard of liberty in whatsoever place he did enter, and gained whatsoever force he could in all his march toward the land of Gideon. And it came to pass that thousands did flock unto his standard, and did take up their swords in the defense of their freedom, that they might not come into bondage. . . .*

**And it came to pass that Moroni and Pahoran went down with their armies into the land of Zarahemla, and went forth against the city, and did meet the men of Pachus, insomuch that they did come to battle.**

**And behold, Pachus was slain and his men were taken prisoners, and Pahoran was restored to his judgment-seat.** *(Alma 62:3–5, 7–8; emphasis added)*

Again, Moroni became the great motivator as he recruited supporters on his journey to rescue Pahoran and Zarahemla. His return restored the elected leaders to power and ended the rebellion.

## Moroni's Battle to Retake Nephihah

Captain Moroni quickly returned to the battlefield. Six thousand men were sent as reinforcements to both Helaman and Lehi. Moroni's new undertaking was to retake the city of Nephihah from the Lamanites. This is a story of enormous success. On his march to the front line of the war, he encountered a Lamanite army.

> *And it came to pass that as they were marching toward the land, they took a large body of men of the Lamanites, and slew many of them, and took their provisions and their weapons of war.*
>
> *And it came to pass after they had taken them, they caused them to enter into a covenant that they would no more take up their weapons of war against the Nephites.*
>
> *And when they had entered into this covenant they sent them to dwell with the people of Ammon, and they were in number about four thousand who had not been slain. (Alma 62:15–17)*

This is another typical example of Captain Moroni's mercy and belief in his fellow men. With a covenant not to take up arms, Moroni released an entire Lamanite army to go live in Nephite lands with the former Lamanites, the people of Ammon. This is almost unbelievable—but not if you understand the mind-set of Moroni. He believed in liberty and offered freedom to his defeated enemies. This was a marvelous opportunity to choose freedom over tyranny. They had experienced the oppression of the Lamanite kings. Who wouldn't make the choice for liberty?

I had a similar experience in the war in Iraq. My best Iraqi friends were high-ranking soldiers of the Iraqi army who had experienced the tyranny of Saddam Hussein. They were men of honor anxious to help the cause of freedom in their homeland. When Moroni gave the choice of freedom over tyranny, it was accepted by four thousand Lamanites. Based on my friendships with former Iraqi military officers, Moroni's offer and the Lamanite acceptance is easy to understand. Moroni marched directly to the city of Nephihah that had been captured by a Lamanite army. Remember that Moroni was a master of military intelligence, which he proved yet again. In the night, he climbed the wall of the city and discovered the Lamanite army camped and sleeping on the eastern part of the city. He quickly mobilized his forces to ascend the wall and descend into the city on the west. The account is as follows.

> *And when the night came, Moroni went forth in the darkness of the night, and came upon the top of the wall to spy*

*out in what part of the city the Lamanites did camp with their army.*

*And it came to pass that they were on the east, by the entrance; and they were all asleep. And now Moroni returned to his army, and caused that they should prepare in haste strong cords and ladders, to be let down from the top of the wall into the inner part of the wall.*

*And it came to pass that Moroni caused that his men should march forth and come upon the top of the wall, and let themselves down into that part of the city, yea, even on the west, where the Lamanites did not camp with their armies. (Alma 62:20–22.)*

The city was easily recaptured and Moroni showed clemency again.

**Thus had Moroni and Pahoran obtained the possession of the city of Nephihah without the loss of one soul;** *and there were many of the Lamanites who were slain. Now it came to pass that many of the Lamanites that were prisoners were desirous to join the people of Ammon and become a free people. . . .*

*Therefore, all the prisoners of the Lamanites did join the people of Ammon, and did begin to labor exceedingly, tilling the ground, raising all manner of grain,*

*and flocks and herds of every kind; and thus were the Nephites relieved from a great burden; yea, insomuch that they were relieved from all the prisoners of the Lamanites. (Alma 62:26–27, 29; emphasis added)*

What an incredible turn of events. Usually the captured Lamanites needed to be imprisoned and fed. Moroni offered them freedom, and they immediately became an asset to his war effort. They joined the Ammonites in providing support to the armies of the chief captain. This victory was successful, and the defection of the Lamanites was a tremendous help to the Nephites. The armies of Moroni, Helaman, and Lehi gained the advantage and eventually drove the Lamanites back into their lands. The end of this epic story is best told by the writers of the Book of Mormon.

*And it came to pass that after Moroni had fortified those parts of the land which were most exposed to the Lamanites, until they were sufficiently strong, he returned to the city of Zarahemla; and also Helaman returned to the place of his inheritance; and there was once more peace established among the people of Nephi.*

**And Moroni yielded up the command of his armies into the hands of**

*his son, whose name was Moronihah; and he retired to his own house that he might spend the remainder of his days in peace.*

***And Pahoran did return to his judgment-seat; and Helaman did take upon him again to preach unto the people the word of God. . . .***

*And the people of Nephi began to prosper again in the land, and began to multiply and to wax exceedingly strong again in the land. And they began to grow exceedingly rich.*

*But notwithstanding their riches, or their strength, or their prosperity, they were not lifted up in the pride of their eyes; neither were they slow to remember the Lord their God; but they did humble themselves exceedingly before him.*

***Yea, they did remember how great things the Lord had done for them, that he had delivered them from death, and from bonds, and from prisons, and from all manner of afflictions and he had delivered them out of the hands of their enemies.***

***And they did pray unto the Lord their God continually, insomuch that the Lord did bless them, according to his word, so that they did wax***

***strong and prosper in the land.*** (Alma 62:42–44, 48–51; emphasis added)

What a fitting tribute to a band of Nephite brothers: Moroni, Lehi, Teancum, Helaman, and Pahoran. Through a remarkable effort, an enormous sacrifice, and an expression of faith, they brought peace to their land. They kept the covenant of their patriarch, Lehi, by remembering the Lord. As a result, they were blessed with success and prosperity.

## Lessons to Learn from Captain Moroni's Example

I believe that one of the reasons Mormon included this part of the Nephite history was to describe the consequences of wicked men to the people in the latter days. The following is one of Mormon's reflective editorials:

*Thus we see how quick the children of men do forget the Lord their God, yea, how quick to do iniquity, and to be led away by the evil one.*

***Yea, and we also see the great wickedness one very wicked man can cause to take place among the children of men.***

*Yea, we see that Amalickiah, because he was a man of cunning device and a man of many flattering words, that he led away the hearts of many people to do wickedly; yea, and to seek to destroy the church of God, and to destroy the foundation of liberty which God had granted unto them, or which blessing God had sent upon the face of the land for the righteous' sake. (Alma 46:8–10; emphasis added)*

Mormon was very clear in these captivating verses. We should "see" what he saw in depraved leaders and not let them flourish in our time. We should take careful note of Mormon's explicit description of wicked men.

***Men of cunning devise—they will be scheming behind the view of the people to bring themselves wealth and power.*** We need to be vigilant and gain knowledge about our leaders and their intentions. It is imperative that we sustain men of honor. Honesty must be a core value of the leaders we support.

***Men of flattering words—they will be fluent in their use of language to convince us that they are honest and thinking of us when they are not.*** It is important for us to critically analyze the rhetoric of people seeking our support. If we are not thoughtful and knowledgeable, they may mislead us into sustaining their wicked schemes.

***Men who seek to destroy the church of God—they will endeavor to make the church***

***and faith in Christ look irrational and uneducated.*** It is their intentions to make people of faith appear emotional and foolish. If we become ashamed to take on the name of Christ they will have accomplished their purpose.

***Men who seek to destroy our foundation of liberty—they will attempt to enslave us by taking our freedoms.*** The individual freedom to worship, speak openly, and own property should be central principles in our government. In the United States, we have the divinely inspired Constitution that guarantees these God-given freedoms. We must know the founding principles therein to ensure that our leaders follow them.

In this story of Captain Moroni, we are given an example of what we should expect from all leaders. We are shown an interesting contrast in leadership. Captain Moroni was almost a mirror opposite to Amalickiah. We should emulate the great chief captain by being courageous, thoughtful, fair, and merciful. Moroni understood the wickedness of Amalickiah and motivated the people. Perhaps his greatest illustration of strength and wisdom was his title of liberty.

*And it came to pass that he [Captain Moroni] rent his coat; and he took a piece thereof, and wrote upon it—**In memory*** *of our God, our religion, and freedom, and our peace, our wives, and our children—and he fastened it upon the end of a pole.*

*And he fastened on his head-plate, and his breastplate, and his shields, and girded on his armor about his loins; and he took the pole, which had on the end thereof his rent coat, (and he called it the title of liberty) and he bowed himself to the earth, and he prayed mightily unto his God for the blessings of liberty to rest upon his brethren, so long as there should a band of Christians remain to possess the land—(Alma 46:12–13; emphasis added)*

What an incredible image of leadership! Captain Moroni is an amazing example of spirituality, honor, and patriotism. He made the title of liberty from his torn coat as a symbol that he was making a covenant, which included the following:

**To remember God**—an obligation to God, the source of all blessings must be first on the title of liberty.

**To support religion and faith**—a dedication to Christ's church and gospel is an overriding principle.

**To honor freedom**—a commitment to liberty is paramount because without the agency of man, life loses its purpose.

**To desire peace**—the warrior's most fond aspiration is lasting peace!

**To remember our wives and children**—Gods greatest gift to man—the family—must be in the covenant. The foundation and justification for war is that it is fought for the children—that they will have a future of opportunity and peace.

**To offer the ultimate sacrifice**—putting on his armor gave us a visual sign of commitment, a willingness to give his life in the battle for freedom.

**To kneel in prayer**—this demonstrated perhaps the most important of all leadership qualities—humility and faith.

Isn't this declaration of war magnificent? The Nephites under Captain Moroni had a rule for war that would benefit all of mankind—in all of history. It is obviously different from the Lamanites, who attacked because they were beset by hate and wanted to profit from slavery. The rule of war was simple.

*Now the Nephites were taught to defend themselves against their enemies, even to the shedding of blood if it were necessary; yea, and they were also taught never to give an offense, yea, and never to raise the sword except it were against an enemy, except it were to preserve their lives.*

*And this was their faith, that by so doing God would prosper them in the land, or in other words, if they were faithful in keeping the commandments of God that he would prosper them in the land; yea, warn them to flee, or to prepare for war, according to their danger; (Alma 48:14–15; emphasis added)*

Again, these statements are extremely clear! We have been taught through the stories of Captain Moroni the true justification for war: to defend liberty and to protect our families. And finally, any act of war must be part of our faith. By keeping the commandments of God, He will bring prosperity to our land. This was proven true under the protection of Captain Moroni, and it is just as true for us today. Remember the result of Moroni's hard work.

*But behold there never was a happier time among the people of Nephi, since the days of Nephi, than in the days of Moroni, yea, even at this time, in the twenty and first year of the reign of the judges. (Alma 50:23; emphasis added)*

It is readily apparent to me that the awe-inspiring Nephite chief captain was perhaps the greatest of all military generals—not just of the Nephites but in all of recorded history.

Without question, his story deserved to be highlighted in the Book of Mormon. Even though I have pointed this out earlier in this chapter, it needs to be repeated. Here is Mormon's ultimate compliment to the *greatest* of Nephite captains—Moroni.

*And Moroni was a strong and a mighty man; he was a man of a perfect understanding; yea, a man that did not delight in bloodshed; a man whose soul did joy in the liberty and the freedom of his country, and his brethren from bondage and slavery;*

*Yea, a man whose heart did swell with thanksgiving to his God, for the many privileges and blessings which he bestowed upon his people; a man who did labor exceedingly for the welfare and safety of his people.*

*Yea, and he was a man who was firm in the faith of Christ, and he had sworn with an oath to defend his people, his rights, and his country, and his religion, even to the loss of his blood. . . .*

*And also, that God would make it known unto them whither they should go to defend themselves against their enemies, and by so doing, the Lord would deliver them; and this was the faith of Moroni, and his heart did glory in it; not in the shedding of blood but in doing good, in preserving his people, yea, in keeping the commandments of God, yea, and resisting iniquity.*

**Yea, verily, verily I say unto you, if all men had been, and were, and ever would be, like unto Moroni, behold, the very powers of hell would have been shaken forever; yea, the devil would never have power over the hearts of the children of men.** *(Alma 48:11–13, 16–17; emphasis added]*

May we emulate the imposing example of Captain Moroni in our lives and teach every generation the truths he illustrated for us.

## Sources

1. "Introduction to the Holocaust," http://www.ushmm.org.
2. Dan Stone, ed. *The Historiography of the Holocaust* (New York: Palgrave-Macmillan, 2004), 383–96.
3. David Glantz, "The Soviet German War: Myths and Realities, A Survey Essay," Helion and Company Limited, Solihul, England.
4. "Stalin, Joseph," http://www.enotes.com/stalin-joseph-reference/stalin-joseph.
5. Bruce Walker, "Remembering the Mass-murderer Mao," http://thenewamerican.com/history/world/2166-remembering-the-mass-murderer-mao.

# Six

# SECRET COMBINATIONS— THE GADIANTON ROBBERS

*Wherefore, O ye Gentiles, it is wisdom in God that these things
should be shown unto you, that thereby ye may repent of your sins,
and suffer not that these murderous combinations
shall get above you, which are built up to get power and gain. . . .
Wherefore, the Lord commandeth you, when ye shall see these things
come among you that ye shall awake to a sense of your awful situation,
because of this secret combination which shall be among you.*
MORONI, SON OF MORMON, IN ETHER 8:23–24

This chapter is a departure from the others in that the main character is not a great and faithful warrior. He is Gadianton, one of the most evil of all men. He was a primary founder of a group of conspirators who sought to overthrow the leadership of both the Nephites and the Lamanites. His faction gained enormous power, influenced the Nephites and Lamanites for over four hundred years, and ultimately destroyed the Nephite nation. Mormon tells us this when he first wrote about the band of Gadianton. This was his reflection.

*And behold, in the end of this book [The Book of Mormon] ye shall see that this Gadianton [Secret Combination Founder] did prove the overthrow, yea, almost the entire destruction of the people of Nephi. (Helaman 2:13)*

The murderous system that Gadianton

designed with the aid of Satan was often called secret combinations by Book of Mormon authors. Reading the quotes stated previously, it is easy to see that God has given us a grave warning regarding these combinations of wicked men. In a very simple but direct statement the Lord is telling us: *Do not let this system of wickedness function among you. It will destroy your faith, your freedom, and, subsequently, any orderly way of life.* The purpose of this chapter is to give an account of the development of these secret combinations and the terrible tragedy they brought to the promised land. Once this wickedness is illustrated and understood, it will be easy to see why the Lord wants us to guard against it.

## The Setting—
## A Time of Dissension and Secrecy

The time of this historical account is approximately 50 BC. The story of this great iniquity begins with the chief judge of the Nephites, Pahoran. He had supported Moroni and defeated the king-men. Several years after the defeat of the Lamanite armies, Pahoran died, leaving three sons—Pahoran, Pacumeni, and Paanchi—who sought the judgeship. The people elected Pahoran but Paanchi rebelled. Paanchi was tried for treason and condemned to death. Among his supporters was a murderous

dissenter named Kishkumen. He slipped secretly into the hall of justice and murdered Pahoran, the newly elected chief judge while he sat in his judgment seat. Kishkumen then successfully escaped. A band of conspirators took an oath of secrecy to cover up this murder and other crimes. Within a short time, a cunning and crafty man named Gadianton rose up to be their leader. From that time forward, the band took his name and was called the Gadianton robbers (Helaman 1–2).

Our brief discussion will illustrate the characteristics of these clandestine organizations and how they influenced the Nephites and the Lamanites. Alma the Younger, Nephite chief judge and prophet, was one of the first to identify the wickedness of these conspirators. He read about them in a history written upon twenty-four gold plates, which told the story of the Jaredites, a civilization that started around 2000 BC. He was an aging prophet at the time and was instructing his son Helaman about the role of prophet and historian. Alma made these comments concerning the danger of these secret combinations twenty years before the formation of the Gadiantons among the Nephites.

*Therefore I command you, my son Helaman, that ye be diligent in fulfilling all my words, and that ye be diligent in keeping the commandments of God as they are written.*

*And now, I will speak unto you concerning those twenty-four plates, that ye keep them, that the mysteries and the works of darkness, and their secret works, or the secret works of those people who have been destroyed, may be made manifest unto this people; yea, all their murders, and robbings, and their plunderings, and all their wickedness and abominations, may be made manifest unto this people; yea, and that ye preserve these interpreters.*

**For behold, the Lord saw that his people began to work in darkness, yea, work secret murders and abominations; therefore the Lord said, if they did not repent they should be destroyed from off the face of the earth.** *(Alma 37:20–22; emphasis added)*

Alma read about the secret works of darkness in the ancient record and was genuinely worried that these conspiracies would become known among the Nephites and cause their downfall. He told his son about his grave concern.

*For behold,* **there is a curse upon all this land***, that destruction shall come upon all those workers of darkness,*

*according to the power of God, when they are fully ripe; therefore I desire that this people might not be destroyed.*

**Therefore ye shall keep these secret plans of their oaths and their covenants from this people,** *and only their wickedness and their murders and their abominations shall ye make known unto them; and ye shall teach them to abhor such wickedness and abominations and murders; and ye shall also teach them that these people were destroyed on account of their wickedness and abominations and their murders.*

*For behold, they murdered all the prophets of the Lord who came among them to declare unto them concerning their iniquities; and the blood of those whom they murdered did cry unto the Lord their God for vengeance upon those who were their murderers; and thus the judgments of God did come upon these workers of darkness and secret combinations.*

**Yea, and cursed be the land forever and ever unto those workers of darkness and secret combinations, even unto destruction, except they repent before they are fully ripe.**

*And now, my son, remember the words which I have spoken unto you;*

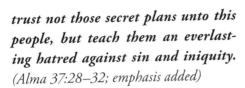

*trust not those secret plans unto this people, but teach them an everlasting hatred against sin and iniquity.*
(Alma 37:28–32; emphasis added)

## Secret Plots of Murder and Crime

This band of wicked men was bound together by four common elements: an oath of secrecy, deceit to gain power, murder, and criminal behavior to get wealth. Each of these characteristics will be discussed separately.

The first Nephite encounter with this group was the murder of the Chief Judge Pahoran and the attempted murder of Chief Judge Helaman by a man named Kishkumen.

> *And it came to pass that Helaman, who was the son of Helaman, was appointed to fill the judgment-seat, by the voice of the people.*
>
> *But behold, Kishkumen, who had murdered Pahoran, did lay wait to destroy Helaman also; and he was upheld by his band, who had entered into a covenant that no one should know his wickedness.*
>
> *For there was one Gadianton, who was exceedingly expert in many words, and also in his craft, to carry on the secret work of murder and of robbery; therefore he became the leader of the band of Kishkumen.*
>
> *Therefore he did flatter them, and also Kishkumen, that if they would place him in the judgment-seat he would grant unto those who belonged to his band that they should be placed in power and authority among the people; therefore Kishkumen sought to destroy Helaman.* (Helaman 2:2–5; emphasis added)

The plot to kill Helaman was thwarted by a loyal Nephite who had infiltrated the Kishkumen band and discovered the scheme. The scriptures explain how the conspiracy was foiled.

> *And it came to pass that he met Kishkumen, and he gave unto him a sign; therefore Kishkumen made known unto him the object of his desire, desiring that he would conduct him to the judgment-seat that he might murder Helaman.*
>
> *And when the servant of Helaman had known all the heart of Kishkumen, and how that it was his object to murder, and also that it was the object of all those who belonged to his band to murder, and to rob, and to gain power, (and this was their secret plan, and their combination) the servant of Helaman*

*said unto Kishkumen: Let us go forth unto the judgment-seat.*

*Now this did please Kishkumen exceedingly, for he did suppose that he should accomplish his design; but behold, the servant of Helaman, as they were going forth unto the judgment-seat, did stab Kishkumen even to the heart, that he fell dead without a groan. And he ran and told Helaman all the things which he had seen, and heard, and done. And it came to pass that Helaman did send forth to take this band of robbers and secret murderers, that they might be executed according to the law. (Helaman 2:7–10; emphasis added)*

We learn interesting details from these brief passages in Helaman 2. First, notice how they identified each other with secret signs. Second, observe that the secret band was motivated by the desire for power and wealth through murder and deception. Again we see the emergence of an evil man who was "exceedingly expert in many words, and also in his craft" (v. 4). Gadianton convinced the members of his band to make him leader. He then placed the members of his covert group in key positions of power with the purpose of gaining wealth. This process became extremely successful and within a few years, they were in control of most of the Nephite nation—the process was flattery, false promises, deception, and murder.

A fascinating word used in this text is also used today. Notice that the author said Gadianton was expert in his *craft*. I worked in military intelligence and studied modern covert activities carried out by nations hostile to the United States. These intelligence gathering methods are often called espionage. They have some very common tactics. The people who design the activities of these undercover networks call their plans and methods "tradecraft." The word *craft* seems to have been brought through the centuries into our time.

When stationed in Iraq with the United States Army during 2003, I observed how this same clandestine process worked for Saddam Hussein, Iraqi dictator from 1979 to 2003. His political Ba'ath Party gained power by cruelty and murder. Saddam moved up through the Ba'ath Party to a top leadership position. During a meeting of party leaders, he gained control by accusing those who opposed him of treason. The leaders of opposition were then executed without trial. He often tortured or killed people who resisted his regime. He even went so far as to torture his Olympic athletes when they failed to win. There was actually a torture chamber at the Olympic training facility.

I spoke with an Iraqi Air Force colonel

shortly after the fall of Baghdad. At the end of our discussion, he volunteered some advice to us as the conquering force. After complimenting us for having the most powerful army in history and flattering us about how quickly we conquered Iraq, he made the following comment. "You Americans can win the war but will never control the Iraqi people." We inquired as to why and he replied, "Because you don't torture people." Our response was that he missed the point: "We came here to bring freedom and eliminate torture." Centuries of cruel leaders and oppression had brought him to his conclusion. This well-educated, high-ranking military officer actually believed that successful governance in their country could only be based on oppression and fear. What a sad commentary.

In Saddam's Iraq, it was a real opportunity to be in the Ba'ath Party. For example, high-ranking military promotions were based on Ba'ath Party membership. There were a number of resorts built throughout the country for senior Ba'ath Party members to enjoy. There was even a "Special Republican Guard" army appointed to protect the resorts and facilities from public intrusion. I lived on one of the resorts in Baghdad. It was exceptionally gaudy. It had seven man-made lakes filled with exotic fish. There were thirty-four palaces

decorated with Italian marble interiors and luxurious top-of-the-line furniture and Persian rugs. There was even a children's playground made in miniature to look like a "hobbit" village right out of J. R. R. Tolkien's books. One might compare the palaces to five-star hotels complete with costly furnishings and chandeliers. One of the most audacious buildings was called the "Victory Over America Palace." Saddam had told his people that he won the first Gulf war in 1992. His outrageous reasoning was that the Americans had retreated and gone home. The truth was that his army was totally decimated. However, he still built a victory palace in his own honor. He fashioned incredible lies designed to deceive his people into believing he was invincible.

During one of my interviews with an Iraqi regime leader, he laughed at what he thought was my naiveté. We knew that Saddam had smuggled war supplies through the United Nations investigators at the border. I asked him how this was done. He laughed and said the co-conspirators who shipped the military equipment simply posted on the large shipment crates that they were filled with food and medical supplies. The UN border guards never checked. The conspiracy included bribes to those who were shipping the prohibited war materials and possibly the border guards as well. These secret acts of trickery kept this wicked government in power for a decade.

Having viewed firsthand the evil designs that created a wicked political machine in Iraq makes it easy for me to understand how the Gadianton robbers through murder, bribery, fear, and the promise of power eventually took over the Nephite nation.

## Nephite Wickedness Enables Evil Bands to Thrive

The strength of the Nephite nation was determined by its righteousness. The enemies from within and from without could only gain power if the Nephites turned away from the Lord. Helaman taught the gospel to the people, and Chief Captain Moronihah maintained safety and peace by driving the Gadiantons into the wilderness. When Helaman the second died, his son Nephi became the spiritual leader and the chief judge. The peace lasted fifteen years, and then a Lamanite army took much of the Nephite territory, slaughtering thousands. The prophet Nephi explained how pride and wickedness reduced the strength of the Nephite nation.

*Now this great loss of the Nephites, and the great slaughter which was among them, would not have happened had it not been for their wickedness and their abomination which was among them; yea, and it was among those also who professed to belong to the church of God.*

***And it was because of the pride of their hearts,*** *because of their exceeding riches, yea, it was because of their oppression to the poor, withholding their food from the hungry, withholding their clothing from the naked, and smiting their humble brethren upon the cheek, making a mock of that which was sacred, denying the spirit of prophecy and of revelation, murdering, plundering, lying, stealing, committing adultery, rising up in great contentions, and deserting away into the land of Nephi, among the Lamanites—*

***And because of this their great wickedness, and their boastings in their own strength, they were left in their own strength;*** *therefore they did not prosper, but were afflicted and smitten, and driven before the Lamanites, until they had lost possession of almost all their lands.*

*But behold, Moronihah did preach many things unto the people because of their iniquity, and also Nephi and Lehi, who were the sons of Helaman, did preach many things unto the people, yea, and did prophesy many things unto them concerning their iniquities, and what should come unto them if they did not repent of their sins. (Helaman 4:11–14; emphasis added)*

### The Source of the Evil Scheme Was Satan

The Nephites did repent, but their repentance lasted for less than five years, and they drifted back into iniquity. This time it was more than pride because they began to subscribe to the rules of conspiracy and accepted the Gadianton robbers into their land. Nephi explained how the Nephites fell into this satanic snare.

> *For behold, the Lord had blessed them so long with the riches of the world that they had not been stirred up to anger, to wars, nor to bloodshed; **therefore they began to set their hearts upon their riches; yea, they began to seek to get gain that they might be lifted up one above another; therefore they began to commit secret murders, and to rob and to plunder, that they might get gain.***
>
> *And now behold, those murderers and plunderers were a band who had been formed by Kishkumen and Gadianton. And now it had come to pass*

*that **there were many, even among the Nephites, of Gadianton's band. But behold, they were more numerous among the more wicked part of the Lamanites. And they were called Gadianton's robbers and murderers.** (Helaman 6:17–18)*

This infiltration into the lands of the Nephites and Lamanites caused an outright theft of freedom. The following phrase describes the loss of freedom: "they began to seek to get gain that they might be lifted up one above another" (v. 17) Note how this came from within—no armies and no revolutions. The wickedness of the people caused the secret combinations to grow in strength. When Satan gains power over nations through wicked men, it is much like placing gasoline on a fire. The wickedness of the people combined with the terrible iniquity of these organizations allowed them to explode into power among both the Lamanites and the Nephites.

> *And now it came to pass that when the Lamanites found that there were robbers among them they were exceedingly sorrowful; and they did use every means in their power to destroy them off the face of the earth.*
>
> ***But behold, Satan did stir up the***

*hearts of the more part of the Nephites, insomuch that they did unite with those bands of robbers, and did enter into their covenants and their oaths, that they would protect and preserve one another in whatsoever difficult circumstances they should be placed, that they should not suffer for their murders, and their plunderings, and their stealings.*

*And it came to pass that they did have their signs, yea, their secret signs, and their secret words; and this that they might distinguish a brother who had entered into the covenant, that whatsoever wickedness his brother should do he should not be injured by his brother, nor by those who did belong to his band, who had taken this covenant.*

*And thus they might murder, and plunder, and steal, and commit whoredoms and all manner of wickedness, contrary to the laws of their country and also the laws of their God.*

*And whosoever of those who belonged to their band should reveal unto the world of their wickedness and their abominations, should be tried, not according to the laws of their country, but according to the laws of their wickedness, which had been*

*given by Gadianton and Kishkumen. (Helaman 6:20–24; emphasis added)*

A primary message in these passages is that the source of the oaths and covenants is Satan. The Gadianton band created an oath that allowed murder and theft to thrive with no fear of exposure. The goal of secrecy was well defined. They could commit multiple crimes and be protected by their covenant. They could not be brought before the honest courts of the land because their deception prevented the truth from coming to the light. Inside the secret society, on the other hand, was a different code of justice. If a band member broke the laws of Gadianton, it called for the ultimate punishment—death. Just imagine the horror this would bring into the lives of people foolishly recruited into their depraved association. This same corruption is what allowed Adolf Hitler to exterminate six million Jews. His protective officers were called the SS. It is evident that secrecy was their ultimate weapon against truth and fairness. They committed the ruthless murder of millions without fear of retribution or exposure.

The scriptures in Helaman tell us in detail how Satan entices these men and works his way into their hearts.

*Now behold, those secret oaths and covenants did not come forth unto Gadianton from the records which were delivered unto Helaman; but behold, they were put into the heart of Gadianton by that same being who did entice our first parents to partake of the forbidden fruit. . . .*

*Yea, it is that same being who put it into the heart of Gadianton to* still carry on the work of darkness, and of secret murder; and he has brought it forth from the beginning of man even down to this time.

*And behold, it is he who is the author of all sin. And behold, he doth* carry on his works of darkness and secret murder, and doth hand down their plots, and their oaths, and their covenants, and their plans of awful wickedness, from generation to generation according as he can get hold upon the hearts of the children of men.

*And now behold, he had got great hold upon the hearts of the Nephites; yea, insomuch that they had become exceedingly wicked; yea, the more part of them had turned out of the way of righteousness, and did trample* under their feet the commandments of God, and did turn unto their own ways, and did build up unto themselves idols of their gold and their silver.

*And it came to pass that all these iniquities did come unto them in the space of not many years, insomuch that* a more part of it had come unto them in the sixty and seventh year of the reign of the judges over the people of Nephi. (Helaman 6:26, 29–32; emphasis added)

Note that the crafty son of darkness took control of the "more part" of the Nephite people in "the space of not many years." A reasonable estimate is less than ten years. Two chief judges were murdered in one year. The situation was so bad that the Nephites became more wicked and accepting of the wicked band of Gadiantons than the Lamanites. It is particularly interesting that the Lamanites were more concerned about ridding themselves of the robbers than the Nephites were. It was a brief ray of hope when the Lamanites were successful in dealing with the robbers. This was a natural place for the editor, Mormon, to make one of his many reflections—again, it begins with the familiar words, *"And thus we see."*

*And thus we see that the Spirit of the Lord began to withdraw from the Nephites, because of the wickedness and the hardness of their hearts.*

*And thus we see that the Lord began to pour out his Spirit upon the*

*Lamanites, because of their easiness and willingness to believe in his words.*

**And it came to pass that the Lamanites did hunt the band of robbers of Gadianton; and they did preach the word of God among the more wicked part of them,** *insomuch that this band of robbers was utterly destroyed from among the Lamanites.*

*And it came to pass on the other hand,* **that the Nephites did build them up and support them, beginning at the more wicked part of them, until they had overspread all the land of the Nephites,** *and had seduced the more part of the righteous until they had come down to believe in their works and partake of their spoils, and to join with them in their secret murders and combinations.*

**And thus they did obtain the sole management of the [Nephite] government,** *insomuch that they did trample under their feet and smite and rend and turn their backs upon the poor and the meek, and the humble followers of God.*

*And thus we see that they were in an awful state, and ripening for an everlasting destruction.* (Helaman 6:35–40; emphasis added)

What an amazing turn of events! The Lamanites became more righteous and drove out the band of robbers. They even taught the gospel to the wicked of the band. The Lamanites also came into the Nephite lands to preach the gospel. The most prominent to come was Samuel, who called the Nephites to repentance and prophesied about the birth of the Savior (Helaman 13–15). While the Lamanites became faithful, the opposite was true of the Nephites. They embraced the wickedness and allowed the wicked secrecy laden band to take "sole management of the government." Mormon makes an important statement regarding their behavior. Those who suffered the most were the "humble followers of God." Knowing that Satan was the inspiration for the depraved leaders of the Nephites, one can see that persecution of the church would become commonplace.

The prophet Nephi and his brother Lehi tried to teach the Nephites with little success. Nephi then called upon the Lord to bring a famine to humble the people, and his request was granted. The famine lasted four years, and the people repented and were blessed. However, in a short time, approximately four more years, a civil war started among the Nephites because of dissension and the return of the Gadiantons. For ten years, the wicked band continued to gain strength. There was a brief period of repentance after the signs of the birth of the Savior.

However, after one generation, about thirty years, the problem with the Gadianton robbers became so grave that the Nephites joined with the Lamanites in a terribly destructive war to drive the robbers out.

*And it came to pass in the thirteenth year [AD 13] there began to be wars and contentions throughout all the land; for the Gadianton robbers had become so numerous, and did slay so many of the people, and did lay waste so many cities, and did spread so much death and carnage throughout the land,* **that it became expedient that all the people, both the Nephites and the Lamanites, should take up arms against them.**

*Therefore, all the Lamanites who had become converted unto the Lord did unite with their brethren, the Nephites, and were compelled, for the safety of their lives and their women and their children, to take up arms against those Gadianton robbers, yea, and also to maintain their rights, and the privileges of their church and of their worship, and their freedom and their liberty.*

*And it came to pass that before this thirteenth year had passed away the Nephites were threatened with utter destruction because of this war, which*

*had become exceedingly sore. (3 Nephi 2:11–13; emphasis added)*

During this tough sequence of wars, the leader of the band of robbers, Giddianhi, wrote a letter to the chief judge of the Nephites, Lachoneus. In the letter, Giddianhi offered to spare the Nephites if they surrender their lands and joined with the secret band. The haughtiness and arrogance of the robber leader is evident.

**Lachoneus, most noble and chief governor of the land,** *behold, I write this epistle unto you, and do give unto you exceedingly great praise because of your firmness, and also the firmness of your people, in maintaining that which ye suppose to be your right and liberty; yea, ye do stand well, as if ye were supported by the hand of a god, in the defense of your liberty, and your property, and your country, or that which ye do call so. And it seemeth a pity unto me, most noble Lachoneus, that ye should be so foolish and vain as to suppose that ye can stand against so many brave men who are at my command.*

*And I, knowing of their unconquerable spirit, having proved them in the field of battle, and knowing of their everlasting hatred toward you because of the many wrongs which ye have done unto them, therefore if they should come down against you they would visit you with utter destruction. . . .*

**Therefore I write unto you, desiring that ye would yield up unto this my people, your cities, your lands, and your possessions, rather than that they should visit you with the sword and that destruction should come upon you. Or in other words, yield yourselves up unto us, and unite with us and become acquainted with our secret works, and become our brethren that ye may be like unto us—not our slaves, but our brethren and partners of all our substance.**

*And behold, I swear unto you, if ye will do this, with an oath, ye shall not be destroyed; but if ye will not do this, I swear unto you with an oath, that on the morrow month I will command that my armies shall come down against you, and they shall not stay their hand and shall spare not, but shall slay you, and shall let fall the sword upon you even until ye shall become extinct.*

*And behold, I am Giddianhi; and I am the governor of this the secret society of Gadianton; which society and the works thereof I know to be good; and they are of ancient date and they have been handed down unto us.*

**And I write this epistle unto you, Lachoneus, and I hope that ye will deliver up your lands and your possessions, without the shedding of blood, that this my people may recover their rights and government, who have dissented away from you because of your wickedness in retaining from them their rights of government, and except ye do this, I will avenge their wrongs. I am Giddianhi.** *(3 Nephi 3:2–4, 6–10; emphasis added)*

What an interesting diatribe! Here is a commander of a rogue band of robbers threatening the utter destruction of the Nephite nation and offering a treaty. Giddianhi boasts of his army and the superiority of his soldiers. He was, however, an impostor and could not be trusted. The purpose of the evil band was to plunder and get gain. Could they be trusted to set up an honorable government? Absolutely not! They were a bloodthirsty secret society that had made a covenant with Satan to destroy all righteousness. Giddianhi tried to make it sound so good. He was concerned about the welfare of the Nephites. This was a total fabrication. What we need to see from this letter is that wicked men lie. Their honor had been forsaken. Murder and deceit were at the core of their philosophy. Once men join the band of secrecy, lying is commonplace, and they become pathologically good at it. They become cunning and deceitful leaders, desire authority, and will commit all manner of wickedness to get power and expand their influence.

There is no record of a written reply from Lachoneus. He was a man of God and knew of the evil designs of the Gadianton robbers. While he did not respond in writing, he did make one of the most remarkable plans in all of Nephite history. He and his great military commander, Gidgiddoni, were extraordinary leaders. They asked the people to turn to the Lord. An editorial from Mormon explains just how great they were.

*Yea, he [Lachoneus] said unto them: As the Lord liveth, except ye repent of all your iniquities, and cry unto the Lord, ye will in no wise be delivered out of the hands of those Gadianton robbers. And so great and marvelous were the words and prophecies of Lachoneus that they did cause fear to come upon all the people; and they did exert themselves in their might to do according to the words of Lachoneus.*

*And it came to pass that Lachoneus did appoint chief captains over all the armies of the Nephites, to command them at the time that the robbers should come*

*down out of the wilderness against them. Now the chiefest among all the chief captains and the great commander of all the armies of the Nephites was appointed, and his name was Gidgiddoni.*

***Now it was the custom among all the Nephites to appoint for their chief captains, (save it were in their times of wickedness) some one that had the spirit of revelation and also prophecy; therefore, this Gidgiddoni was a great prophet among them, as also was the chief judge.*** *(3 Nephi 3:15–19; emphasis added)*

The plan of Lachoneus and Gidgiddoni is recorded in Third Nephi 3. Lachoneus first told his people to turn to the Lord, and then he said to bring the people into a common area, in the central part of the Nephite lands, for protection.

***Now behold, this Lachoneus, the governor, was a just man, and could not be frightened by the demands and the threatenings of a robber; therefore he did not hearken to the epistle of Giddianhi,*** *the governor of the robbers, but he did cause that his people should cry unto the Lord for strength against the time that the robbers should come down against them.*

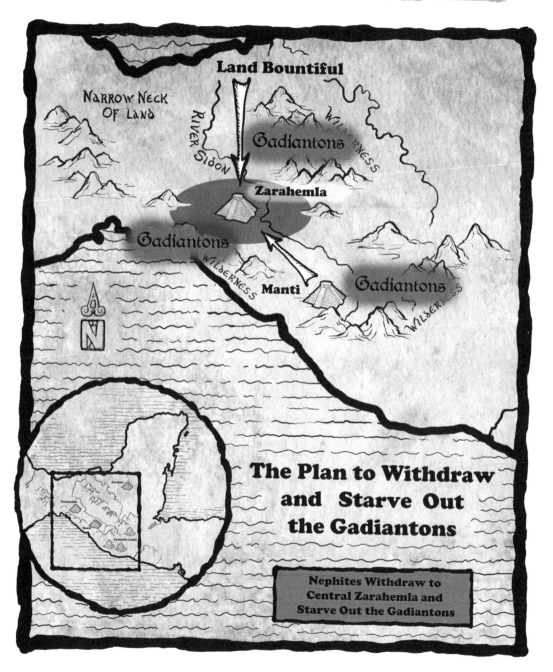

Land Bountiful

NARROW NECK OF LAND

RIVER SIDON

WILDERNESS

Gadiantons

Zarahemla

Gadiantons

WILDERNESS

Manti

Gadiantons

WILDERNESS

N

**The Plan to Withdraw and Starve Out the Gadiantons**

**Nephites Withdraw to Central Zarahemla and Starve Out the Gadiantons**

*Yea, he sent a proclamation among all the people, that they should gather together their women, and their children, their flocks and their herds, and all their substance, save it were their land, unto one place. And he caused that fortifications should be built round about them, and the strength thereof should be exceedingly great. And he caused that armies, both of the Nephites and of the Lamanites, or of all them who were numbered among the Nephites, should be placed as guards round about to watch them, and to guard them from the robbers day and night. (3 Nephi 3:12–14; emphasis added)*

What a unique plan! He was going against historical military strategy. In the past, they had searched out the enemy to destroy it. After the plan to collect the people in a central area was presented and showed success, the people wanted to chase the robbers in the wilderness and asked Gidgiddoni for a change in policy. He responded in this way:

*Now the people said unto Gidgiddoni: Pray unto the Lord, and let us go up upon the mountains and into the wilderness, that we may fall upon the robbers and destroy them in their own lands.*

*But Gidgiddoni saith unto them: The Lord forbid; for if we should go up against them the Lord would deliver us into their hands; therefore we will prepare ourselves in the center of our lands, and we will gather all our armies together, and we will not go against them, but we will wait till they shall come against us; therefore as the Lord liveth, if we do this he will deliver them into our hands.*

*And it came to pass in the seventeenth year, in the latter end of the year, the proclamation of Lachoneus had gone forth throughout all the face of the land, and they had taken their horses, and their chariots, and their cattle, and all their flocks, and their herds, and their grain, and all their substance, and did march forth by thousands and by tens of thousands, until they had all gone forth to the place which had been appointed that they should gather themselves together, to defend themselves against their enemies.*

*And the land which was appointed was the land of Zarahemla, and the land which was between the land Zarahemla and the land Bountiful, yea, to the line which was between the land Bountiful and the land Desolation. (3 Nephi 3:20–23; emphasis added)*

The plan was an inspiration from God to Lachoneus. Captain Gidgiddoni was also a prophet and knew the plan was right for the time. The plan was carried out, and the people were protected by the Nephite army, fortified with body armor under the design and direction of Gidgiddoni, the chief captain. The record tells us how this plan worked.

*And it came to pass that in the latter end of the eighteenth year those armies of robbers had prepared for battle, and began to come down and to sally forth from the hills, and out of the mountains, and the wilderness, and their strongholds, and their secret places, and began to take possession of the lands.*

*But behold, there were no wild beasts nor game in those lands which had been deserted by the Nephites, and there was no game for the robbers save it were in the wilderness.*

*And the robbers could not exist save it were in the wilderness, for the want of food; for the Nephites had left their lands desolate, and had gathered their flocks and their herds and all their substance, and they were in one body. Therefore, there*

*was no chance for the robbers to plunder and to obtain food, save it were to come up in open battle against the Nephites. (3 Nephi 4:1–4)*

The plan worked very well because the enemy was starving. The Gadiantons were not an organized society that raised food or produced goods and services. As shown in the map, they were concentrated in the mountainous wilderness. They were a band of robbers who thrived on theft and crime. Even though they surrounded the Nephites, they were powerless. Tens of thousands of Nephites had gathered to a central land under the direction of Lachoneus, a prophet. They were protected by a chief captain who was a prophet. In short, they had turned to God and followed his direction. The plan lasted two years, and the Gadianton system failed. Consequently, they were forced to come to battle on Nephite terms. A tremendous conflict ensued, and the report of the encounter is very sobering.

The Gadiantons had clad themselves in frightful clothing—they had a loincloth made of lambskin that was dyed in blood. Their heads were shaved and covered in an armored head plate. The writer describes their appearance as "great and terrible" (3 Nephi 4:7). The beginning of the battle was unusual—note that the armies of the robbers were godless and ferocious, while the Nephites were humble and prayerful.

*And it came to pass that the armies of the Nephites,* **when they saw the appearance of the army of Giddianhi, had all fallen to the earth, and did lift their cries to the Lord their God,** *that he would spare them and deliver them out of the hands of their enemies.*

**And it came to pass that when the armies of Giddianhi saw this they began to shout with a loud voice, because of their joy, for they had supposed that the Nephites had fallen with fear because of the terror of their armies. But in this thing they were disappointed, for the Nephites did not fear them; but they did fear their God and did supplicate him for protection;** *therefore, when the armies of Giddianhi did rush upon them they were prepared to meet them; yea, in the strength of the Lord they did receive them.*

*And the battle commenced in this the sixth month; and great and terrible was the battle thereof, yea, great and terrible was the slaughter thereof, insomuch that there never was known so great a slaughter among all the people of Lehi since he left Jerusalem. (3 Nephi 4:8–11)*

What an amazing sight! This would be awe inspiring—an entire Nephite army on its knees in prayer. No wonder they were successful. The Gadiantons were counting on fear and hate to bring victory. This was an astounding contrast in military character. The Gadiantons were driven by secrecy, murder, and hate. They dressed in clothing designed to bring fear to the enemy. In contrast, the Nephites were motivated by love of family and knelt in prayer led by a prophet of God. This major conflict is described by the author as the largest battle in the six hundred year history of the Nephite nation.

My religious experience in Iraq helps me appreciate this marvelous Nephite prayer. While I can't say that we started battle on our knees, I can say that there was more religion among the soldiers than most would believe. I have included two pictures of soldiers in prayer that I got from the Internet. They are not Latter-day Saints. The first shows a group of soldiers approaching the Lord in prayer. The second picture illustrates a priceless act. It is a group of United States Marines kneeling in prayer over a fallen comrade. My experience was that, along with patriotism, faith was the soldiers' common denominator. The danger in war and the possibility of death brings soldiers close to their God. The fight for liberty brings strong patriotism. Seeing a nation liberated and watching

*Both photos may be found at*
*http://media.photobucket.com*

the people react to freedom is a deeply spiritual experience.

Following the great battle between the Nephites and the Gadiantons, Gidgiddoni pursued the defeated enemy into the wilderness and completed the victory.

> *And now, Gidgiddoni being aware of their design, and knowing of their weakness because of the want of food, and the great slaughter which had been made among them, therefore he did send out his armies in the night-time, and did cut off the way of their retreat, and did place his armies in the way of their retreat.*
>
> *And this did they do in the night-time, and got on their march beyond the robbers, so that on the morrow, when the robbers began their march, they were met by the armies of the Nephites both in their front and in their rear. And the robbers who were on the south were also cut off in their places of retreat. And all these things were done by command of Gidgiddoni. (3 Nephi 4:24–26)*

This brief report tells about the impressive leadership of Gidgiddoni. His tactics were excellent. He moved under the cover of darkness to intercept the retreating enemy. The enemy was totally defeated, and the prisoners were treated with mercy. Prisoners were required to make a covenant not to return to their previous behavior and then were allowed to join the general population. We have seen this before in the history of Captain Moroni. The merciful treatment of prisoners and respect for the enemy is a trait of the great Nephite generals.

Following their impressive victory, the Nephites celebrated. The description of the festivity illustrates the joy among the Nephites and the proper way to celebrate a military victory.

*And they did rejoice and cry again with one voice, saying: May the God of Abraham, and the God of Isaac, and the God of Jacob, protect this people in righteousness, so long as they shall call on the name of their God for protection.*

***And it came to pass that they did break forth, all as one, in singing, and praising their God for the great thing which he had done for them, in preserving them from falling into the hands of their enemies.*** *Yea, they did cry: Hosanna to the Most High God. And they did cry: Blessed be the name of the Lord God Almighty, the Most High God.*

***And their hearts were swollen with joy, unto the gushing out of many tears, because of the great goodness of God in delivering them out of the hands of their enemies; and they knew it was because of their repentance and their humility that they had been delivered from an everlasting***

***destruction.*** *(3 Nephi 4:30–33; emphasis added)*

I have a note in the margin of my scriptures regarding this group of passages. It says "right thinking." Indeed this is the appropriate way to celebrate a military victory. They demonstrated humility and gratitude. Most of all, we see them giving credit to God for the victory. Can you imagine how much any nation would prosper with this type of thinking among the army and the citizens? Can you imagine how eager God would be to protect this same grateful country?

At this time, about AD 21, the Nephites did repent and turn to the Lord. Virtually every soul was converted to a sincere belief in Christ.

*And now behold, there was not a living soul among all the people of the Nephites who did doubt in the least the words of all the holy prophets who had spoken; for they knew that it must needs be that they must be fulfilled.*

*And they knew that it must be expedient that Christ had come, because of the many signs which had been given, according to the words of the prophets; and because of the things which had come to pass already they knew that it must needs be that all things should come to pass according to that which had been spoken. Therefore they did forsake all their sins, and their abominations, and their whoredoms, and did serve God with all diligence day and night. (3 Nephi 5:1–3)*

The Lord blessed them. This period when Lachoneus and Gidgiddoni were the principle leaders was very prosperous and reflects the inspiration and greatness of these two remarkable leaders. The prosperity lasted less than a decade, however, and the account is only three chapters long. It is summarized by the following passages.

*And they began again to prosper and to wax great; and the twenty and sixth and seventh years passed away, and there was great order in the land; and they had formed their laws according to equity and justice. And now there was nothing in all the land to hinder the people from prospering continually, except they should fall into transgression.*

***And now it was Gidgiddoni, and the judge, Lachoneus, and those who had been appointed leaders, who had established this great peace in the land.*** *And it came to pass that there were many cities built anew, and there were many old cities repaired. And there*

*were many highways cast up, and many roads made, which led from city to city, and from land to land, and from place to place. And thus passed away the twenty and eighth year, and the people had continual peace. (3 Nephi 6:4–9; emphasis added)*

## The Collapse of the Nephite Government

The clear repentant nature of the Nephites lasted only eight years. The cycle of pride began to appear among the people and is described very clearly. Notice how "inequality" followed "pride."

*But it came to pass in the twenty and ninth year there began to be some disputings among the people; and some were lifted up unto pride and boastings because of their exceedingly great riches, yea, even unto great persecutions; for there were many merchants in the land, and also many lawyers, and many officers.*

*And the people began to be distinguished by ranks, according to their riches and their chances for learning; yea, some were ignorant because of their poverty, and others did receive great learning because of their riches.*

*Some were lifted up in pride, and*

*others were exceedingly humble; some did return railing for railing, while others would receive railing and persecution and all manner of afflictions, and would not turn and revile again, but were humble and penitent before God.*

***And thus there became a great inequality in all the land, insomuch that the church began to be broken up; yea, insomuch that in the thirtieth year the church was broken up in all the land save it were among a few of the Lamanites who were converted unto the true faith;*** *and they would not depart from it, for they were firm, and steadfast, and immovable, willing with all diligence to keep the commandments of the Lord.*

***Now the cause of this iniquity of the people was this—Satan had great power, unto the stirring up of the people to do all manner of iniquity, and to the puffing them up with pride, tempting them to seek for power, and authority, and riches, and the vain things of the world.***

*And thus Satan did lead away the hearts of the people to do all manner of iniquity; therefore they had enjoyed peace but a few years. (3 Nephi 6:10–16; emphasis added)*

This is such a distressing commentary. In less than two years, there was a collapse of their peace and integrity. This is a great description of the process of pride. The main descriptor is the inequality among the people. The rich should have been grateful and humble because of the opportunity to increase their wealth and prosperity. However, they began to be prideful and created inequalities: "And the people began to be distinguished by ranks, according to their riches and their chances for learning" (3 Nephi 6:12). The role of Satan is to cause dissension and hate, and that's exactly what he did in a very short time. This situation was not ignored by the good people as the scriptures report; many rose up and spoke of the inequalities.

***And there began to be men inspired from heaven and sent forth, standing among the people in all the land, preaching and testifying boldly of the sins and iniquities of the people, and testifying unto them concerning the redemption which the Lord . . .***

*Now there were many of the people who were exceedingly angry because of those who testified of these things; and those who were angry were chiefly the chief judges, and they who had been high priests and lawyers; yea, all those who were lawyers were angry with those who* *testified of these things. . . . Now there were **many of those who testified of the things pertaining to Christ who testified boldly, who were taken and put to death secretly by the judges** . . .*

*And they [the lawyers and judges] did enter into a covenant one with another, yea, even into that covenant which was given by them of old, which covenant was given and administered by the devil, to combine against all righteousness. Therefore they did combine against the people of the Lord, and enter into a covenant to destroy them. . . .*

*And they did set at defiance the law and the rights of their country; and they did covenant one with another to destroy the governor, and to establish a king over the land, that the land should no more be at liberty but should be subject unto kings.* (3 Nephi 6:20–21, 23, 28–30; emphasis added)

This story seems to be repeated often in the history of the Nephites. Because of pride and a desire for power, secret covenants were made among the participants. What a dreadful conclusion to a marvelous period of peace. The people just could not handle prosperity. The result was appalling—the total collapse of the Nephite government.

*Now all this was done, and there were no wars as yet among them; and all this iniquity had come upon the people because they did yield themselves unto the power of Satan. **And the regulations of the government were destroyed, because of the secret combination of the friends and kindreds of those who murdered the prophets.***

*And they did cause a great contention in the land, insomuch that the more righteous part of the people had nearly all become wicked; yea, there were but few righteous men among them. And thus six years had not passed away since the more part of the people had turned from their righteousness, like the dog to his vomit, or like the sow to her wallowing in the mire.* (3 Nephi 7:5–8; emphasis added)

This commentary is so fascinating. There was no war! The chaos of war did not cause this problem. This collapse came through the designs of Satan and his secret combinations. The sorrow in the expression of the writer comes through a simile: "the people had turned from their righteousness, like the dog to his vomit, or like the sow to her wallowing in the mire" (3 Nephi 7:8).

The behavior of the people led to virtual anarchy. They moved into tribes to

protect themselves from these deceitful secret combinations.

> *And the people were divided one against another; and they did separate one from another into tribes, every man according to his family and his kindred and friends; and thus they did destroy the government of the land. And every tribe did appoint a chief or a leader over them; and thus they became tribes and leaders of tribes. Now behold, there was no man among them save he had much family and many kindreds and friends; therefore their tribes became exceedingly great. (3 Nephi 7:2–4)*

### Secret Combinations Brought Nephite Destruction

Shortly after the collapse of the Nephites into tribes, the Savior appeared to the Nephites. Many of the wicked were destroyed at His coming. His message to the people was so successful that the people lived in peace and harmony for almost two hundred years. After this time, contention and strife returned among the people and pride began to appear again. A commentary from Mormon tells us how the cycle of pride came among the people and they forget the Lord.

> *And now I, Mormon, would that ye should know that the people had multiplied, insomuch that they were spread upon all the face of the land, and that they had become exceedingly rich, because of their prosperity in Christ.*
>
> *And now, in this two hundred and first year there began to be among them those who were lifted up in pride, such as the wearing of costly apparel, and all manner of fine pearls, and of the fine things of the world. And from that time forth they did have their goods and their substance no more common among them. And they began to be divided into classes; and they began to build up churches unto themselves to get gain, and began to deny the true church of Christ. (4 Nephi 1:23–26)*

Mormon recorded that they again separated into two main groups. Those who followed the prophets were called Nephites, and those who opposed the gospel were called Lamanites. As this dissension continued the Gadiantons reappeared in about AD 260. In the next generation, up to AD 300, the Gadianton robbers strengthened their place among the people:

> *And it came to pass that when three hundred years had passed away, both the people of Nephi and the Lamanites had*

*become exceedingly wicked one like unto another.*

*And it came to pass that the robbers of Gadianton did spread over all the face of the land; and there were none that were righteous save it were the disciples of Jesus. And gold and silver did they lay up in store in abundance, and did traffic in all manner of traffic. (4 Nephi 1:45–46)*

The Lamanites became so strong that around AD 340, they had defeated the Nephites in their capital city, Zarahemla. We will cover these wars in detail in the following chapter, when we discuss the life of Mormon. Now, however, I want to point out the role the Gadiantons played near the end of the Nephite civilization. Mormon recorded that the Gadiantons were thriving and joined with the Lamanites in the final battles. Together, these two groups were so powerful that the Nephites gave them all of the land southward shortly after winning it back.

*And my heart did sorrow because of this the great calamity of my people, because of their wickedness and their abominations. But behold, we did go forth against the Lamanites and the robbers of Gadianton, until we had again taken possession of the lands of our inheritance.*

*And the three hundred and forty and*

*ninth year had passed away. And in the three hundred and fiftieth year we made a treaty with the Lamanites and the robbers of Gadianton, in which we did get the lands of our inheritance divided. And the Lamanites did give unto us the land northward, yea, even to the narrow passage which led into the land southward. And we did give unto the Lamanites all the land southward. (Mormon 2:27–29)*

A few years later the Lamanites and the Gadiantons broke the treaty and came with a huge army that brought destruction to the Nephites. However, these few verses verify the statement given earlier by Mormon. Remember, he said that the Gadianton robbers would bring about the downfall of the Nephites. Bear in mind that when the story of the Gadianton robbers first appeared, Mormon added a comment to the record. As the last great Nephite chief captain, he personally saw the destruction of the Nephites and could not help himself by giving a clue to the future. Here is his reflection.

*And behold, in the end of this book [the Book of Mormon] ye shall see that this Gadianton did prove the overthrow, yea, almost the entire destruction of the people of Nephi. (Helaman 2:13)*

## A Message for the People of the Latter Days

A serious message about secret combinations is written clearly in the record of the Jaredite nation, which preceded the Nephite nation. The Jaredites traveled to the promised land in the Americas about the time of the Tower of Babel. They were totally destroyed through warring factions led by secret combinations. Their history came from twenty-four gold plates translated by the Nephite prophets. The record was placed in the Book of Mormon by Moroni, the son of Mormon. This Jaredite history is called the Book of Ether. Moroni was the last writer in the Book of Mormon—about AD 400.

After writing about the secret combinations of the Jaredites, Moroni commented on the problems created by these covert bands. He recorded the following statement in Ether 8.

*And it came to pass that they [the enemies of the Jaredite prophets] formed a secret combination, even as they of old; which combination is most abominable and wicked above all, in the sight of God;*

***For the Lord worketh not in secret combinations,*** *neither doth he will that man should shed blood, but in all things hath forbidden it, from the beginning of man. And now I, Moroni, do not write the manner of their oaths and combinations, for it hath been made known unto me that they are had among all people, and they are had among the Lamanites.*

***And they have caused the destruction of this people of whom I am now speaking, and also the destruction of the people of Nephi.*** *And whatsoever nation shall uphold such secret combinations, to get power and gain, until they shall spread over the nation, behold, they shall be destroyed; for the Lord will not suffer that the blood of his saints, which shall be shed by them, shall always cry unto him from the ground for vengeance upon them and yet he avenge them not.*

***Wherefore, O ye Gentiles, it is wisdom in God that these things should be shown unto you, that thereby ye may repent of your sins, and suffer not that these murderous combinations shall get above you,*** *which are built up to get power and gain—and the work, yea, even the work of destruction come upon you, yea, even the sword of the justice of the Eternal God shall fall upon you, to your overthrow and destruction if ye shall suffer these things to be.*

***Wherefore, the Lord commandeth you, when ye shall see these***

*things come among you that ye shall awake to a sense of your awful situation, because of this secret combination which shall be among you; or wo be unto it, because of the blood of them who have been slain; for they cry from the dust for vengeance upon it, and also upon those who built it up.*

*For it cometh to pass that whoso buildeth it up seeketh to overthrow the freedom of all lands, nations, and countries; and it bringeth to pass the destruction of all people, for it is built up by the devil, who is the father of all lies; even that same liar who beguiled our first parents, yea, even that same liar who hath caused man to commit murder from the beginning; who hath hardened the hearts of men that they have murdered the prophets, and stoned them, and cast them out from the beginning.*

*Wherefore, I, Moroni, am commanded to write these things that evil may be done away, and that the time may come that Satan may have no power upon the hearts of the children of men, but that they may be persuaded to do good continually, that they may come unto the fountain of all righteousness and be saved. (Ether 8:18–26; emphasis added)*

Moroni was very specific about the appalling problems brought about by these secret combinations. The thoughts of Moroni are heartfelt and descriptive. My analysis of this dangerous system of secrecy comes in a simplified list.

- Secret combinations are abominable in the sight of God.
- They have existed from the beginning of time and are directed by Satan.
- The Lord has forbidden these secret societies.
- Their tactics include the shedding of blood to create fear and terror.
- The purpose of these deceitful groups is to get power and gain wealth.
- Their methods will destroy the liberty of the people through corruption.
- Nations that allow these combinations to exist will be destroyed from within.
- The Lord will grant the destruction of these corrupt nations because of the cries of the murdered saints. The Book of Mormon provides two examples—the Nephites and the Jaredites.
- The ultimate motive for these secret organizations is to overthrow the freedom of all nations.

This serious message of Moroni is aimed

directly at the readers of the Book of Mormon, the people of the latter days. He says: "Wherefore, O ye Gentiles, it is wisdom in God that these things should be shown unto you, that thereby ye may repent of your sins, and suffer not that these murderous combinations shall get above you" (Ether 8:23). Moroni's advice to us is to repent and stand up against these wicked groups that desire to take our liberty. His final statement is an unmistakable warning: "The Lord commandeth you, when ye shall see these things come among you that ye shall awake to a sense of your awful situation" (Ether 8:24).

Is this warning well placed? Are there problems within our nations today? Believe me—secret combinations are thriving in the promised land, the Americas. First, a number of Central and South American nations are beset with corruption. This corruption is fueled by murderous drug cartels set up to gain wealth from illegal drugs. In many cases, the cartels of drug producers and distributors are wealthier than their governments. It is virtually impossible to police these criminals because of bribes, threats and deceptive lies. The most deplorable conduct of these cartels is murder. Local leaders and police that confront them are often murdered. In addition, the families and loved ones of the leaders become the target of the criminals and are often murdered to create fear and bring compliance

to their wicked ways. To add to the disorder, the children of influential people are often kidnapped for ransom. These countries are in a state of chaos because of criminals who flourish by using the methods of secret combinations described by Moroni.

The United States is also seriously influenced by this wickedness. The practice of kidnapping has come into Arizona, where Phoenix has become one of the kidnapping capitals of the world.

The lives of American children are polluted by the addictions caused by the use of illegal drugs. The cure for these addictions is very difficult and often hopeless. The cartels are so powerful below the southern border of the United States that they have threatened to assassinate Arizona county sheriffs and police who are thwarting their drug traffic. Do we need to heed the warning of Moroni about secret combinations? Absolutely!

Are these secret combinations thriving in the United States? Without question! The easiest way to identify these people is by their behavior. Moroni told us their design is to take away our liberty. Within our government, power has been generated by creating a huge bureaucracy that controls the people. These bureaucrats are not elected by the people but have enormous power because behind closed doors they can create rules and regulations that take sovereignty and freedom from the people. The United States Congress and Senate often conduct their business in secrecy, away from the eyes of the citizens. Huge pieces of legislation containing thousands of pages of regulation can be created in back rooms and voted on before they can be read and analyzed by the general population. Policy and laws are created privately without the voice of opposition. Legislation is then voted into law without the opportunity for the people to respond and present alternative propositions.

It is painful to point out that just like the Nephites of old, we are losing our rule of law. The Gadiantons corrupted Nephite judges. Today, our legislators often ignore the principle law of the land, the Constitution of the United States. Laws that take away property and freedom are designed to control the people. The prosperity and wealth of the people is taken by taxes and distributed like bribes to obtain power.

The way of the Lord is to allow people to mature and grow through sharing their wealth voluntarily. Every person should have equal opportunity to grow and prosper. The core values of the people should be such that they work hard to create wealth, which they can share by employing people and providing excellent products and services. Equality should not be forced on the people by laws.

People should turn to Christ and follow his commandments. A truly Christian society will share the blessings of God with each other. If Moroni was allowed to speak, he would talk about individual liberty and the opportunity for all to mature, prosper, and serve the Lord. Like the great prophets Alma, Helaman, and Nephi, Christians should move among the people and teach them that obedience to the laws of God will bring prosperity and safety from those who would take away freedom and enslave the people.

At present, there are organizations outside the Americas that desire to destroy the freedom of all lands. There is a threat to the Christian nations of the world by Muslim extremists who function much like the secret combinations described in the Book of Mormon. These Muslim extremists function behind the scenes in secrecy. The most classic example is the secret cell of murderers who attacked the World Trade Center towers in New York City in September 2001. They infiltrated the country and went underground while plotting the murder of thousands of Americans. Their desire was to create terror and fear while destroying the financial systems of the free world. It is important for us to follow the warnings of Moroni and investigate these organizations that seek to establish a single faith which denies the divinity of Christ.

The Muslim people are not to blame. Most are family people who want to have decent work and raise their families. However, a few people of the Muslim community foster hate and seek to establish fear and terror in the world by murdering innocent people and creating chaos.

In summary, it is time for us to examine the behavior of the secret combinations inside and outside our borders. As in the Book of Mormon, we must find and support leaders who clearly understand the danger of secret societies and nations that desire to undermine freedom. Moreover, it is imperative that we follow the covenants enumerated by Lehi and many other Nephite prophets. We should turn to Christ and follow the commandments. God will in turn bless us with prosperity and give our leaders the inspiration necessary to protect us from these dangerous and wicked people. The solution seems simple, but it is true. Follow the commandments of God, turn your faith to Christ, do not let these secret combinations get a foothold within the promised land, and be vigilant in missionary work by bringing the gospel to the world. As Moroni warned, we should "awake to a sense of [our] awful situation" (Ether 8:24). We have been slowly losing our freedoms to these secret combinations for many years. To reverse this trend, we must demand truth and honor from our leaders and our courts. Just like the Nephites, the Lord will bless us with prosperity if we turn to Him for help and keep His commandments. However, if we do not heed the warning of Moroni and allow secrecy and iniquity to thrive, we will lose our freedom and the Lord with withdraw His support for our beloved promised land.

# Seven

# MORMON—THE LAST NEPHITE CHIEF CAPTAIN

*And my soul was rent with anguish, because of the slain of my people, and I cried:*
*O ye fair ones, how could ye have departed from the ways of the Lord!*
*O ye fair ones, how could ye have rejected that Jesus, who stood with open arms to receive you!*
*Behold, if ye had not done this, ye would not have fallen. But behold, ye are fallen,*
*and I mourn your loss.*
MORMON 6:16–18

The Book of Mormon was compiled, edited, and named after the great Nephite prophet and chief captain—Mormon. The Book of Mormon is a compilation of books. Within this group is a smaller book also named the book of Mormon, consisting of only nine chapters. It includes the story of Mormon and the history of the Nephites during his life. The quoted statement above reflects Mormon's love for the Nephite people and the sorrow he felt after their nation was literally destroyed by a coalition of Lamanites and Gadianton robbers.

His lamentation is based on the idea that the annihilation of the Nephite nation was unnecessary. They would have continued as a free and prosperous people if they would have followed the admonition of the prophets and kept the commandments. The Nephite people had violated the covenant that they made with the Lord: the Lord would bless them with freedom and prosperity if they kept his commandments. If not, they would be swept from the promised land (1 Nephi 2:20–21).

In this chapter, I will tell the story of Mormon

with my reflections as a fellow soldier. Mormon is undeniably one of the most important spiritual giants to have ever lived. I undertake this opportunity to discuss his life and writings with a great deal of humility, knowing how honorable and courageous he was.

## The Setting

Mormon was born about 310 years after the birth of Christ. Ammaron was the Nephite prophet and record keeper. The Nephites had been through a prolonged period of affluence that began after the visit of Christ and lasted almost two hundred years. Prosperous cities and buildings stretched from the northern lands all the way to the south. Mormon traveled this land as a youth with his father, and he felt like the people were as numerous as the "sand of the sea" (Mormon 1:6–7). Mormon was called at a young age to serve the Lord. Ammoron, the prophet, came to visit Mormon.

*And about the time that Ammaron hid up the records unto the Lord,* **he came unto me, (I being about ten years of age, and I began to be learned somewhat after the manner of the learning of my people) and Ammaron said unto me: I perceive that thou art a sober child, and art quick to observe;**

*Therefore, when ye are about twenty and four years old I would that ye should remember the things that ye have observed concerning this people; and when ye are of that age go to the land Antum, unto a hill which shall be called Shim; and there have I deposited unto the Lord all the sacred engravings concerning this people.*

*And behold, ye shall take the plates of Nephi unto yourself, and the remainder shall ye leave in the place where they are; and ye shall engrave on the plates of Nephi all the things that ye have observed concerning this people. (Mormon 1:2–4)*

This assignment must have seemed overwhelming. He needed to learn the written language and follow in the steps of the prophet Ammoron by recording the history of his people. Mormon's father was also named Mormon, and we are not told about his father, but I assume he must have been a very impressive and influential man. The prophet Ammoron may have been a close friend of Mormon's father and probably spent time with him at his home and grew to know the extraordinary young man of the house. Father Mormon was certainly a righteous parent who educated his son in the ways of the Nephites and taught him the gospel. He most likely taught his son to love the Nephite culture and the greatness of the nation by taking his eleven-year-old son on a trip throughout the Nephite lands.

## Mormon's Spiritual Mission Begins

Mormon starts in the first chapter of his book by giving his own story. His personal history is brief but very clear. Because he refers to the dates on all major events, it is possible to give his age during each experience. Hopefully, referring to his age at each part of his life will build a more personal understanding of his story and enable us to compare our experiences to his.

There was a war during Mormon's early years, and the Lamanites were driven back to their lands. However, Mormon tells us that the people did not give the Lord credit for their military success.

> But wickedness did prevail upon the face of the whole land, insomuch that the Lord did take away his beloved disciples [Nephite apostles], and the work of miracles and of healing did cease because of the iniquity of the people. And there were no gifts from the Lord, and the Holy Ghost did not come upon any, because of their wickedness and unbelief.
>
> **And I, being fifteen years of age and being somewhat of a sober mind, therefore I was visited of the Lord,**

**and tasted and knew of the goodness of Jesus.**

> And I did endeavor to preach unto this people, but my mouth was shut, and I was forbidden that I should preach unto them; for behold they had willfully rebelled against their God; and the beloved disciples were taken away out of the land, because of their iniquity.
>
> But I did remain among them, but I was forbidden to preach unto them, because of the hardness of their hearts; and because of the hardness of their hearts the land was cursed for their sake.
>
> And these Gadianton robbers, who were among the Lamanites, did infest the land, insomuch that the inhabitants thereof began to hide up their treasures in the earth; and they became slippery, because the Lord had cursed the land, that they could not hold them, nor retain them again.
>
> And it came to pass that there were sorceries, and witchcrafts, and magics; and the power of the evil one was wrought upon all the face of the land, even unto the fulfilling of all the words of Abinadi, and also Samuel the Lamanite. (Mormon 1:13–19; emphasis added)

There is no doubt Mormon was an

exceptional young man. From these few verses, we can understand why he understood the behavior of the people and the reaction of the Lord. I suspect that he knew the disciples who were Nephite apostles and had a very personal relationship with all of them. They must have been superb leaders and helped Mormon understand the consequences of the Nephite wickedness rampant in the land. The Disciples probably influenced him to write about this iniquity. He indicated that the problems with the Gadianton robbers was so bad that people hid their treasures and still lost their money because it was "slippery." This is such a poignant way of describing how the land was "cursed." In addition, he described the evils of witchcrafts. One unmistakable comment in the last verse gives us insight into the spiritual strength of the young Mormon; he knew the Nephite scriptures and the prophecies regarding his time. He was keenly aware these wicked and evil practices were foretold by the prophets Abinadi and Samuel. Mormon is a prominent example to us in teaching our children. They would be blessed to emulate Mormon and study the scriptures at a young age. It would be a wonderful blessing if children were just like Mormon: they love the scriptures and are influenced by the Lord at a young age.

Mormon was so spiritual that he received a visit from the Savior at the age fifteen. He was undoubtedly a humble young man and fits the word he described himself: "sober." His description of the visit is very poetic. He said he was "visited of the Lord, and tasted and knew of the goodness of Jesus" (Mormon 1:15). Like other great prophets and saints who received a witness, his first desire was to preach the gospel. His effort to teach the people illustrates another remarkable character trait of Mormon—he was faithful and brave. To attempt to go among this wicked people as a mere boy was an amazing act of faith and displayed marvelous courage. However, the people were so wicked, he was forbidden to continue preaching.

## Mormon's Military Mission Begins

There is no question—Mormon was an impressive young man. However, it is difficult to imagine the traits he needed to be chosen as the chief captain and leader of all the Nephite armies at age sixteen. Mormon tells us of his appointment in simple terms.

*And it came to pass in that same year there began to be a war again between the Nephites and the Lamanites. **And notwithstanding I being young, was large in stature;** therefore the people of*

*Nephi appointed me that I should be their leader, or the leader of their armies.*

*Therefore it came to pass that in my sixteenth year I did go forth at the head of an army of the Nephites, against the Lamanites; therefore three hundred and twenty and six years had passed away. (Mormon 2:1–2; emphasis added)*

Mormon was much more than "large in stature." Mormon was not an obscure young man from the "north country." He must have been well known among the national leaders and the military. Perhaps his father was a chief captain and trained his son in military strategy at a young age. It may have been that the young Mormon was well respected among the educated elite or the primary decision makers of the Nephite nation. There is no question, however, that he must have been a remarkable and respected young man to be chosen to lead all the armies of the Nephites when only sixteen. And how did he describe himself? Take note, he didn't give himself a glowing résumé; he simply said, "And notwithstanding I being young, was large in stature; therefore the people of Nephi appointed me that I should be their leader, or the leader of their armies." (Mormon 2:1). I find this statement astonishing. He was so humble and modest that he recognized only one simple trait in himself: "large in stature."

Within a year, Lamanite armies came into the land and Mormon's armies attempted to stop them with no success. In the first battle, his armies were frightened and retreated. In the second battle, he fortified the city of Angola and was driven entirely out of the city and the land of David. His armies retreated again to the city of Joshua near the western sea. Mormon attempted to gather the people in defense but was defeated again. The beginning of Mormon's command was—by any measure—a failure. After three years and three major defeats, Mormon gave an accounting of the situation with the following commentary.

*And it came to pass that we did gather in our people as fast as it were possible, that we might get them together in one body.*

*But behold, the land was filled with robbers and with Lamanites; and notwithstanding the great destruction which hung over my people, they did not repent of their evil doings; therefore there was blood and carnage spread throughout all the face of the land, both on the part of the Nephites and also on the part of the Lamanites; and it was one complete revolution throughout all the face of the land. (Mormon 2:7–8)*

Essentially, Mormon felt that bringing together an organized defensive effort was virtually impossible because of the chaotic situation brought about by the people's evil practices.

## Mormon's First Victory

In the middle of this hectic situation, Mormon finally assembled an effective army. The year was AD 330 and Mormon was twenty years old. He had been the chief captain for four years and finally experienced a victory. He recorded the victory in the following verses.

*And now, the Lamanites had a king, and his name was Aaron; and he came against us with an army of forty and four thousand. And behold, I withstood him with forty and two thousand. And it came to pass that I beat him with my army that he fled before me. And behold, all this was done, and three hundred and thirty years had passed away.*

*And it came to pass that the Nephites began to repent of their iniquity, and began to cry even as had been prophesied by Samuel the prophet; for behold no man could keep that which was his own, for the thieves, and the robbers, and the murderers, and the magic art, and the witchcraft which was in the land. Thus there began*

*to be a mourning and a lamentation in all the land because of these things, and more especially among the people of Nephi.*

*And it came to pass that when I, Mormon, saw their lamentation and their mourning and their sorrow before the Lord, my heart did begin to rejoice within me, knowing the mercies and the long-suffering of the Lord, therefore supposing that he would be merciful unto them that they would again become a righteous people. (Mormon 2:9–12)*

His first victory brought great suffering and Mormon hoped that the people would repent. Their sorrow was a sign that they might turn to the Lord. A depressing time for him, Mormon recognized that the Nephites were not going to change, and they didn't change for fourteen years. There were undoubtedly more battles and efforts to defeat the Lamanites, but the Nephites refused to repent. Mormon's description of this time must have been very hard for him to record.

***But behold this my joy was vain, for their sorrowing was not unto repentance,*** *because of the goodness of God; but it was rather the sorrowing of the damned, because the Lord would not always suffer them to take happiness in sin.*

*And they did not come unto Jesus with broken hearts and contrite spirits, but they did curse God, and wish to die. Nevertheless they would struggle with the sword for their lives.*

*And it came to pass that my sorrow did return unto me again, **and I saw that the day of grace was passed with them, both temporally and spiritually;** for I saw thousands of them hewn down in open rebellion against their God, and heaped up as dung upon the face of the land. And thus three hundred and forty and four years had passed away. (Mormon 2:13–15; emphasis added)*

His discouragement is apparent in his words. He could see that their "day of grace was passed" and that they were headed for devastation (Mormon 2:15). The following year, the Lamanites came again and drove the Nephites into the northern lands where Ammoron had hidden the records of the Nephites. Mormon retrieved the plates of Nephi for their protection. He made a comment here about the historical record. Remember, he had two sets of plates: the complete historical record of the Nephites on the plates of Nephi and an abridged record he made on a set of golden plates.

*And upon the plates of Nephi I did*

*make a full account of all the wickedness and abominations; but upon these plates I did forbear to make a full account of their wickedness and abominations, for behold, a continual scene of wickedness and abominations has been before mine eyes ever since I have been sufficient to behold the ways of man.*

*And wo is me because of their wickedness; for my heart has been filled with sorrow because of their wickedness, all my days; nevertheless, I know that I shall be lifted up at the last day. (Mormon 2:18–19)*

Again, Mormon's heart had been continually filled with grief. He couldn't even rejoice in military victories because the people failed to repent. In the time that followed, the people were hunted and driven by the Lamanites and the Gadianton robbers. There were utter confusion and slaughter.

## Mormon's Second Major Victory— A Military Masterpiece

In previous Lamanite victories, the Nephite people were driven several hundred miles into the land north, which was above the narrow neck of land. The Lamanites were coming with another great army. The map below illustrates

Mormon's Military Masterpiece

⬆ Movement of Mormon's army

how far the Nephites had been driven into the northern areas. In brief, the Nephites had lost two-thirds of their lands.

When Mormon was about thirty-six years old, he went among the people to motivate them and build an army to contend against the Lamanites. Mormon was an inspiring motivator and brought his army to remember their wives and families. He records his efforts in this way.

*And it came to pass that I did speak unto my people, and did urge them with great energy, that they would stand boldly before the Lamanites and fight for their wives, and their children, and their houses, and their homes. And my words did arouse them somewhat to vigor, insomuch that they did not flee from before the Lamanites, but did stand with boldness against them.*

*And it came to pass that we did contend with an army of thirty thousand against an army of fifty thousand. And it came to pass that we did stand before them with such firmness that they did flee from before us.*

*And it came to pass that when they had fled we did pursue them with our armies, and did meet them again, and did beat them; nevertheless the strength of the Lord was not with us; yea, we were left to ourselves, that the Spirit of the Lord did not abide in us; therefore we had become weak like unto our brethren.*

*And my heart did sorrow because of this the great calamity of my people, because of their wickedness and their abominations. But behold, we did go forth against the Lamanites and the robbers of Gadianton, until we had again taken possession of the lands of our inheritance. (Mormon 2:23–27)*

This was his second major victory against numerous defeats. It appears from the account that it took Mormon some time to build and train his army, which then stopped the northward movement of the Lamanites. He then moved south against the Lamanites in a two-year war. It was a tremendous victory against unbelievable odds. His modest army of thirty thousand was confronted by a Lamanite army of fifty thousand men. Mormon defeated the Lamanite army and then moved south. He ultimately recaptured the lands of "inheritance," which was probably the land of Zarahemla.

Mormon was humble and took no credit for the conquest. From a military standpoint, this victory was unprecedented. He had moved his enemy probably 150 miles to the south and had taken back many great cities. However, his remarks following the triumph reflect disappointment because he could not see a spiritual change in his people: "Nevertheless the strength of the Lord was not with us; yea, we were left to ourselves, that the Spirit of the Lord did not abide in us" (Mormon 2:26). They had peace throughout the land for a few years, and then a treaty was made that gave back the lands they had just won. Mormon was now forty years old.

> *And in the three hundred and fiftieth year we made a treaty with the Lamanites and the robbers of Gadianton, in which we did get the lands of our inheritance divided.*
>
> *And the Lamanites did give unto us the land northward, yea, even to the narrow passage which led into the land southward. And we did give unto the Lamanites all the land southward.*
> *(Mormon 2:28–29)*

From a military perspective, this treaty is hard to understand. Why did they give back so much land and move all of their people north of the narrow neck of land? We are not told. However, I would speculate that the Lamanites had become so strong that this was a concession to stop the onslaught of endless war. Another possibility for accepting the treaty may have been a military strategy that was made by Mormon and the political leaders. In this theory, the land they gave up was too hard to defend, and if they moved north, they could set up fortifications around their cities and use the narrow passage as an obstacle to the enemy. The narrow neck of lack was a natural boundary and could be used to set up a blockade. We have no written indication of why this treaty was successful, but we are told that for ten years there was no attempt by the Lamanites to bring armies northward.

During this relatively short time of peace, the Lord told Mormon to become a missionary and go among the people to preach repentance. This was not a successful endeavor, and Mormon said that they "did harden their hearts" (Mormon 3:1–3). I would also envision that this was the time when Mormon completed his writings on the plates of Mormon. He was forty years old when the decade of peace began, and looking at his history, there was little time to read the many records and prepared his edited version under the direction of the Lord. This undertaking was not simple. After reading the records and deciding which part of the history to include, he needed to smelt the ore, prepare the plates, and then etch the record onto the thin golden sheets. This was considerably more difficult than using paper and pen and infinitely more difficult than using our modern computers. Mormon's personal record of his fifty-plus years is only seven chapters or eleven English pages. The other records he wrote on the plates translated into 445 pages of English. This enormous task took many years to complete. I speculate that he completed most of his writing during this ten-year interlude of peace.

## Mormon's Third Major Victory Ends in a Spiritual Catastrophe

Following ten years of peace, the Lamanite king wrote a letter to Mormon telling him that the Lamanites would come north and enter the Nephite lands with their armies. From a military point of view, this is very awkward. The letter eliminates the element of surprise. This might have been an indication of respect for Mormon because of their previous treaty. The Lamanites now intended to break the treaty without reason. On the other hand, it may have meant that the Lamanites expected more concessions from the Nephites. Remember, in the earlier treaty, the Nephites gave up half of their lands without a fight. Mormon's account is very brief.

*And it came to pass that after this tenth year had passed away, making, in the whole, three hundred and sixty years from the coming of Christ, the king of the Lamanites sent an epistle unto me, which gave unto me to know that they were preparing to come again to battle against us.*

*And it came to pass that I did cause my people that they should gather themselves together at the land Desolation, to a city which was in the borders, by the narrow pass which led into the land southward. And there we did place our armies, that we might stop the armies of the Lamanites, that they might not get possession of any of our lands; therefore we did fortify against them with all our force.*

*And it came to pass that in the three hundred and sixty and first year the Lamanites did come down to the city of Desolation to battle against us; and it came to pass that in that year we did beat them, insomuch that they did return to their own lands again. (Mormon 3:4–7)*

The military strategy of Mormon was successful. Under Mormon's direction, they built massive fortifications near the narrow passage and in the city of Desolation. The Nephites were triumphant, and a year later the Lamanites tried again and were beaten back.

***And now, because of this great thing which my people, the Nephites, had done, they began to boast in their***

*own strength, and began to swear before the heavens that they would avenge themselves of the blood of their brethren who had been slain by their enemies.* And they did swear by the heavens, and also by the throne of God, that they would go up to battle against their enemies, and would cut them off from the face of the land.

*And it came to pass that I, Mormon, did utterly refuse from this time forth to be a commander and a leader of this people, because of their wickedness and abomination.* Behold, I had led them, notwithstanding their wickedness I had led them many times to battle, and had loved them, according to the love of God which was in me, with all my heart; and my soul had been poured out in prayer unto my God all the day long for them; nevertheless, it was without faith, because of the hardness of their hearts.

*And thrice have I delivered them out of the hands of their enemies, and they have repented not of their sins.* (Mormon 3:9–13; emphasis added)

Mormon's third victory was hollow. Once again, the Nephites did not repent, and this time it was worse. They boasted in their own strength and wanted revenge against their enemy. They desired to move into the lands of their enemy and destroy them. This is a major reversal in the practice of Nephite warfare. They had been told by the prophets how God wanted them to conduct war and why. The rules of war were given under the leadership of Captain Moroni almost four hundred years earlier. They operated under a strict code—given by God—regarding war.

*Nevertheless, the Nephites were inspired by a better cause, for they were not fighting for monarchy nor power but they were fighting for their homes and their liberties, their wives and their children, and their all, yea, for their rites of worship and their church.*

*And they were doing that which they felt was the duty which they owed to their God; for the Lord had said unto them, and also unto their fathers, that:* **Inasmuch as ye are not guilty of the first offense, neither the second, ye shall not suffer yourselves to be slain by the hands of your enemies.**

*And again, the Lord has said that:* Ye shall defend your families even unto bloodshed. **Therefore for this cause were the Nephites contending with the Lamanites, to defend themselves, and their families, and their lands, their** *country, and their rights, and their religion. (Alma 43:45–47; emphasis added)*

God's law regarding war required a defensive philosophy, which included the security of their land. The offensive practice of war, to attack for advantage or revenge, was forbidden. Entrance into the lands of the enemy was not a Nephite practice.

Previously, the Nephites had respect for their enemy and even let them return to their lands or even stay among the Nephites if they took an oath. They considered their enemies to be misguided children of God and deserved reverence or mercy after being defeated. In the entire history of the Nephites, this was the first time they initiated the act of war for revenge. Consequently, Mormon refused to be their leader. The Lord spoke to him regarding vengeance.

*And when they had sworn by all that had been forbidden them by our Lord and Savior Jesus Christ, that they would go up unto their enemies to battle, and avenge themselves of the blood of their brethren, behold the voice of the Lord came unto me, saying:*

**Vengeance is mine, and I will repay; and because this people**

*repented not after I had delivered them, behold, they shall be cut off from the face of the earth.*

*And it came to pass that I utterly refused to go up against mine enemies; and I did even as the Lord had commanded me; and I did stand as an idle witness to manifest unto the world the things which I saw and heard, according to the manifestations of the Spirit which had testified of things to come. (Mormon 3:14–16; emphasis added)*

Mormon testified that vengeance would cause the destruction of the Nephite nation. Mormon now considered himself a spectator and he stood as witness against his own people. These are his observations about the years following his resignation as the Nephite military commander.

**And it was because the armies of the Nephites went up unto the Lamanites that they began to be smitten; for were it not for that, the Lamanites could have had no power over them.**

*But, behold, the judgments of God will overtake the wicked; and it is by the wicked that the wicked are punished; for it is the wicked that stir up the hearts of the children of men unto bloodshed. . . .*

*And it is impossible for the tongue to describe, or for man to write a perfect description of the horrible scene of the blood and carnage which was among the people, both of the Nephites and of the Lamanites; and every heart was hardened, so that they delighted in the shedding of blood continually.*

***And there never had been so great wickedness among all the children of Lehi, nor even among all the house of Israel, according to the words of the Lord, as was among this people. . . .***

***And from this time forth did the Nephites gain no power over the Lamanites, but began to be swept off by them even as a dew before the sun.***
*(Mormon 4:4–5, 11–12, 18; emphasis added)*

Mormon knew the Nephites' end was near and that their wickedness and anger would lead them into poor decisions. Indeed, they would "be swept off by [the Lamanites] even as a dew before the sun" (Mormon 4:18). The battles between the two nations raged on with both sides driven by hate and revenge. The Lamanites sacrificed Nephite women and children to their idols. And eventually the Nephites became even more depraved. Mormon again was constrained to give details of the dreadful battles.

*And now behold, I, Mormon, do not desire to harrow up the souls of men in casting before them such an awful scene of blood and carnage as was laid before mine eyes; but I, knowing that these things must surely be made known, and that all things which are hid must be revealed upon the house-tops—*

*But now, behold, **they are led about by Satan, even as chaff is driven before the wind, or as a vessel is tossed about upon the waves, without sail or anchor, or without anything wherewith to steer her; and even as she is, so are they.*** (Mormon 5:8, 18; emphasis added)*

The scene was so bad that Mormon constrained his writing. He found it easier to use poetic metaphors to explain how terrible the situation was. In the midst of this great horror, Mormon used masterful literary expressions to explain how the people were influenced by Satan. What a marvelously talented and spiritual writer! Mormon was a wonderful prophet and wanted his people to be blessed through the gospel of Jesus Christ. But he was forced to observe their downfall as a bystander. Satan was directing the hatred and caused them be driven as chaff in the wind or as a ship without an anchor.

## Nephite Wickedness Exceeded that of the Lamanites

In a letter to his son Moroni, recorded in the Moroni 9, Mormon told of the depravity of both the Lamanites and the Nephites. This commentary is so disheartening. War can develop the more noble parts of man's character, but only when it is used to defend family and freedom. However, when Satan gains control of the hearts of men, they are truly as chaff in the wind. Man can sink to the lowest levels of human depravity when driven by hate and revenge. Each act of revenge becomes replicated or made worse by each side until the heart of man totally denies the spirit of Christ and becomes dark and loathsome.

Knowing the darkness and evil nature of some of our enemies when I was in Iraq caused us great concern. Often, the enemy captured our soldiers and tortured them. They would often behead them and show it on film through the Middle Eastern news media. Knowing this horrific possibility, we had an understanding among our fellow soldiers that we would not surrender. The maltreatment and the cruelty would be too much for our families to witness. The ugliness of war can take the honor from the enemy. The humane treatment of prisoners of war must be a part of an honorable defense of true liberty. This policy proved to be helpful during the first Gulf War in 1992. The Iraqi soldiers surrendered by the thousands, knowing that their suffering in the desert would end and that they would be treated in a humane and lawful manner by the Americans and their allies.

Here are some excerpts from Mormon's letter to Moroni wherein he describes the dark images of war.

*And now I write somewhat concerning the sufferings of this people. For according to the knowledge which I have received from Amoron, behold, the Lamanites have many prisoners, which they took from the tower of Sherrizah; and there were men, women, and children.*

*And the husbands and fathers of those women and children they have slain; and they feed the women upon the flesh of their husbands, and the children upon the flesh of their fathers; and no water, save a little, do they give unto them.*

*And notwithstanding this great abomination of the Lamanites, it doth not exceed that of our people in Moriantum. For behold, many of the daughters of the Lamanites have they taken prisoners; and after depriving them of that which was most dear and precious above all things, which is chastity and virtue—*

*And after they had done this thing,*

*they did murder them in a most cruel manner, torturing their bodies even unto death; and after they have done this, they devour their flesh like unto wild beasts, because of the hardness of their hearts; and they do it for a token of bravery. (Moroni 9:7–10)*

Mormon didn't dwell on this and neither will I, except to say that the hate and revenge had removed the mercy and common decency on both sides. The Nephites, as he says, had become even worse than the Lamanites and the Gadianton robbers. When following Satan's path, man's inhumanity knows no bounds.

## Mormon Leads His People in Their Final Battle

Near the end, Mormon changed his mind and decided to help his people as their commander again. This decision by Mormon bespeaks the great love he had for his people. In their darkest hour and even in their most wicked time, he couldn't abandon them. This loyal Nephite was full of devotion for his people. Love, loyalty, and forgiveness would be at the top of a list of Mormon's character traits. As their commander, he orchestrated the last battle at the mountain called Cumorah.

*And I, Mormon, wrote an epistle unto the king of the Lamanites, and desired of him that he would grant unto us that we might gather together our people unto the land of Cumorah, by a hill which was called Cumorah, and there we could give them battle. And it came to pass that the king of the Lamanites did grant unto me the thing which I desired.*

*And it came to pass that we did march forth to the land of Cumorah, and we did pitch our tents around about the hill Cumorah; and it was in a land of many waters, rivers, and fountains; and here we had hope to gain advantage over the Lamanites.*

*And when three hundred and eighty and four years had passed away, we had gathered in all the remainder of our people unto the land of Cumorah. (Mormon 6:2–5)*

Mormon was now seventy-four years old. He was born in AD 310, and it was now AD 384. The leadership was very difficult knowing the depravity and the iniquity of his people. Moroni, Mormon's son, was one of Mormon's chief captains. In a letter to his son, Mormon told of the problems in his command.

*O my beloved son . . . How can we*

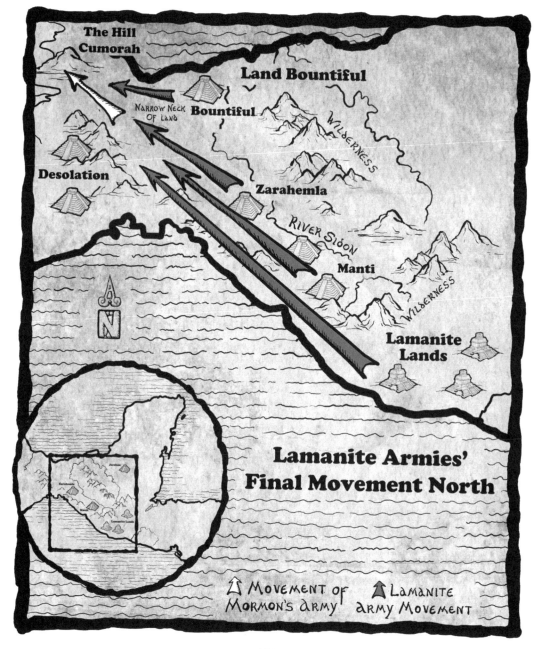

The Hill Cumorah

Land Bountiful

Narrow Neck of Land

Bountiful

Wilderness

Desolation

Zarahemla

River Sidon

Manti

Wilderness

Lamanite Lands

**Lamanite Armies' Final Movement North**

⬆ Movement of Mormon's Army     ⬆ Lamanite Army Movement

The Final Battle and Destruction of the Nephites

Movement of Nephite Army

Movement of Lamanite Armies

212

*expect that God will stay his hand in judgment against us? Behold, my heart cries: Wo unto this people. Come out in judgment, O God, and hide their sins, and wickedness, and abominations from before thy face! . . .*

*O the depravity of my people! They are without order and without mercy. Behold, I am but a man, and I have but the strength of a man, and I cannot any longer enforce my commands.*

*And they have become strong in their perversion; and they are alike brutal, sparing none, neither old nor young; and they delight in everything save that which is good; and the suffering of our women and our children upon all the face of this land doth exceed everything; yea, tongue cannot tell, neither can it be written.*

*And now, my son, I dwell no longer upon this horrible scene. Behold, thou knowest the wickedness of this people; thou knowest that they are without principle, and past feeling; and their wickedness doth exceed that of the Lamanites. Behold, my son, I cannot recommend them unto God lest he should smite me.* (Moroni 9:11, 14, 18–21)

Writing this must have been so frustrating and painful. His commands were being ignored

because the army was wicked and "without order." Ultimately, his greatest fears had materialized. His people had become so perverse that Mormon knew they would be destroyed; their wickedness was greater than the Lamanites.

The people were gathered at Cumorah for the final battle. Mormon told of the terror in the hearts of his people and explained this was much more than an army. Virtually all of the remaining Nephites were there, including their families.

*And it came to pass that my people, with their wives and their children, did now behold the armies of the Lamanites marching toward them; and with that awful fear of death which fills the breasts of all the wicked, did they await to receive them.*

*And it came to pass that they came to battle against us, and every soul was filled with terror because of the greatness of their numbers.*

*And it came to pass that they did fall upon my people with the sword, and with the bow, and with the arrow, and with the ax, and with all manner of weapons of war.* (Mormon 6:7–9)

The armies of the Lamanites far outnumbered the Nephites. The worst problem was not the numbers. The Nephites had abandoned the Lord, and He had left them to their own strength. No wonder every soul was filled with terror. It is apparent how personal this was for Mormon as he described the aftermath of the battle. He shows his concern for the Nephites by him giving the names of his captains and their losses. This part of the Mormon's record is laborious; however, as a soldier, I must include it all because Mormon did. Out of personal respect and love, he included many of their names.

*And it came to pass that my men were hewn down, yea, even my ten thousand who were with me, and I fell wounded in the midst; and they passed by me that they did not put an end to my life.*

*And when they had gone through and hewn down all my people save it were twenty and four of us, (among whom was my son Moroni) and we having survived the dead of our people, did behold on the morrow, when the Lamanites had returned unto their camps, from the top of the hill Cumorah, the ten thousand of my people who were hewn down, being led in the front by me.*

*And we also beheld the ten thousand of my people who were led by my son Moroni. And behold, the ten thousand of Gidgiddonah had fallen, and he also in*

*the midst. And Lamah had fallen with his ten thousand; and Gilgal had fallen with his ten thousand; and Limhah had fallen with his ten thousand; and Jeneum had fallen with his ten thousand; and Cumenihah, and Moronihah, and Antionum, and Shiblom, and Shem, and Josh, had fallen with their ten thousand each*

*And it came to pass that there were ten more who did fall by the sword, with their ten thousand each; yea, even all my people, save it were those twenty and four who were with me, and also a few who had escaped into the south countries, and a few who had deserted over unto the Lamanites, had fallen; and their flesh, and bones, and blood lay upon the face of the earth, being left by the hands of those who slew them to molder upon the land, and to crumble and to return to their mother earth. (Mormon 6:10–15)*

There were twenty-three Nephite captains, including Mormon and his son, Moroni. Each unit had 10,000 men, which made a total of 230,000 soldiers. All were slain—even their wives and children. To calculate the total number killed, we must consider that each Nephite soldier brought his family to Cumorah. Each family probably included one elderly parent, a wife, and at least one child.

This means that there were, at the very least, three additional people slain for every Nephite soldier killed. A reasonable estimate would be that nearly 900,000 Nephite men, women, and children were killed in this horrific battle. That only includes the Nephites. When the slain Lamanites are counted in the total, it is reasonable to assume that over 1.5 million lives were lost.

Mormon tells us that only twenty-four men were left, including himself and Moroni. Why were Mormon and Moroni among the last to survive? I would venture two reasons. First, the great leaders probably had guards around them who were the best warriors. Second, and most likely, the Lord protected them from death. Mormon was wounded and passed over for dead. Also, Moroni was certainly spared because he had a future task to complete for the Lord. Mormon lamented his lost civilization in just a few verses. The sorrow is apparent in his words.

*And my soul was rent with anguish, because of the slain of my people, and I cried: O ye fair ones, how could ye have departed from the ways of the Lord! O ye fair ones, how could ye have rejected that Jesus, who stood with open arms to receive you!*

*Behold, if ye had not done this, ye would not have fallen. But behold, ye are fallen, and I mourn your loss. O ye fair sons and daughters, ye fathers and mothers, ye husbands and wives, ye fair ones, how is it that ye could have fallen!*

*But behold, ye are gone, and my sorrows cannot bring your return. And the day soon cometh that your mortal must put on immortality, and these bodies which are now moldering in corruption must soon become incorruptible bodies; and then ye must stand before the judgment-seat of Christ, to be judged according to your works; and if it so be that ye are righteous, then are ye blessed with your fathers who have gone before you.*

*O that ye had repented before this great destruction had come upon you. But behold, ye are gone, and the Father, yea, the Eternal Father of heaven, knoweth your state; and he doeth with you according to his justice and mercy. (Mormon 6:16–22; emphasis added)*

Mormon loved his people so much. He spoke almost as a father: "O ye fair ones." These passages seem like a prayer in their behalf. As an apostle and prophet, he wanted to speak in their behalf but had difficulty in expressing his desire for mercy: "But behold, ye are gone, and my sorrows cannot bring your return" (v. 20).

Ultimately, Mormon trusted in God to give them His mercy when he said that "the Eternal Father of heaven, knoweth your state; and he doeth with you according to his justice and mercy" (v. 22). Isn't this true of many fathers and their children? There comes a time when nothing more can be done than to trust in God, that he also loves them, and will be there when you can't be.

Mormon knew that this devastating end of the Nephite nation was foretold. He had abridged the history of the Nephites and was familiar with the many prophecies concerning the future demise of the Nephites if they turned away from the Lord. This painful end of the Nephite civilization was foretold by Christ (3 Nephi 27:32), Nephi (1 Nephi 12:14–23; 2 Nephi 26:10–11), Alma (45:10–14) and Samuel the Lamanite (Helaman 13:8–10). Mormon's dreadful lot was to have known these prophesies, to observe their fulfillment, and then to record it.

## A Message to the People of the Latter Days—Repent and Prepare for the Judgement

As with other chapters, I will end the discussion of Mormon's story with messages that he personally wanted to give us. Mormon bore his testimony to his readers after realizing he couldn't help the Nephites any longer. Remember when he refused to be their leader and became a witness? During that moment, he stopped telling the history and spoke personally to his readers with these statements.

*And it came to pass that I utterly refused to go up against mine enemies; and I did even as the Lord had commanded me; and I did stand as an idle witness to manifest unto the world the things which I saw and heard, according to the manifestations of the Spirit which had testified of things to come.*

***Therefore I write unto you, Gentiles***, *and also unto you, house of Israel, when the work shall commence, that ye shall be about to prepare to return to the land of your inheritance;* ***Yea, behold, I write unto all the ends of the earth; yea, unto you, twelve tribes of Israel,*** *who shall be judged according to your works by the twelve whom Jesus chose to be his disciples in the land of Jerusalem.*

***And I write also unto the remnant of this people,*** *who shall also be judged by the twelve whom Jesus chose in this land; and they shall be judged by the other twelve whom Jesus chose in the land of Jerusalem.*

*And these things doth the Spirit manifest unto me; therefore I write unto you all.* **And for this cause I write unto you, that ye may know that ye must all stand before the judgment-seat of Christ,** *yea, every soul who belongs to the whole human family of Adam; and ye must stand to be judged of your works, whether they be good or evil;*

*And also that ye may believe the gospel of Jesus Christ, which ye shall have among you;* **and also that the Jews, the covenant people of the Lord, shall have other witness** *besides him whom they saw and heard, that Jesus, whom they slew, was the very Christ and the very God.*

**And I would that I could persuade all ye ends of the earth to repent and prepare** *to stand before the judgment-seat of Christ. (Mormon 3:16–22; emphasis added)*

It is as if he just paused in his writings and bore his testimony to the future inhabitants of the earth. Notice how he addressed this message to three groups of people.

**First, the Gentiles,** the latter-day inhabitants of the American continents who are mostly of European descent. They came to the Americas, as described by Nephi, the son of Lehi. They were not from Jerusalem and consequently were called Gentiles by the Book of Mormon prophets.

**Second, the twelve tribes of Israel**—and all the ends of the earth. It is certain that he wanted to remember the descendants of Abraham who were scattered over all the earth.

**Third, the remnant of this people** (Lamanites). He knew the Lamanites would not be destroyed and would inhabit these American continents.

Mormon was specific in his message to these groups. First, Mormon testified about the judgments of God. "I write unto you, that ye may know that ye must all stand before the judgment-seat of Christ, yea, every soul who belongs to the whole human family of Adam; and ye must stand to be judged of your works, whether they be good or evil" (Mormon 3:20).

The second message was to encourage all people to accept the gospel of Jesus Christ, especially the Jews. "And also that ye may believe the gospel of Jesus Christ, which ye shall have among you; and also that the Jews, the covenant people of the Lord, shall have other witness besides him whom they saw and heard" (Mormon 3:21). Note here that he talks about the Jews having another witness of Christ—the Book of Mormon.

The third message was to repent. This is

understandable because Mormon had watched his people being destroyed because of their failure to return to God. "And I would that I could persuade all ye ends of the earth to repent and prepare to stand before the judgment-seat of Christ" (Mormon 3:22).

## A Message to the Latter-Day Lamanites and Jews

In many places in the Book of Mormon, the Nephites' hearts went out to the Lamanites. They desired to give them the gospel of Jesus Christ. The missions of the sons of Mosiah were probably the most notable and successful effort to bring the message of Christ to the Lamanites. Mormon recorded these labors in his abridgement of the plates of Nephi onto his golden plates. In the following verses, Mormon—in his own personal writings—turned to the Lamanites, knowing that they would remain on the American continents as a mere remnant of the great civilizations that Mormon had witnessed and chronicled.

*And now behold, this I speak unto their seed [the Lamanites], and also to the Gentiles [Americans] who have care for the house of Israel, that realize and know from whence their blessings come*

*[those who have the Bible]. . . .*

*Now these things are written unto the remnant of the house of Jacob [the Lamanites]; and they are written after this manner, because it is known of God that wickedness will not bring them forth unto them; and they are to be hid up unto the Lord that they may come forth in his own due time.*

*And this is the commandment which I have received; and behold, they shall come forth according to the commandment of the Lord, when he shall see fit, in his wisdom. . . .*

*And also that the seed of this people may more fully believe his gospel, which shall go forth unto them from the Gentiles. (Mormon 5:10, 12–13, 15)*

This is Mormon's testimony that the Book of Mormon will come forth as commanded by the Lord "in his own due time" (Mormon 5:12). Mormon wants the Lamanites and the Gentiles to remember that their prosperity and blessings come from God. He prophesies that the Lamanites will become a loathsome people and would be mistreated and scattered by the Gentiles (Mormon 5:20–21). However, he points out that the Lord would remember his covenant with them by bringing them the gospel. These desires of the great prophet have truly come to pass. The Lamanites in the Americas are coming to Christ and joining his Church by the tens of thousands. The missionary program of The Church of Jesus Christ of Latter-day Saints is having its greatest success among the descendants of the Lamanites, who Mormon called the remnant of the house of Jacob. The Lord has not forgotten "the prayers of the righteous" (Mormon 5:21).

## A Message about the Gathering of Israel and the Restoration of the Gospel

Mormon was so impressed, after writing the words of Christ to the Nephites, that he made the following remarks about the sayings that would come forth. He knew his record of Christ's visit, along with his abridgment of other prophets' and his personal writings, would come forth in the latter days as the Book of Mormon. He also understood the writings of the great Old Testament prophets. Consequently, he stated the following:

*And now behold, I say unto you that when the Lord shall see fit, in his wisdom, that these sayings shall come unto the Gentiles according to his word, then ye may know that the covenant which the Father hath made with the children of Israel,*

*concerning their restoration to the lands of their inheritance, is already beginning to be fulfilled.*

*And ye may know that the words of the Lord, which have been spoken by the holy prophets, shall all be fulfilled; and ye need not say that the Lord delays his coming unto the children of Israel.*

*And ye need not imagine in your hearts that the words which have been spoken are vain, for behold, the Lord will remember his covenant which he hath made unto his people of the house of Israel. (3 Nephi 29:1–3)*

It is interesting that, after recording Christ's words to the Nephites, Mormon's thoughts turned to the covenants made to the House of Israel. The question could be asked, why here? Perhaps he had a vision of the future and wanted to tell us. He was specific regarding the Book of Mormon. He said that the coming forth of these sayings (the Book of Mormon) would signal the beginning of the return of the Jews to their land of inheritance—Jerusalem. Mormon wanted us to know that the Lord keeps His word, that He will fulfill His part of the covenant made with Israel. Indeed, we live in a day when we can see the gathering of Israel to the lands around Jerusalem happening before our eyes.

In the same chapter, Mormon wrote about

the negative response to Christ's efforts to bring forth the gospel in the latter days.

*And when ye shall see these sayings coming forth among you, then ye need not any longer spurn at the doings of the Lord, for the sword of his justice is in his right hand; and behold, at that day, if ye shall spurn at his doings he will cause that it shall soon overtake you.*

**Wo unto him that spurneth at the doings of the Lord; yea, wo unto him that shall deny the Christ and his works! Yea, wo unto him that shall deny the revelations of the Lord, and that shall say the Lord no longer worketh by revelation, or by prophecy, or by gifts, or by tongues, or by healings, or by the power of the Holy Ghost!**

**Yea, and wo unto him that shall say at that day, to get gain, that there can be no miracle wrought by Jesus Christ;** *for he that doeth this shall become like unto the son of perdition, for whom there was no mercy, according to the word of Christ!*

*Yea, and ye need not any longer hiss, nor spurn, nor make game of the Jews, nor any of the remnant of the house of Israel; for behold, the Lord remembereth his covenant unto them, and he will do*

*unto them according to that which he hath sworn.*

*Therefore ye need not suppose that ye can turn the right hand of the Lord unto the left, that he may not execute judgment unto the fulfilling of the covenant which he hath made unto the house of Israel. (3 Nephi 29:4–9; emphasis added)*

Latter-day revelation from God is the central feature in the restoration of the gospel. It appears that Mormon knew that people would "spurn" or mock the Lord's restoration. People of the latter days would ridicule revelation and miracles. Knowing this was going to happen obviously annoyed Mormon because he warned against these behaviors. Again, Mormon's words cannot be misunderstood. "Yea, wo unto him that shall deny the revelations of the Lord, and that shall say the Lord no longer worketh by revelation" (3 Nephi 29:6).

### A Message on Faith, Hope, and Charity

Moroni recorded one of his father's sermons in his writings, as found in Moroni 7. We are not told when the sermon was given, only that it was given by Mormon. I commend to you the entire chapter. I will relate only a small portion. The sermon is much like the writings of Paul to the

Corinthians in chapter 13. The Lord revealed these great truths to Mormon so he could give them to the Nephites, just as he revealed them to Paul for the Christians of Corinth.

> *Wherefore, I would speak unto you that are of the church, that are the peaceable followers of Christ, and that have obtained a sufficient hope by which ye can enter into the rest of the Lord, from this time henceforth until ye shall rest with him in heaven.*
>
> *And now my brethren, I judge these things of you because of your peaceable walk with the children of men. For I remember the word of God which saith by their works ye shall know them; for if their works be good, then they are good also. (Moroni 7:3–5)*

In many of his writings that I have included, Mormon speaks of sin and repentance. In this sermon, he is addressing the Saints who wish to improve their lives and are on a better path. It appears they are already doing good works and want to do even better. I admire his poetic abilities. He admires these saints because of their "peaceable walk with the children of men." Again I commend to you this entire chapter where Mormon speaks on how to know good from evil with a "perfect knowledge." He also

bears witness of angels and their mission among men. I will concentrate on his words about faith, hope, and charity. He begins with statements on faith.

> *Behold I say unto you, Nay; for it is by faith that miracles are wrought; and it is by faith that angels appear and minister unto men; wherefore, if these things have ceased wo be unto the children of men, for it is because of unbelief, and all is vain.*
>
> *For no man can be saved, according to the words of Christ, save they shall have faith in his name; wherefore, if these things have ceased, then has faith ceased also; and awful is the state of man, for they are as though there had been no redemption made.*
>
> *But behold, my beloved brethren, I judge better things of you, for I judge that ye have faith in Christ because of your meekness; for if ye have not faith in him then ye are not fit to be numbered among the people of his church. (Moroni 7:37–39)*

Mormon starts his sermon by explaining that faith is the source of miracles. It is the first principle of the gospel, and no man can be saved without faith in Christ. He describes meekness as a character trait of people with faith. They

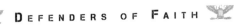
must become humble, accepting, and obedient. The second key principle in the sermon is hope.

> *And again, my beloved brethren, I would speak unto you concerning hope. How is it that ye can attain unto faith, save ye shall have hope?*
>
> *And what is it that ye shall hope for? Behold I say unto you that ye shall have hope through the atonement of Christ and the power of his resurrection, to be raised unto life eternal, and this because of your faith in him according to the promise.*
>
> *Wherefore, if a man have faith he must needs have hope; for without faith there cannot be any hope. And again, behold I say unto you that he cannot have faith and hope, save he shall be meek, and lowly of heart. (Moroni 7:40–43)*

Mormon's logic is impeccable. Faith brings hope in Christ and His Atonement. Life with its accompanying difficulties is so much easier for a faithful Christian. We all know people with debilitating diseases. They are a witness of how hope makes life bearable. Christ abides with us because of faith and then gives us hope. Again we see how Mormon thinks. He gives us the character traits of people of hope. They are "meek and lowly of heart." Losing loved ones through death will happen to all people.

Knowing that Christ can grant us eternal life is the ultimate blessing of hope.

Mormon moves on to discuss charity.

> *If so, his faith and hope is vain, for none is acceptable before God, save the meek and lowly in heart; and if a man be meek and lowly in heart, and confesses by the power of the Holy Ghost that Jesus is the Christ, he must needs have charity; for if he have not charity he is nothing; wherefore he must needs have charity.*
>
> *And charity suffereth long, and is kind, and envieth not, and is not puffed up, seeketh not her own, is not easily provoked, thinketh no evil, and rejoiceth not in iniquity but rejoiceth in the truth, beareth all things, believeth all things, hopeth all things, endureth all things.*
>
> *Wherefore, my beloved brethren, if ye have not charity, ye are nothing, for charity never faileth. Wherefore, cleave unto charity, which is the greatest of all, for all things must fail—But charity is the pure love of Christ, and it endureth forever; and whoso is found possessed of it at the last day, it shall be well with him. (Moroni 7:44–47)*

This revealed truth from the prophet is both beautiful and inspirational. Charity is the definitive characteristic of a healthy and active Christian. The desire of a Christian's heart should be to reflect the "true love of Christ" as we "peaceably walk with the children of men." Mormon's final verse as recorded in chapter seven demonstrates his own charity.

*Wherefore, my beloved brethren, pray unto the Father with all the energy of heart, that ye may be filled with this love, which he hath bestowed upon all who are true followers of his Son, Jesus Christ; that ye may become the sons of God; that when he shall appear we shall be like him, for we shall see him as he is; that we may have this hope; that we may be purified even as he is pure. Amen. (Moroni 7:48)*

## A Message about Children

In a letter to his son, Mormon speaks of his love for his son and for all children.

*My beloved son, Moroni, I rejoice exceedingly that your Lord Jesus Christ hath been mindful of you, and hath called you to his ministry, and to his holy work.*

*I am mindful of you always in my prayers, continually praying unto God the Father in the name of his Holy Child, Jesus, that he, through his infinite*

*goodness and grace, will keep you through the endurance of faith on his name to the end. (Mormon 8:2–3)*

Speaking as a father, he expressed his love and told of his prayers in behalf of Moroni. He was mindful, as all parents should be, that his son should endure to the end. Mormon is such a marvelous example. We should all express our love to our children and should do so often. Mormon continued his discussion about the Lord's love for children.

*But little children are alive in Christ, even from the foundation of the world; if not so, God is a partial God, and also a changeable God, and a respecter to persons. . . .*

*And I am filled with charity, which is everlasting love; wherefore, all children are alike unto me; wherefore, I love little children with a perfect love; and they are all alike and partakers of salvation. (Moroni 8:12, 17)*

What I find remarkable here is Mormon's personal expression of love for children. We don't know how many children or grandchildren he had, but we can read his words and know that he had a marvelous experience with children. He calls his love for little children "perfect." Why would he be so outspoken regarding children? Speaking as a soldier, I have a possible answer.

Children are amazing and so beautiful. Never was this so evident to me than in a war zone. I carried pictures of my children with me. I recognized early in my experience that in war we do not go to battle for ourselves. We fight for children—our children and the children we liberate. Children were everywhere in Iraq. It didn't matter where we stopped. They were there by the dozens. It seemed that they just came out of the cracks in the sidewalk and wanted to touch us. Even when we were in full battle dress and carrying weapons, they had no fear. It was breathtaking.

To illustrate this, I have included two pictures of children taken at a place we stopped south of Baghdad. Notice the smiles on their faces. When we first drove around Baghdad only days after it was liberated, people flooded the streets to see our convoys. Children would give us the "thumbs up" sign to indicate support and jump up and down when we returned the sign.

Another sweet experience with children took place in downtown Baghdad. We were near a major hotel. While some members of the unit had assignments in the hotel, we spoke with people on the street. One man across a quiet street from me had a small boy, perhaps five years old, with him. He motioned to the little boy to look at us. I crossed over and talked with him in his broken English. He said he wanted his son to meet some Americans and also that he was grateful our armies had liberated Baghdad. He was in the area because he worked at the hotel in the reservations area. This father told me that Saddam Hussein had executed his uncle. I inquired about a white bandage wrapped around the boy's hand, and he told me it had been burned. Just then another man came up and said he also had children and took a picture out of his wallet to show me. I took two pictures from my wallet, one of my family and another of my son and his fiancé. He easily understood the picture of my family, but it was difficult to communicate in English that the second picture was an engagement photo. People were now gathering around us—perhaps eight to ten people. The second man looked at my pictures and suddenly they disappeared in the crowd. It was interesting how the people passed around these two simple pictures. I could easily appreciate the love for their families, and they seemed happy to share that love with me even though it was not verbally communicated. It took me several minutes to retrieve the photos, and we then had to leave because a crowd, even a small one, was not safe. On a quiet street in Baghdad, I had found two things that we shared

in common—a love of freedom and affection for families and, in particular, for children.

Family and children become so important when a soldier is separated from them by war. I remember one time when I came home on leave and was lucky enough to attend my youngest son's mission farewell. I sat with my sweet wife in the middle of the congregation and could not stop the tears. The meaning of the gospel, the love of our fellow saints, and the appreciation for an honorable son was simply overwhelming.

Mormon must have had a similar circumstance when he saw the children of the cities he liberated. They would have been drawn to him as a liberating warrior, just as the Iraqi children were attracted to us. Mormon's love for children was "perfect" and was probably developed during his intimate experience with his family and own children. There is no question in my mind that Mormon knew this important principle: *A soldier does not fight wars for himself—he fights for the freedom of his family and for the children of future generations.* This is especially true for the children of the liberated nation. It takes generations for a liberated country to change, and the children will be the benefactors of that freedom.

## A Message to the Latter-Day Gentiles (Americans)

One of the most important passages from Mormon and the one I have placed last is a warning to the Gentiles. By "Gentiles," he is referring to non-Lamanites living in the promised land. Mormon told them to remember the source of their blessings and gave a serious and frightful warning:

*And then, O ye Gentiles, how can ye stand before the power of God, except ye shall repent and turn from your evil ways? Know ye not that ye are in the hands of God? Know ye not that he hath all power, and at his great command the earth shall be rolled together as a scroll?*

***Therefore, repent ye, and humble yourselves before him, lest he shall come out in justice against you—lest a remnant of the seed of Jacob shall go forth among you as a lion, and tear you in pieces, and there is none to deliver.*** *(Mormon 5:22–24; emphasis added)*

This message was given in the later years of Mormon's life when he was more than seventy years old. Could he have been more direct? He expressed his desire that the Gentiles of the latter days needed to turn to the Lord or face the consequences much like the Nephites of his time. They need to be humble, grateful, and know that their prosperity is a gift from God. Mormon finished his warning by letting America know that it would be possible for the

Lamanites to again "rise as a lion." The message is clear. Repent and be kind and helpful to the Lamanites of the latter days.

Mormon gave a similar warning to the Gentiles after he had finished the account of the Savior's mission to the Nephites in Bountiful. Only two verses long, his message is poignant and spoken directly to the Gentiles (all Americans, including South, North, and Central Americans who are not Lamanites).

***Hearken, O ye Gentiles, and hear the words of Jesus Christ, the Son of the living God, which he hath commanded me that I should speak concerning you, for, behold he commandeth me that I should write, saying:***

***Turn, all ye Gentiles, from your wicked ways; and repent of your evil doings,*** *of your lyings and deceivings, and of your whoredoms, and of your secret abominations, and your idolatries, and of your murders, and your priestcrafts, and your envyings, and your strifes, and from all your wickedness and abominations, and come unto me, and be baptized in my name, that ye may receive a remission of your sins, and be filled with the Holy Ghost, that ye may be numbered with my people who are of the house of Israel. (3 Nephi 30:1–2; emphasis added)*

Mormon's warnings cannot be mistaken or misunderstood. Some of these transgressions are individual, while others refer to nations. One thing is absolutely true. These clear passages were addressed to us because Christ commanded Mormon to write them as a direct warning to the Gentiles. I repeat again, because Mormon did, this is all Americans—South, North, and Central Americans who are not Lamanites. Due to its prophetic nature, we should not take this warning lightly. Similar warnings were given to the Jaredites and the Nephites, and they failed to heed the warnings. We cannot allow the same destructive consequence to come upon us. As a soldier and military officer, there is but one way to look at these statements. It would be as if the great Chief Captain Mormon were standing before us dressed in his armor and ready for battle, saying: **"Attention! These are your orders! I got them directly from your Savior. Repent and turn to the Lord!"**

# Eight

# MORONI—GUARDIAN OF THE PROMISED LAND

*Behold, the Lord hath shown unto me great and marvelous things*
*concerning that which must shortly come, at that day when these things shall come forth*
*among you. Behold, I speak unto you as if ye were present, and yet ye are not.*
*But behold, Jesus Christ hath shown you unto me, and I know your doing.*
MORMON 8:35

Moroni lived in the fourth century AD and was the last author of the Book of Mormon. He was the son of Mormon, the last Nephite chief captain. He was also a military warrior serving under the direction of his father. Moroni commanded over ten thousand men of the Nephite army, which was destroyed in the final catastrophic battle of between the Nephites and the Lamanites in AD 420.

Moroni was the last Nephite prophet of the Book of Mormon and the one who buried the Nephites' ancient records, which were engraven on golden plates. He secured a place to hide the plates in a hill outside of Palmyra, New York. He was the angel of the Restoration of the gospel of Jesus Christ and appeared to Joseph Smith on the September 21, 1823 (see Joseph Smith—History 1:27–54).

Moroni's chronicle is one of heroism, honor, and testimony. He was shown a vision of the future and had knowledge of latter-day behavior. Moroni's witness to mankind of the Savior will live throughout the eternities. It is an honor to tell his story.

## The Setting

Prior to the final battles between the Nephites and Lamanites, Mormon transferred the golden plates containing the Nephites' history to his son Moroni with an admonition to complete the final history (Mormon 6:6). Moroni told us that after the final battle, the few who escaped were hunted and killed by the Lamanites. He started his writing by saying, "I, Moroni, do finish the record of my father, Mormon. Behold, I have but few things to write, which things I have been commanded by my father" (Mormon 8:1). From these comments, it appears that he thought he had but a few days to live and would only finish the history with a few brief comments. However, he lived for many years and added the equivalent of fifty English pages to the final text. A close examination of his writings shows Moroni made a concluding statement ending his contribution to the plates three times. However, he continued writing, and we see his confidence grow as his ability to write and communicate was magnified by the Lord. I will tell his story using his three recorded sections to organize my commentary.

## Moroni's Initial Remarks— A Simple Declaration

Moroni tells about the difficulty of his remaining time by saying the Lamanites had killed his father and were searching for him. It is a sad observation of a man who had seen everything taken from him: his family, possessions, and country. His freedom was also taken; he had to flee for his life and constantly hide from the Lamanites.

Most soldiers in the United States military are trained in what is called "escape and evasion." The training is given as a precaution because many soldiers in combat will be separated from their units and face being captured. For example, the Army Special Forces and the Navy Seals are especially well trained in escape and evasion because of the difficult assignments they are given to operate behind enemy lines. Air force and army pilots are also given a heavy dose of this training. If they are shot down over enemy territory, they would need to evade the enemy until they could be rescued or until they could find their way back across enemy lines to their own forces.

Ponder for just a moment how horrendous Moroni's plight was. His army of ten thousand was totally defeated, and the Nephite nation had been virtually destroyed. Moroni couldn't flee south because the Lamanites were in control of the land. Fleeing north would have also been difficult because of the Gadianton robbers, who controlled the wilderness. Moreover, from our modern knowledge, we know that north of Moroni's location was the Aztec nation. It was a flourishing, bloodthirsty band that would consider him an outsider.

The following few verses describe Moroni's feelings of hopelessness.

*And my father also was killed by them, and I even remain alone to write the sad tale of the destruction of my people. But behold, they are gone, and I fulfill the commandment of my father. And whether they will slay me, I know not. Therefore I will write and hide up the records in the earth; and whither I go it mattereth not. . . .*

*And behold, it is the hand of the Lord which hath done it. And behold also, the Lamanites are at war one with another; and the whole face of this land is one continual round of murder and bloodshed; and no one knoweth the end of the war. And now, behold, I say no more concerning them, for there are none save it be the Lamanites and robbers that do exist upon the face of the land.* (Mormon 8:3–4, 8–9)

This is an extremely disheartening commentary. By reading between the lines, we can understand how he feels lost and without

purpose. He finished his first attempt at completing the historical record at the end of his father's book with a very simple declaration.

*And whoso receiveth this record, and shall not condemn it because of the imperfections which are in it, the same shall know of greater things than these. Behold, I am Moroni; and were it possible, I would make all things known unto you. Behold, I make an end of speaking concerning this people. I am the son of Mormon, and my father was a descendant of Nephi.* (Mormon 8:12–13)

Take note of how he concludes his text. He was concerned readers would see his "imperfections" and discount the greatness of the spiritual work in the Book of Mormon. Of all the writers in the book of Mormon, he seems to feel a sense of inadequacy in writing and wants the reader to forgive his lack of eloquence. Moroni then ends the record by telling us of his Nephite heritage.

## The Second Set of Remarks—A Spiritual Witness to the People of Today

When Moroni returned, he wrote with more force and energy than before. First, he explained that the entire landscape was beset with murder and chaos. Perhaps he found a safe place to hide and rest from his desperate flight from the Lamanites. He left a clue as to what might have happened when Moroni wrote that there were no believers left.

> *And behold, it is the hand of the Lord which hath done it. And behold also, the Lamanites are at war one with another; and the whole face of this land is one continual round of murder and bloodshed; and no one knoweth the end of the war. And now, behold, I say no more concerning them, for there are none save it be the Lamanites and robbers that do exist upon the face of the land.*
>
> **And there are none that do know the true God save it be the disciples of Jesus, who did tarry in the land until the wickedness of the people was so great that the Lord would not suffer them to remain with the people; and whether they be upon the face of the land no man knoweth.** *But behold, my father and I have seen them, and they have ministered unto us. (Mormon 8:8– 11; emphasis added)*

The statement of interest here is about the three Nephite disciples who were allowed to tarry on earth until the return of the Savior.

They labored among the people until the wickedness was so appalling that the Spirit caused them to stop their ministry. Moroni told us they had previously helped him and his father. It is possible they returned to assist Moroni. They may have helped him escape and find a safe place to recuperate, rest, and prepare to write more. Moroni does not tell us what happened; but it is evident that, like a distance runner, he got a second wind.

Moroni began again with a straightforward introduction. "And I am the same who hideth up this record unto the Lord" (Mormon 8:14). As he continued, it is obvious that he had been energized by a unique experience. The new dialogue made it clear Moroni had seen a vision of the future and had more energy to write. He first testified of the coming forth of the Nephite history (the Book of Mormon) in the latter days and of the people who would bring it forth.

> *And I am the same who hideth up this record unto the Lord; the plates thereof are of no worth, because of the commandment of the Lord. For he truly saith that no one shall have them to get gain; but the record thereof is of great worth; and whoso shall bring it to light, him will the Lord bless. . . .*
>
> **And blessed be he that shall bring this thing to light; for it shall be**

*brought out of darkness unto light, according to the word of God; yea, it shall be brought out of the earth, and it shall shine forth out of darkness, and come unto the knowledge of the people; and it shall be done by the power of God.*

*And if there be faults they be the faults of a man. But behold, we know no fault; nevertheless God knoweth all things; therefore, he that condemneth, let him be aware lest he shall be in danger of hell fire. (Mormon 8:14, 16–17; emphasis added)*

It seems evident Moroni had seen a vision of Joseph Smith, the latter-day prophet given the task to translate the plates of Mormon and publish the Book of Mormon. Moroni seems to know that many will disparage the works of the Lord recorded in the Book of Mormon.

For just a moment, put yourself in Moroni's place. You have seen the destruction of a great nation; you have risked your life in war and seen ten thousand of those you commanded, along with their families, destroyed in battle; you have lost your family and all that you hold dear; you have seen a vision of the future regarding the great works of the Lord in the latter days; and you have also seen how foolish people under the influence of Satan will disparage the future works of God. Wouldn't you just be mystified when you saw how the people of the latter days

refuse to recognize the distinctly marvelous works of God? Wouldn't you want to shout to the world to wake up and investigate the truth being given freely by God? Is it any wonder that Moroni warns the people who reject the works of God by saying they "shall be in danger of hell fire" (Mormon 8:17)?

Moroni gave another insight from this vision when he cautioned those in the future who would punish the house of Israel during the Middle Ages and the latter days.

*And he that shall breathe out wrath and strifes against the work of the Lord, and against the covenant people of the Lord who are the house of Israel, and shall say: We will destroy the work of the Lord, and the Lord will not remember his covenant which he hath made unto the house of Israel—the same is in danger to be hewn down and cast into the fire; For the eternal purposes of the Lord shall roll on, until all his promises shall be fulfilled. (Mormon 8:21–22)*

It is obvious Moroni had seen the mistreatment of the Lord's covenant people in vision. Can you visualize his mind-set after seeing how the Jews were driven from their lands in the rise of the Muslim empires? Can you feel his heartache when viewing the Middle Ages and the slaughter in Jerusalem and the carnage of the Jews in Spain? Imagine his thoughts as he saw The Church of Jesus Christ of Latter-day Saints driven from state to state in search of religious freedom. What horror he must have experienced in viewing the treatment and murder of six million Jews in Europe under the German leader Adolf Hitler. Perhaps he even saw how today the return of the Jews to their homeland is threatened by nuclear destruction from radical Middle Eastern leaders in modern Persia, now called Iran.

It was certainly disheartening for Moroni to know that so many terrible things would happen to the covenant people of Israel. He was perhaps most upset by the treatment of the remnant of the house of Israel in the Americas. The remaining Lamanites living in the Americas were enslaved and mistreated by Spain and Portugal in South and Central America. Moreover, the American Indians of North America were driven from their lands and placed in reservations. Moroni certainly had reason to speak of those who injure his people when he wrote, "The same is in danger to be hewn down and cast into the fire; for the eternal purposes of the Lord shall roll on, until all his promises shall be fulfilled" (Mormon 8:21–22).

Moroni continued to speak of the House of Israel, the Lord's covenant people. He told us

to "search the prophecies of Isaiah" (Mormon 8:23). This is not new to the Book of Mormon—this is a restatement of the words of Christ to the Nephites during his miraculous visit following his resurrection. Jesus said, "Ye remember that I spake unto you, and said that when the words of Isaiah should be fulfilled—behold they are written, ye have them before you, therefore search them" (3 Nephi 20:11). Moroni wanted to remind us of the importance of Isaiah's writings. He had read Isaiah, knew his prophesies, and seen their fulfillment in vision. Moroni gave us an idea of what Isaiah's words were referring to when he said the following:

> Search the prophecies of Isaiah. Behold, I cannot write them. **Yea, behold I say unto you, that those saints who have gone before me, who have possessed this land, shall cry, yea, even from the dust will they cry unto the Lord; and as the Lord liveth he will remember the covenant which he hath made with them.**
>
> And he knoweth their prayers, that they were in behalf of their brethren. And he knoweth their faith, for in his name could they remove mountains; and in his name could they cause the earth to shake; and by the power of his word did they cause prisons to tumble to the earth;

*yea, even the fiery furnace could not harm them, neither wild beasts nor poisonous serpents, because of the power of his word.*

**And behold, their prayers were also in behalf of him that the Lord should suffer to bring these things forth [Joseph Smith]. And no one need say they shall not come, for they surely shall, for the Lord hath spoken it; for out of the earth shall they come, by the hand of the Lord, and none can stay it; and it shall come in a day when it shall be said that miracles are done away; and it shall come even as if one should speak from the dead.** *(Mormon 8:23–26; emphasis and reference added)*

Moroni is speaking of the Book of Mormon, which would be hidden in the earth and would come forth as from the "dust" (Isaiah 29:4). He was mindful of the great Book of Mormon prophets who desired that their history would come forth as a blessing to the Lamanites and all the House of Israel. The following are the actual words of Isaiah and tell of voices that will speak from out of the "*ground*" and be low in the "*dust.*"

**And thou shalt be brought down, and shalt speak out of the ground, and thy speech shall be low out of the** *dust, and thy voice shall be, as of one that hath a familiar spirit, out of the ground, and thy speech shall whisper out of the dust....*

*Wherefore the Lord said, Forasmuch as this people draw near me with their mouth, and with their lips do honour me, but have removed their heart far from me, and their fear toward me is taught by the precept of men:*

**Therefore, behold, I will proceed to do a marvellous work among this people, even a marvellous work and a wonder: for the wisdom of their wise men shall perish, and the understanding of their prudent men shall be hid. And in that day shall the deaf hear the words of the book, and the eyes of the blind shall see out of obscurity, and out of darkness.** *(Isaiah 29:4, 13–14, 18; emphasis added)*

Moroni testified the words of Isaiah would come to pass. Isaiah's message told of "*the book*" that would come forth in the latter days to bring light to the darkness. Now we know, because Moroni told us, these voices from the dust are the prophets of the Book of Mormon. Without question, Isaiah was right. The work of the Lord is a "marvellous work and a wonder."

Moroni also spoke about the behavior of the

people in the latter days. Briefly he told of the circumstances that would exist.

*And it shall come in a day when the blood of saints shall cry unto the Lord, because of secret combinations and the works of darkness.*

*Yea, it shall come in a day when the power of God shall be denied. . . . Yea, it shall come in a day when there shall be heard of fires, and tempests, and vapors of smoke in foreign lands; And there shall also be heard of wars, rumors of wars, and earthquakes in divers places.*

*Yea, it shall come in a day when there shall be great pollutions upon the face of the earth. . . . Yea, it shall come in a day when there shall be churches built up that shall say: Come unto me, and for your money you shall be forgiven of your sins. O ye wicked and perverse and stiffnecked people, why have ye built up churches unto yourselves to get gain? . . .*

*Behold, the Lord hath shown unto me great and marvelous things concerning that which must shortly come, at that day when these things shall come forth among you. Behold, I speak unto you as if ye were present, and yet ye are not.*

*But behold, Jesus Christ hath shown you unto me, and I know your doing.* (Mormon 8: 27–35)

Moroni saw the restoration of the gospel and was speaking directly to us. He saw the innocent blood of the Latter-day Saints spilled by violent mobs. It is possible that he saw the many wars during the 1800s, possibly the bombs of World War II, and the smoke of nuclear explosions in the 1900s. He was appalled by the indulgences paid to churches to absolve men from sin. Moreover, he was disgusted with the latter-day churches that wanted money. I seriously recommend that we read every verse of Mormon 8 and give it our explicit attention. The Savior showed Moroni our day in vision, and he is speaking directly to us. Moroni's desire is that the latter-day readers of his writings will recognize their waywardness and repent. He continued:

*And I know that ye do walk in the pride of your hearts; and there are none save a few only who do not lift themselves up in the pride of their hearts, unto the wearing of very fine apparel, unto envying, and strifes, and malice, and persecutions, and all manner of iniquities; and your churches, yea, even every one, have become polluted because of the pride of your hearts.*

*For behold, ye do love money, and your substance, and your fine apparel, and the adorning of your churches, more than ye love the poor and the needy, the sick and the afflicted.*

*O ye pollutions, ye hypocrites, ye teachers, who sell yourselves for that which will canker, why have ye polluted the holy church of God? **Why are ye ashamed to take upon you the name of Christ?** Why do ye not think that greater is the value of an endless happiness than that misery which never dies—because of the praise of the world? . . . Yea, why do ye build up your secret abominations to get gain. . . .*

***Behold the sword of vengeance hangeth over you;** and the time soon cometh that he avengeth the blood of the saints upon you, for he will not suffer their cries any longer (Mormon 8:36–28, 40–41).*

This is no small talk. It is serious and must not be taken lightly. Moroni wants Christians to stand up for correct principles and not be "ashamed" to take up the cause of the Savior. Moroni saw our day, and we must respond to his call to repentance and return to the Lord's ways. Then we need to help others to know the truth and return to the ways of God.

## Moroni Speaks to Those Who Deny the Miracles of Christ

In chapters eight and nine of his father's book, Moroni is extremely energized. His vision of the latter days was a great motivation to him. He saw those who did not believe in Christ and addressed them directly.

***And now, I speak also concerning those who do not believe in Christ.** Behold, will ye believe in the day of your visitation—behold, when the Lord shall come, yea, even that great day when the earth shall be rolled together as a scroll, and the elements shall melt with fervent heat, yea, in that great day when ye shall be brought to stand before the Lamb of God—then will ye say that there is no God?*

*Then will ye longer deny the Christ, or can ye behold the Lamb of God? Do ye suppose that ye shall dwell with him under a consciousness of your guilt? (Mormon 9:1–3; emphasis added)*

It is simple for Moroni. He knew the truth and had an understanding of the purpose of God. He came right to the point and gave us a definitive warning. He knew there would be a judgment, that the Savior knows us all personally, and that He would see into our unrepentant souls. Next, he spoke to the same people but on another topic. He stated that true faith must include a belief in miracles.

*And again I speak unto you who deny the revelations of God, and say that they are done away, that there are no revelations, nor prophecies, nor gifts, nor healing, nor speaking with tongues, and the interpretation of tongues;*

***Behold I say unto you, he that denieth these things knoweth not the gospel of Christ; yea, he has not read the scriptures; if so, he does not understand them.*** *For do we not read that God is the same yesterday, today, and forever, and in him there is no variableness neither shadow of changing?*

*And now, if ye have imagined up unto yourselves a god who doth vary, and in whom there is shadow of changing, then have ye imagined up unto yourselves a god who is not a God of miracles. But behold, I will show unto you a God of miracles, even the God of Abraham, and the God of Isaac, and the God of Jacob; and it is that same God who created the heavens and the earth, and all things that in them are. . . .*

*Who shall say that it was not a miracle that by his word the heaven and the earth should be; and by the power of his word man was created of the dust of the earth; and by the power of his word have miracles been wrought?*

*And who shall say that Jesus Christ did not do many mighty miracles? And there were many mighty miracles wrought by the hands of the apostles. . . .* ***Behold, I say unto you that whoso believeth in Christ, doubting nothing, whatsoever he shall ask the Father in the name of Christ it shall be granted him; and this promise is unto all, even unto the ends of the earth.*** *(Mormon 9:7–11, 17–18, 21; emphasis added)*

After giving his witness of the gifts of God, he prepared for another end to his writing. Remember at the last ending, he said not to reject his message because of his "imperfections." He repeated himself with this ending.

*Behold, I speak unto you as though I spake from the dead; for I know that ye shall have my words. Condemn me not because of mine imperfection, neither my father, because of his imperfection, neither them who have written before him; but rather give thanks unto God that he hath made manifest unto you our imperfections, that ye may learn to be more wise than we have been. (Mormon 9:30–31)*

In this conclusion, Moroni followed the lead of many Nephite prophets before him—a request that the Lord would bless the Lamanites and restore them to the gospel.

> *But the Lord knoweth the things which we have written, and also that none other people knoweth our language; and because that none other people knoweth our language, therefore he hath prepared means for the interpretation thereof.*
>
> *And these things are written that we may rid our garments of the blood of our brethren, who have dwindled in unbelief. And behold, these things which we have desired concerning our brethren, yea, even their restoration to the knowledge of Christ, are according to the prayers of all the saints who have dwelt in the land.*
>
> *And may the Lord Jesus Christ grant that their prayers may be answered according to their faith; and may God the Father remember the covenant which he hath made with the house of Israel; and may he bless them forever, through faith on the name of Jesus Christ. Amen. (Mormon 9:34–37)*

## Moroni's Third and Final Record

Moroni once again returned to complete his work. First, he included the book of Ether from twenty-four plates that were found by the people of Limhi in approximately 120 BC. King Mosiah had translated the record and it was then included with the many records of the Nephites. The Lord influenced Moroni to include this record on the Plates of Mormon, which had been handed down to him. The record was a history of the Jaredites who left for the promised land at the time of the Tower of Babel. The Jaredites became a great nation and then were corrupted by secret combinations. They were destroyed in massive battles where millions of people were slain. Moroni's comment regarding this people was similar to his father's when he said. "And thus we see that the Lord did visit them in the fullness of his wrath, and their wickedness and abominations had prepared a way for their everlasting destruction (Ether 14:25).

In the words of Ether, the last prophet of the Jaredites, they were "drunken with anger" (Ether 15:22) and were overpowered by the influence of Satan.

> *But behold, the Spirit of the Lord had ceased striving with them, and Satan had full power over the hearts of the people; for they were given up unto the hard-*

ness of their hearts, and the blindness of their minds that they might be destroyed; wherefore they went again to battle. *(Ether 15:19)*

Their entire civilization composed of millions of people was reduced to a handful of angry men who desired revenge and fought to the death. Moroni gave us the detailed record of this people. At one point in the record, he stopped his writing to reflect on the principle of faith. It is without a doubt one of the most touching reflections in all of the Book of Mormon. Speaking of the last Jaredite prophet Ether, Moroni said, "And it came to pass that Ether did prophesy great and marvelous things unto the people, which they did not believe, because they saw them not" (Ether 12:5). Saddened by how the Jaredites had rejected the prophet, Moroni wrote the following expressions on faith.

*And now, I, Moroni, would speak somewhat concerning these things; **I would show unto the world that faith is things which are hoped for and not seen; wherefore, dispute not because ye see not, for ye receive no witness until after the trial of your faith.***

*For it was by faith that Christ showed himself unto our fathers, after he had risen from the dead; and he showed not himself unto them until after they had faith in him; wherefore, it must needs be that some had faith in him, for he showed himself not unto the world.*

*But because of the faith of men he has shown himself unto the world, and glorified the name of the Father, and prepared a way that thereby others might be partakers of the heavenly gift, that they might hope for those things which they have not seen.*

***Wherefore, ye may also have hope, and be partakers of the gift, if ye will but have faith.*** *(Ether 12:6–9; emphasis added)*

What an amazing insight into faith! He gives the definition of faith: it is a function of hope and consists of knowledge about things that can't be seen. Moreover, he reminds us that the journey toward faith is not easy and is beset with trials. Moroni's defining statement on faith is amazingly candid: "wherefore, dispute not because ye see not, for ye receive no witness until after the trial of your faith" (v. 6). He is telling us that faith is not easily acquired. Our ability to see the unseen or have a witness of hope will only come after we have been tested. Faith comes through a dedicated effort under difficult circumstances. In Moroni's life, the trial was his horrible defeat as a commander in battle, the loss of his entire family to death, and constant fear of the enraged Lamanites' desire to take his life. His monumental tasks included finishing the Book of Mormon while fleeing the Lamanites, searching for food, and humbly praying for the faith to write a witness of Christ to the whole world. Do any of us have more trials than Moroni?

Our trial may be a troubled family, a severely painful disease, a physical or mental illness, a loved one who requires constant care, or even a calling in the Church that seems insurmountable. It doesn't matter what the trial is, the Lord has promised he will be with us. The Lord was always with Moroni and relieved his suffering while also magnifying his abilities. Moroni is a wonderful illustration of monumental faith under the most difficult circumstances.

I commend this entire chapter (Ether 12) to you. Moroni described numerous examples of faith taken from the stories in the Book of Mormon. These reflections humbled Moroni, and he again spoke to the Lord about his limitations in writing. Remember he had done this twice before as he made earlier ends to his history. Now, in his third and final record, he repeated his feelings.

*And I said unto him: Lord, the Gentiles will mock at these things, because of our weakness in writing; for Lord thou hast made us mighty in word by faith, but thou hast not made us mighty in writing; for thou hast made all this people that they could speak much, because of the Holy Ghost which thou hast given them;*

*And thou hast made us that we could write but little, because of the awkwardness of our hands. Behold, thou hast not made us mighty in writing like unto the brother of Jared, for thou madest him that the things which he wrote were mighty even as thou art, unto the overpowering of man to read them.*

***Thou hast also made our words powerful and great, even that we cannot write them; wherefore, when we write we behold our weakness, and stumble because of the placing of our words; and I fear lest the Gentiles shall mock at our words.***

*And when I had said this, the Lord spake unto me, saying: Fools mock, but they shall mourn; and my grace is sufficient for the meek, that they shall take no advantage of your weakness; And if men come unto me I will show unto them their weakness. I give unto men weakness that they may be humble;* ***and my grace is sufficient for all men that humble themselves before me; for if they humble***

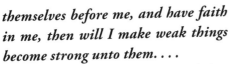 

*themselves before me, and have faith in me, then will I make weak things become strong unto them. . . .*

*And I, Moroni, having heard these words, was comforted, and said: O lord, thy righteous will be done, **for I know that thou workest unto the children of men according to their faith.** (Ether 12:23–27, 29; emphasis added)*

The Lord had taken a humble writer and made him strong. This is a great lesson for all of God's children. The Lord's response to Moroni is the same for all children of faith: "and my grace is sufficient for all men that humble themselves before me" (Ether 12:27). The Lord took his modest servant Moroni and magnified his abilities right before our eyes. We can see clearly that Moroni grew in his abilities to write. He concluded his thoughts on faith, speaking clearly to those Gentile elites whom he thought might mock him. His eloquence in writing is very evident.

*And now I, Moroni, bid farewell unto the Gentiles, yea, and also unto my brethren whom I love, until we shall meet before the judgment-seat of Christ, where all men shall know that my garments are not spotted with your blood.*

***And then shall ye know that I have***

*seen Jesus, and that he hath talked with me face to face, and that he told me in plain humility, even as a man telleth another in mine own language, concerning these things. . . .*

*And now, I would commend you to seek this Jesus of whom the prophets and apostles have written, that the grace of God the Father, and also the Lord Jesus Christ, and the Holy Ghost, which beareth record of them, may be and abide in you forever. Amen. (Ether 12:38–39, 41; emphasis added)*

## Moroni Concludes by Writing His Own Book

Moroni begins his own book by telling of his dangerous peril. He had found time to conclude his father's book and add the Book of Ether to the plates while constantly fearing for his life and escaping the Lamanites. He stated his peril this way.

*Now I, Moroni, after having made an end of abridging the account of the people of Jared, I had supposed not to have written more, but I have not as yet perished; and I make not myself known to the Lamanites lest they should destroy me.*

*For behold, their wars are exceedingly fierce among themselves; and because of their hatred they put to death every Nephite that will not deny the Christ.*

*And I, Moroni, will not deny the Christ; wherefore, I wonder whithersoever I can for the safety of mine own life. (Moroni 1:1–3)*

In the middle of this terribly frightening situation, Moroni retained his connection to the Savior. He wrote for the purpose of helping the Lamanites, even though they desired to take his life.

*Wherefore, I write a few more things, contrary to that which I had supposed; for I had supposed not to have written anymore; but I write a few more things, that perhaps they may be of worth unto my brethren, the Lamanites, in some future day, according to the will of the Lord. (Moroni 1: 4)*

Isn't it interesting how many of the Nephite prophets had forgiven the Lamanites and wanted the Lord to bless them? Even with the Lamanites searching for him, and his life in jeopardy, Moroni remembered his "brethren, the Lamanites." In the book of Moroni, chapters two through six are about the administration of the priesthood and the sacrament.

He then included chapters seven through nine, which are letters and writings of his father, Mormon.

Chapter ten is Moroni's final testimony, and it illustrates the masterful eloquence of Moroni. It is straightforward, bold, clearly written, and marvelously beautiful. Moroni begins his last chapter with some of the most quoted scripture of the latter days. Every missionary has shown these verses to countless investigators and born testimony that the Lord will answer prayers and give witness of the truthfulness of the Book of Mormon.

*And I seal up these records, after I have spoken a few words by way of exhortation unto you.*

*Behold, I would exhort you that when ye shall read these things, if it be wisdom in God that ye should read them, that ye would remember how merciful the Lord hath been unto the children of men, from the creation of Adam even down until the time that ye shall receive these things, and ponder it in your hearts.*

*And when ye shall receive these things, I would exhort you that ye would ask God, the Eternal Father, in the name of Christ, if these things are not true; and if ye shall ask with a sincere heart, with real intent, having faith in Christ, he will manifest the truth of it unto you, by the power of the Holy Ghost.*

***And by the power of the Holy Ghost ye may know the truth of all things.*** *(Moroni 10:2–5; emphasis added)*

Moroni had such deep feelings about spiritual gifts that, in the middle of this chapter, he wrote twenty verses about these gifts from God and ended with these thoughts on miracles.

***And now I speak unto all the ends of the earth—that if the day cometh that the power and gifts of God shall be done away among you, it shall be because of unbelief.***

*And wo be unto the children of men if this be the case; for there shall be none that doeth good among you, no not one. For if there be one among you that doeth good, he shall work by the power and gifts of God. (Moroni 10:24–25; emphasis added)*

Moroni testified many times of the power of faith and repeated his declaration here while speaking to the ends of the earth. Moroni's final testimony about the truth of the Book of Mormon is bold, clear, and commanding. As you read this, remember the words of Isaiah

about a voice from the dust (Isaiah 29). Moroni gave his witness that the words of Isaiah would come to pass.

*And I exhort you to remember these things; for the time speedily cometh that ye shall know that I lie not, for ye shall see me at the bar of God; and the Lord God will say unto you:* ***Did I not declare my words unto you, which were written by this man, like as one crying from the dead, yea, even as one speaking out of the dust?***

*I declare these things unto the fulfilling of the prophecies. And behold, they shall proceed forth out of the mouth of the everlasting God; and his word shall hiss forth from generation to generation.* ***And God shall show unto you, that that which I have written is true.*** *(Moroni 10:27–29; emphasis added)*

What a bold and marvelous witness at the end of the Book of Mormon. Moroni leaves no doubt in this passage of magnificent literature. Sooner or later, we will all know that the words of the book are true. We can know the truth now by asking in humble prayer, or we will know later as we stand before the bar of God.

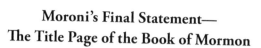
## Moroni's Final Statement—
## The Title Page of the Book of Mormon

Without question, Moroni's principle mission was to complete the history of the Nephite people and prepare the plates to come forth in the latter days. His written message was a resounding testimony of Jesus Christ and of the Book of Mormon. His last written word was probably the title page of the Book of Mormon. It may not be read often, but it is extremely important. Therein he states the purpose of the Book of Mormon and gives a brief synopsis. Moroni's short personal introduction to the book follows.

### THE BOOK OF MORMON

*AN ACCOUNT WRITTEN BY THE HAND OF MORMON UPON PLATES TAKEN FROM THE PLATES OF NEPHI*

*Wherefore, it is an abridgment of the record of the people of Nephi, and also of the Lamanites—Written to the Lamanites, who are a remnant of the house of Israel; and also to Jew and Gentile—Written by way of commandment, and also by the spirit of prophecy and of revelation—Written and sealed up, and hid up unto the Lord, that they might not be destroyed—To come forth by the gift and power of God unto the interpretation thereof—Sealed by the hand of Moroni, and hid up unto the Lord, to come forth in due time by way of the Gentile—The interpretation thereof by the gift of God.*

*An abridgment taken from the Book of Ether also, which is a record of the people of Jared, who were scattered at the time the Lord confounded the language of the people, when they were building a tower to get to heaven— Which is to show unto the remnant of the House of Israel what great things the Lord hath done for their fathers; and that they may know the covenants of the Lord, that they are not cast off forever—And also to the convincing of the Jew and Gentile that Jesus is the Christ, the Eternal God, manifesting himself unto all nations—And now, if there are faults they are the mistakes of men; wherefore, condemn not the things of God, that ye may be found spotless at the judgment-seat of Christ.*

Moroni told us here that the book is a record of three people: the Nephites, Lamanites, and the Jaredites. It is written to the Lamanites, the Jews, and the Gentiles. For the Lamanites, the purpose is to show them the wonderful things the Lord has done for them and to know the covenants that they have received from God. For the Jew and the Gentile, the purpose is to testify that Jesus is the Christ and will manifest himself unto all nations. His approach here is simple and straightforward. Notice again Moroni mentions his fear that his writing contains mistakes, so he warns the reader not to condemn the work of God. Moroni's witness is amazingly clear. His testimony cannot be missed—it is on the first and last page of the Book of Mormon. The words of Moroni ring true to all who sincerely read the book.

## Moroni Returns to Bring the Everlasting Gospel to Joseph Smith

Moroni was so faithful and powerful in his final testimony that the Lord extended his mission into the latter days. He was the great angel seen by the Apostle John. He brought the everlasting gospel in the form of the Book of Mormon.

*And I saw another angel fly in the midst of heaven, having the everlasting gospel to preach unto them that dwell on the earth, and to every nation, and kindred, and tongue, and people, saying with a loud voice, Fear God, and give glory to him; for the hour of his judgment is come: and worship him that made heaven, and earth, and the sea, and the fountains of waters. (John the Revelator, in Revelation 14:6–7)*

Moroni buried the golden plates in a hillside in upstate New York around AD 421. He appeared to the seventeen-year-old Joseph Smith on September 21, 1823, which was roughly fourteen hundred years after his death. (See

Joseph Smith—History 1:27–54.) His purpose in this appearance was to reveal to the young prophet the knowledge of the ancient record he had buried. Joseph Smith described the visitation this way.

*While I was thus in the act of calling upon God, I discovered a light appearing in my room, which continued to increase until the room was lighter than at noonday, when immediately a personage appeared at my bedside, standing in the air, for his feet did not touch the floor.*

*He had on a loose robe of most exquisite whiteness. It was a whiteness beyond anything earthly I had ever seen; nor do I believe that any earthly thing could be made to appear so exceedingly white and brilliant. His hands were naked, and his arms also, a little above the wrist; so, also, were his feet naked, as were his legs, a little above the ankles. His head and neck were also bare. I could discover that he had no other clothing on but this robe, as it was open, so that I could see into his bosom.*

*Not only was his robe exceedingly white, but his whole person was glorious beyond description, and his countenance truly like lightning. The room was exceedingly light, but not so very bright as*

*immediately around his person. When I first looked upon him, I was afraid; but the fear soon left me.*

**He called me by name, and said unto me that he was a messenger sent from the presence of God to me, and that his name was Moroni; that God had a work for me to do;** *and that my name should be had for good and evil among all nations, kindreds, and tongues, or that it should be both good and evil spoken of among all people.*

**He said there was a book deposited, written upon gold plates, giving an account of the former inhabitants of this continent, and the source from whence they sprang. He also said that the fulness of the everlasting Gospel was contained in it, as delivered by the Savior to the ancient inhabitants.** *(Joseph Smith—History 1:30–34; emphasis added)*

This modern description of a resurrected and glorified being paints a magnificent picture for our minds. In this first visit, Moroni quoted scriptures from the Old Testament and revealed to Joseph where the plates were placed. Moroni appeared to Joseph three times in the night with the same message. The next day while working with his father on the farm, Joseph became

exhausted, and his father told him to return home. As Joseph was returning home, Moroni appeared a fourth time, repeated his message, and then told Joseph to go back to his father.

*I obeyed; I returned to my father in the field, and rehearsed the whole matter to him. He replied to me that it was of God, and told me to go and do as commanded by the messenger. I left the field, and went to the place where the messenger had told me the plates were deposited; and owing to the distinctness of the vision which I had had concerning it, I knew the place the instant that I arrived there.*

*Convenient to the village of Manchester, Ontario county, New York, stands a hill of considerable size, and the most elevated of any in the neighborhood. On the west side of this hill, not far from the top, under a stone of considerable size, lay the plates, deposited in a stone box. This stone was thick and rounding in the middle on the upper side, and thinner toward the edges, so that the middle part of it was visible above the ground, but the edge all around was covered with earth.*

*Having removed the earth, I obtained a lever, which I got fixed under the edge of the stone, and with a little exertion raised it up. I looked in, and there indeed did I behold the plates, the Urim and Thummim, and the breastplate, as stated by the messenger. The box in which they lay was formed by laying stones together in some kind of cement. In the bottom of the box were laid two stones crossways of the box, and on these stones lay the plates and the other things with them.*

*I made an attempt to take them out, but was forbidden by the messenger, and was again informed that the time for bringing them forth had not yet arrived, neither would it, until four years from that time; but he told me that I should come to that place precisely in one year from that time, and that he would there meet with me, and that I should continue to do so until the time should come for obtaining the plates.*

***Accordingly, as I had been commanded, I went at the end of each year, and at each time I found the same messenger there, and received instruction and intelligence from him at each of our interviews, respecting what the Lord was going to do, and how and in what manner his kingdom was to be conducted in the last days.*** *(Joseph Smith—History 1:50–54; emphasis added)*

Joseph went to the place shown to him in vision, and Moroni appeared once more to show him the plates. The plan was to have Joseph prepare himself spiritually before receiving the plates to translate. Joseph came back on the same date for four years before he was allowed to take the plates and begin translating. Moroni was his mentor, helping him know how the restoration of the gospel would take place and the role Joseph would play. While Joseph Smith was the translator, Moroni was the guardian of the plates, often appearing to Joseph and taking the plates back when there was a problem.

## Moroni Continues His Work as a Guardian Angel—The Prince of America

This mission to reveal the plates and teach Joseph Smith was not Moroni's only task. Orson Hyde, latter-day apostle told the Church of the extended mission of Moroni. He spoke to a gathering in Utah on July 4, 1854, about America's Founding Fathers.

We are met, fellow citizens, to celebrate one of the most important events that ever embellished the pages of political history— an event of which every American heart is proud to boast, in whatever land or country he perchance may roam—I mean the bold, manly, and daring act of our fathers in the Declaration of the Independence and Sovereignty of these United States. . . .

Remember Lexington, and Bunker Hill, and lastly Yorktown, with all the intermediate scenes as narrated in the history of the American Revolution! Remember the immortal Washington, chosen to lead our infant armies through the perils and hardships of an unequal contest, to the climax of victory and the pinnacle of fame! His name, embalmed in the never-dying sympathies of his grateful countrymen, will be heralded in the melody of song, "while the earth bears a plant or the ocean rolls a wave." While Columbia's sons and daughters regret and mourn his exit hence in accents like the following. . . .

In those early and perilous times, our men were few, and our resources limited. Poverty was among the most potent enemies we had to encounter; yet our arms were successful; and it may not be amiss to ask here, by whose power victory so often perched on our banner? It was by the agency of that same angel of God that appeared unto Joseph Smith, and revealed to him the history of the early inhabitants of this country, whose mounds, bones, and remains of towns, cities, and fortifications speak from the dust in the ears of the living with the voice of undeniable truth. *This same angel presides over the destinies of America, and feels a lively interest in all our*

*doings. He was in the camp of Washington; and, by an invisible hand, led on our fathers to conquest and victory; and all this to open and prepare the way for the Church and kingdom of God to be established on the western hemisphere, for the redemption of Israel and the salvation of the world.*

*This same angel was with Columbus, and gave him deep impressions, by dreams and by visions, respecting this New World.* Trammeled by poverty and by an unpopular cause, yet his persevering and unyielding heart would not allow an obstacle in his way too great for him to overcome; and the angel of God helped him—was with him on the stormy deep, calmed the troubled elements, and guided his frail vessel to the desired haven. *Under the guardianship of this same angel, or Prince of America, have the United States grown, increased, and flourished, like the sturdy oak by the rivers of water.*[1]

What marvelous insight into history. The Lord has influenced the development of the Americas from Columbus to the present. Washington and other Founding Fathers often spoke of Divine Providence. The support of God was requested in the Declaration of Independence penned by Thomas Jefferson. Its last sentence puts the entire document into perspective: "And for the support of this declaration, with a firm reliance on the protection of Divine Providence, we mutually pledge to each other our lives, our fortunes and our sacred honor." The work of the Founding Fathers and the Constitution of the United States were endorsed by the Lord in the Doctrine and Covenants. Indeed, it is obvious that God had a formative influence on these documents.

> *And for this purpose have I established the Constitution of this land, by the hands of wise men whom I raised up unto this very purpose, and redeemed the land by the shedding of blood. (Doctrine and Covenants 101:80)*

Elder Hyde pointed out that the angel Moroni was also guiding the fortunes of the revolutionary army. There is ample evidence that he protected the young George Washington from death. Certain American Indians in the French and Indian War spoke of a young British officer that their bullets could not hit. This was later confirmed by multiple sources.

This was confirmed by Mary Draper Ingels, who was held captive by the Shawnee tribe. While in captivity, she overheard some Frenchmen discussing an event that occurred that defied all logic. Having personally met with Washington, she began to inquire of the Frenchmen about him.

They related the account of an Indian chief named Red Hawk who had been in the victory at Duquesne. Red Hawk told of shooting eleven different times at Washington without killing him. At that point, because his gun had never before missed its mark . . . , he ceased firing at him, being convinced that the Great Spirit protected Washington.[2]

Fifteen years after the battle in which Washington fought in the French and Indian War, the tribe's chief, who could have killed Washington, made the following notable comments through a translator.

I am a chief and ruler over my tribes. My influence extends to the waters of the great lakes and to the far blue mountains. **I have traveled a long and weary path that I might see the young warrior of the great battle.** It was on the day when the white man's blood mixed with the streams of our forest that I first beheld this chief [Washington]. I called to my young men and said, mark yon tall and daring warrior? He is not of the red-coat tribe—he hath an Indian's wisdom, and his warriors fight as we do—himself is alone exposed. Quick, let your aim be certain, and he dies. **Our rifles were leveled, rifles which, but for you, knew not how to miss—'twas all in vain; a power mightier far than we shielded you. Seeing you were under the**

**special guardianship of the Great Spirit, we immediately ceased to fire at you.** I am old and soon shall be gathered to the great council fire of my fathers in the land of shades; but ere I go, there is something bids me speak in the voice of prophecy. Listen! **The Great Spirit protects that man [pointing at Washington], and guides his destinies**—he will become the chief of nations, and a people yet unborn will hail him as the founder of a mighty empire. I am come to pay homage to the man who is the particular favorite of Heaven and who can never die in battle."[3]

History records another instance where Washington was protected by an invisible hand and could not be killed. The "guardian angel of America" knew who the Founding Fathers would be and the role that George Washington would play. Is there any question that Moroni would have played a role in the following situation?

During the revolutionary war there was another instance where Washington was protected by an invisible hand. In 1779 during the American Revolution at the Battle of Brandywine, British Major Patrick Ferguson, head of the British sharpshooters, held an American officer dead in his sights at close range, but instead of firing, he obeyed a strong impulse not to shoot. Ferguson did not realize at that time who he had in his sights, but he later discovered from the soldiers with him that it was George Washington he had allowed to live. Ferguson subsequently explained: *"I could have lodged half a dozen balls in him before he was out of my reach...but it was not pleasant to fire at the back of an unoffending individual who was acquitting himself very coolly of his duty—so I let him live."*

As historian Lyman Draper observed in 1881: "Had Washington fallen, it is difficult to calculate its probable effect upon the result of the struggle of the American people. How slight, oftentimes, are the incidents which, in the course of human events, seem to give direction to the most momentous concerns of the human race. This singular impulse of Ferguson illustrates, in a forcible manner, the over-ruling hand of Providence in directing the operation of a man's mind when he himself is least aware of it."[4]

It is evident that Orson Hyde understood that Moroni had played an inspirational role in the Revolutionary War and provided protection to Washington in the founding of our nation. As illustrated above, historians have validated that America and especially Washington was under the protection of the "hand of Providence." Elder Hyde explained the conditions under which Moroni would continue his positive influence.

So sure and certain as the great water courses wend their way to the ocean, and there find their level—so sure as the passing thundercloud hovers around yonder Twin Peaks of the Wasatch Mountains, and upon their grey and barren rocks pours the fury of its storm, just so sure and certain will the guardian angel of these United States fly to a remote distance from their borders, and the anger of the Almighty wax hot against them in causing them to drink from the cup of bitterness and division, and the very dregs, stirred up by the hands of foreign powers, in a manner more cruel and fierce than the enemies of the Saints in the day of their greatest distress and anguish; and all this because they laid not to heart the martyrdom of the Saints and Prophets, avenged not their blood by punishing the murderers, neither succored nor aided the Saints after they were despoiled of their goods and homes.[5]

Remember how upset Moroni was when he saw in vision how the Latter-day Saints would be driven and punished by mobs? Speaking of the day the Book of Mormon would come forth, he said: "And it shall come in a day when the blood of saints shall cry unto the Lord, because of secret combinations and the works of darkness" (Mormon 8:27). Elder Hyde was explaining that the United States had not taken any steps to give redress for the loss of life and property in Missouri or Illinois. Consequently, Elder Hyde said that Moroni would not return to his role as guardian until there was some form of justice. Some feel the American Civil War was the result of the Lord allowing a tremendous affliction to come upon an unrepentant nation.

When Justice is satisfied, and the blood of martyrs atoned for, the guardian angel of America will return to his station, resume his charge, and restore the Constitution of our country to the respect and veneration of the people; for it was given by the inspiration of our God.[6]

Following the American Civil War and the elimination of slavery, the United States of America have enjoyed and influx of immigrants and continuous growth. Certainly, the prosperity of the United States has been remarkable, far beyond any country in the history of the world. Take note of the growth from the Atlantic Ocean to the Pacific Ocean, including Alaska. In the 1900s, the prosperity and wealth of the entire world was focused in the United States. The industrial power and military support of America brought victory in two world wars and tyranny was curtailed. The oppression of communism and has been halted and democracy and religious freedom restored in large portions of the world. Along with this freedom, the gospel of Jesus Christ is spreading throughout the world. Does the guardian angel of America continue to influence America and the world? Most certainly! When the Lord gathers his people in the day of His coming, won't it be marvelous to talk to Moroni and know exactly what he did to influence the growth of the Americas. Most likely, his influences extended beyond the Revolutionary War, the Founding Fathers, and the Constitution. Perhaps he influenced the creative inventions of the modern era, such as the steam engine, electricity, the internal combustion engine, the airplane, the television, the computer, or the Internet. There is no question that the Lord has been there; however, the question might be, was it through the angel Moroni or through some other way?

## Lessons From Moroni's Amazing Journey

Consider the life of Moroni for a moment. He is an outstanding example after which we can all pattern our lives. We will all have challenges that seem impossible overcome, those that appear so overwhelming that we want to give up, or that bring us to our knees in prayer to beg for the Lord's help. An examination of the character traits and marvelous accomplishments of the great prophet will give us insight into how we, in some small way, can emulate his example.

***A competitor who would not quit against terrible odds.*** Moroni was stripped of his nation, family, and freedom. However, Moroni continued to finish the assignment given to him by his father—complete the history.

***A spiritual giant who was given a vision of the future.*** To give depth to his witness the Lord allowed him to see the day his writings would come to the world. Without a strong commitment to the Lord and his commandments, this spiritual gift could never have been given to him.

***A humble servant whose ability to write was magnified through the grace of God according to his faith.*** He voiced his fear that his mistakes would be exaggerated and that his writing would be mocked by the elite of the latter days. The beauty of his writing and the power of his witness are now echoed by missionaries throughout the world.

***A witness for Christ who was so faithful that he was allowed to speak with the resurrected Savior face to face and who's testimony of the Great Redeemer will influence millions and live throughout eternity.***

***A prophet so dedicated that he was given an assignment following death.*** Moroni's mission was extended into the latter days as the angel of the Restoration of the gospel of Jesus Christ and the angel who presides over the destiny of the Americas.

May we as readers of the Book of Mormon focus on the marvelous writings of Moroni, endorse his witness of the Savior, and emulate his faith so that miracles may continue to follow the Latter-day Saints. It is through our faith that the angel of the Restoration, the Prince of the America, can continue his work.

## Sources

1. *Journal of Discourses,* 6:368–69)
2. David Barton, *The Bulletproof George Washington,* 2nd ed. (Aledo: Wallbuilder Press, 2006), 51.
3. Ibid., 54; emphasis added.
4. Ibid., 57; emphasis added.
5. *Journal of Discourses,* 6:369.
6. Ibid.

# Conclusion

# THE BOOK OF MORMON—
# WITNESSES OF CHRIST

odern prophets have emphasized the value and importance of the Book of Mormon in our lives. It is imperative that we frequently refresh our memories of these great witnesses of the book. Joseph Smith, prophet and translator of the Book of Mormon, stated:

> I told the brethren that the Book of Mormon was the most correct of any book on earth, and the keystone of our religion, and a man would get nearer to God by abiding by its precepts, than by any other book. (Introduction: Book of Mormon)

President Ezra Taft Benson, speaking in a 1986 general conference told of the inspirational and personal value the Book of Mormon can have for all readers.

There is a power in the book which will begin to flow into your lives the moment you begin a serious study of the book. You will find greater power to resist temptation. You will find the power to avoid deception. You will find the power to stay on the strait and narrow path. The scriptures are called 'the words of life' (D&C 84:85), and nowhere is that more true than it is of the Book of Mormon. When you begin to hunger and thirst after those words, you will find life in greater and greater abundance. ... [You will also enjoy] increased love and harmony in the home, greater respect between parent and child, [and] increased spirituality and righteousness.

These promises are not idle promises, but exactly what the Prophet Joseph Smith meant when he said the Book of Mormon will help us draw nearer to God. (Conference Report, Oct. 1986; or Ensign, Nov. 1986)

There is no question that the Book of Mormon can have an overwhelming influence on people and change their lives. It is an effective witness of the Savior Jesus Christ. The purpose of my commentaries is to give the reader a soldier's insight into the authors and characters in the Book of Mormon. Reading the Book of Mormon through the eyes of a soldier adds depth and understanding to the process. The majesty of these great prophet-warriors cannot be overlooked. Their courage, patriotism, love of freedom, and military expertise is right there. From the soldier's prayer of Nephi to the military genius of Captain Moroni, the Book of Mormon is filled with stories and witnesses that they are real people with a soldier's love of life and a dedication to freedom. I am humbled by the truths taught by the Book of Mormon authors. While writing this book, I had one primary concern: I prayed that what I wrote would enhance the readers' appreciation for these marvelous warriors and give readers an additional opportunity to examine their testimonies of Christ.

Let us briefly reflect again on the magnitude of these amazing men. One by one, they give examples of honesty, valor, courage, and outstanding character. I witness that they lived and that the Lord has given us their record to enlighten our spirits and give us examples of how to conduct our lives.

*Nephi*, the son of Lehi, was known as "the great protector" of his people and fought with the sword of Laban. He was forced to take up arms against his family members, Laman and Lemuel and their children. He lamented this horrible consequence in a remarkable poetic verse that resembles a humble soldier's prayer (2 Nephi 4:16–35). His witness of Christ is breathtaking: "And we talk of Christ, we rejoice in Christ, we preach of Christ, we prophesy of Christ, and we write according to our prophecies, that our children may know to what source they may look for a remission of their sins" (2 Nephi 25:26). Throughout his incredible and challenging life, Nephi was obedient to the Lord, and his people prospered. His story begins with his obedient retrieval of the brass plates of Laban when he said, "I will go and do the things which the Lord hath commanded" (1 Nephi 3:7). His entire life is an illustration of his last written words: "I must obey" (2 Nephi 33:15).

***Alma the Younger*** went through a misguided youthful path that was altered by a frightful visit of an angel. He became the first chief judge elected by the Nephites. He defended Nephite freedom by leading their armies and eventually fighting Amlici face-to-face with the sword. Ultimately, Alma knew that if the people did not repent, they would be defeated by the vengeful Lamanites. Consequently, he resigned as chief judge and went among the people as a missionary, giving lessons on faith that are a hallmark of scripture. Alma's ultimate desire is eternally admirable: "O that I were an angel, and could have the wish of mine heart, that I might go forth and speak with the trump of God, with a voice to shake the earth, and cry repentance unto every people!" (Alma 29:1).

***Ammon*** was a Nephite prince who refused the opportunity to become king, and thereafter he became a missionary who entered the lands of the Lamanites at the peril of his life. He took the job of a lowly servant, defended the flocks of the Lamanite king, and taught the king about Christ. Through the efforts of Ammon and his brothers, tens of thousands of Lamanites rejected the hateful traditions of their forefathers and became Christians. Ammon's loyalty to his Heavenly Father and to the Lamanite king Lamoni was remarkable. Who can read the

Book of Mormon and forget Ammon's victorious sword fight with the Lamoni's father, which opened the way for the sons of Mosiah to teach throughout all the lands? Lamoni's description of Ammon is a befitting tribute. "Surely there has not been any servant among all my servants that has been so faithful as this man; for even he doth remember all my commandments to execute them" (Alma 18:10).

***The Stripling Warriors*** were a group of 2,060 young teenage boys whose Lamanite parents had taken an oath to not participate in war. Their story is one of courage and valor because they honored their families by joining the Nephite armies to fight for freedom. They were in extreme danger because they were a young, inexperienced unit of warriors. They confronted the battle-hardened Lamanite veterans without fear because of the faith instilled in them by dedicated and spiritual mothers. If captured, they would be murdered by the hateful Lamanites. Helaman, their commander, spoke of their dedication: "Yea, and they did obey and observe to perform every word of command with exactness; yea, and even according to their faith it was done unto them; and I did remember the words which they said unto me that their mothers had taught them" (Alma 57:21). In the subsequent battles, while thousands of Nephites were slain, none of Helaman's band of youthful soldiers was killed; however, all were wounded. Helaman's statement about his stripling warriors is a wonderful testimonial to the unbelievable success of his youthful soldiers. "And we do justly ascribe it to the miraculous power of God, because of their exceeding faith" (Alma 57:26). Helaman's final compliment describes the character of the boys he called his sons and the true source of their strength: "They are young, and their minds are firm, and they do put their trust in God continually" (Alma 57:27).

*Captain Moroni* was one of the greatest military leaders of all time. His exploits and military genius are awe-inspiring. The authors of the Book of Mormon undoubtedly wanted readers to see the contrast between a motivated, righteous, and merciful Nephite military commander when compared to the deceitful, murderous, and merciless Lamanite military leaders. The great captain motivated his people to fight for freedom. "And it came to pass that he rent his coat; and he took a piece thereof, and wrote upon it—In memory of our God, our religion, and freedom, and our peace, our wives, and our children—and he fastened it upon the end of a pole" (Alma 46:12). Moroni went throughout the land, raising the "title of liberty" and inspiring the people to join in the fight for freedom. Mormon, the compiler of the Book of Mormon, paused while recording the great captain's story to comment on his character. His compliment illustrates an example worthy of our emulation. "Yea, verily, verily I say unto you, if all men had been, and were, and ever would be, like unto Moroni, behold, the very powers of hell would have been shaken forever; yea, the devil would never have power over the hearts of the children of men" (Alma 48:17).

The saga of the **Gadianton robbers** is a tale of vicious conspirators. These evil groups of ruthless men were sworn to secrecy and accordingly were called "secret combinations." They gained power by infiltrating the Nephite political system through murder and deceit. Once they gained power, the people lost their freedom and were forced to join in the corruption or lose their lives. Moroni, son of Mormon, saw our day in vision and warned us not to let these vile organizations come among us. "Wherefore, O ye Gentiles, it is wisdom in God that these things should be shown unto you, that thereby ye may repent of your sins, and suffer not that these murderous combinations shall get above you, which are built up to get power and gain. . . . Wherefore, the Lord commandeth you, when ye shall see these things come among you that ye shall awake to a sense of your awful situation, because of this secret combination which shall be among you" (Ether 8:23–24).

**Mormon** was the editor who took the plates of Nephi, abridged them, and recorded his condensed version onto gold plates. He often reflected on the message we should take from the stories and characters in the Book of Mormon. His editorial comments are introduced with "And thus we see." It is as if he was standing before his troops saying: "Attention! Here is the moral to this story." Mormon was a young prophet who had a visit from Christ at the age of fifteen (Mormon 1:15). He was so well trained and respected that he was given command of the entire Nephite army when he was only sixteen years old (Mormon 2:1–2). In his later life, he was consigned to watch the downfall of the Nephite nation, knowing that the efforts to defend themselves by war would fail unless they repented and kept the commandments. He was much more than a military commander—he was a prophet and an outstanding writer. He lamented the collapse of the Nephite nation in a poetic verse that illustrates his love for his people and his deep sorrow of their downfall. "And my soul was rent with anguish, because of the slain of my people, and I cried: O ye fair ones, how could

ye have departed from the ways of the Lord! O ye fair ones, how could ye have rejected that Jesus, who stood with open arms to receive you! Behold, if ye had not done this, ye would not have fallen. But behold, ye are fallen, and I mourn your loss" (Mormon 6:16–18).

**Moroni**, son of Mormon, was the last prophet and author of the Book of Mormon. He was a spiritual giant who completed his writing under almost impossible odds. His life was in constant danger from the Lamanites who had destroyed his nation, killed his family, and would go to any length to stop him from completing his God-given task. He was a humble servant who felt inadequate to write the final history of his people. Because of his faith, the Lord strengthened him, and he became an eloquent author and witness for Christ. Moroni is a marvelous example of how the Lord works with those who love Him. Christ not only spoke to him face-to-face but also gave him a vision of the future. Moroni saw the latter days and speaks directly to us (the Gentiles): "And now I, Moroni, bid farewell unto the Gentiles, yea, and also unto my brethren whom I love, until we shall meet before the judgment-seat of Christ, where all men shall know that my garments are not spotted with your blood. And then shall ye know that I have seen Jesus, and that he hath talked with me face to face, and that he told me in plain humility, even as a man telleth another in mine own language, concerning these things (Ether 12:38–39). Moroni's eternal witness of the truth of Book of Mormon is carried around the world and spoken through the months of countless missionaries. "And when ye shall receive these things, I would exhort you that ye would ask God, the Eternal Father, in the name of Christ, if these things are not true; and if ye shall ask with a sincere heart, with real intent, having faith in Christ, he will manifest the truth of it unto you, by the power of the Holy Ghost. And by the power of the Holy Ghost ye may know the truth of all things" (Moroni 10:4–5).

Remember Mormon's statement about his enormous task of sorting through the records of the Nephites and deciding what to record on his plates of gold?

*And now there are many records kept of the proceedings of this people, by many of this people, which are particular and very large, concerning them.*

***But behold, a hundredth part of the proceedings of this people****, yea, the account of the Lamanites and of the Nephites, and their wars, and contentions, and dissensions, and their preaching, and their prophecies, and their shipping and* their building of ships, and their building of temples, and of synagogues and their sanctuaries, and their righteousness, and their wickedness, and their murders, and their robbings, and their plundering, and all manner of abominations and whoredoms,* ***cannot be contained in this work.***

*But behold, there are many books and many records of every kind, and they have been kept chiefly by the Nephites. (Helaman 3:13–15; emphasis added)*

Our Book of Mormon is less than "a hundredth part" of the history of the Nephites! Why so much about war? Why so many stories of courageous and faithful prophet-warriors? I hope my effort to reflect on their lives and discuss their difficulties with war will help you answer these questions.

As a soldier, I am especially honored to testify that these great warriors were men of God, whose courage and military acumen adds validity and depth to the stories in the Book of Mormon. The Book of Mormon is a true history and contains many marvelous witnesses of Christ. It is a story of covenants kept and broken: when kept, there was great faith and prosperity. And when broken, there was terrible grief and ultimate devastation. The Nephites were protected and their battles were won miraculously when the people were faithful to their covenants. I am a witness that these men were real people and are among the greatest prophets, warriors, patriots, and defenders of liberty in all of written history. Their stories are worthy to be read to all generations, both young and old. The Book of Mormon prophet-warriors validate the witness that Jesus Christ is the Savior of the world.

# ABOUT THE AUTHOR

Douglas J. Bell was raised in American Fork, a small town in central Utah. His parents, Si and Myrtle, were third generation Mormons with a simple approach to life: worship God, love your family, and work hard. Douglas served a mission for The Church of Jesus Christ of Latter-day Saints in the Netherlands, the land of his ancestors.

Following his mission, he completed a bachelor's degree in business management at Brigham Young University. He later received a master's degree in business from the University of Utah and a PhD from Brigham Young University in higher education. Education has given him a lasting impression of academia: when you learn a concept, it is of little worth to anyone unless it can be clearly written and explained using facts, logic, and concise language.

While employed at Brigham Young University, Dr. Bell served as assistant registrar, director of admission, and clinical professor. As a professor in the student development department, he designed the curriculum, taught effective study skills, published two textbooks on effective study, and gave numerous presentations at national educational conventions. As an adjunct professor for the College of Religion, Dr. Bell taught Book of Mormon for five years. He retired from BYU in 2010.

Douglas joined the Utah National Guard in 1969. Using his mission experience, he became a Dutch linguist and was trained as an interrogator. He was later commission to warrant officer. In 2003, he was deployed in Operation Iraqi Freedom with the 142nd Military Intelligence Battalion. The principle assignment while stationed in Baghdad was to interview high ranking military, government, and university officials regarding the activities of the former regime of Saddam Hussein.

While at BYU, he met and married Caryl Williams, a home economics student from Toronto, Canada. They have four children and four grandchildren. Doug and Caryl have an active schedule, which includes hiking three to five miles a day and spending time with family. They have a tremendous love of the outdoors and spend extensive time in two of their favorite canyons, Provo and Zion.